Basics of Game Design

D0145674

Basics of Game Design

Michael E. Moore

CRC Press
Taylor & Francis Group
Boca Raton London New York

CRC Press is an imprint of the
Taylor & Francis Group, an **informa** business

AN A K PETERS BOOK

A K Peters/CRC Press
Taylor & Francis Group
6000 Broken Sound Parkway NW, Suite 300
Boca Raton, FL 33487-2742

© 2011 by Taylor and Francis Group, LLC
A K Peters/CRC Press is an imprint of Taylor & Francis Group, an Informa business

Library of Congress Cataloging-in-Publication Data

Moore, Michael E.
    Basics of game design / Michael Moore.
      p. cm.
    ISBN 978-1-56881-433-9 (pbk. : alk. paper)
    1. Computer games--Design. 2. Computer games--Programming. 3. Video games--Design. I. Title.

QA76.76.C672M6158 2011
794.8'1536--dc22   2010053534

Visit the Taylor & Francis Web site at
http://www.taylorandfrancis.com

and the A K Peters Web site at
http://www.akpeters.com

CONTENTS

PREFACE

The video game industry has grown explosively over the past decade and is now a major provider of home entertainment. Since the North American release of the Nintendo Entertainment System (NES) in 1985, game industry revenues have also grown substantially and, according to the marketing research company NDP Group, grossed almost $20 billion in the United States in 2009. World sales are about equivalent to US sales, so the game industry brought in approximately $40 billion worldwide in 2009. Even during the late economic downturn, the game industry remains healthy financially.

There are many reasons why games have become so popular. One reason is that they are available on many different platforms, including computers, game consoles, cell phones, iPads, and various handheld devices, especially the Sony PlayStation Portable and Nintendo DS. Over the years, as the platform technology improved, games have become much more sophisticated in creating worlds that immerse the player with their almost photorealistic graphics and 3D sound effects that make players feel they are actually on a battlefield or taking on armies of zombies.

Of course, games are not movies. The main difference is that games allow players to actively participate in the events of the game world as opposed to simply sitting back and passively watching things happen. It is this hands-on involvement in a game world where entities seem to behave independently that sets games apart from traditional forms of art and entertainment. Rather than simply watching the hero fight her way through hordes of enemies to reach the lair where the evil villain is hiding, game players can pick up weapons, whip up magic or highly advanced technology, and even lead armies against the villain.

Of course, just as in other forms of art and entertainment, someone has to create the environment and personages inhabiting the world, put words into the characters' mouths, and define how things will run. The art team creates the worlds and entities. The programming team creates the game engine that coordinates all the processes involved in getting the game to appear on the screen as well as handling the world physics and enemy artificial intelligence. The design team not only creates the script for the game but, more importantly, also has the task of assigning values to objects in the game world so that they can interact as desired.

When asking young people what they think the role of game designer is, many respond that the designer simply has to come up with the story for a game and maybe create the dialogue in the game. While the story and dialogue are indeed major components of the game, they are not the only responsibility of the designer. Just as important is the ability of a designer to create the charts and tables (the database) that drive game play. The designer assigns values to items in the game—for example, the damage done by a weapon, how fast it takes to reload, its carrying weight, how many shots it can hold and other information. Unless these values are assigned to objects, nothing happens in the game world. When the player fires a weapon at an onrushing enemy, the game code defines how the weapon is drawn on the screen, what special visual and audio effects appear when the weapon is discharged, and when the projectile hits its target. But unless there are values assigned for damage to the projectile and health to the target, nothing will happen when the projectile intersects the target. The designer has to come up with these values as well as an explanation of how the combat is resolved and how the values interact with one another.

In simple action, arcade and puzzle games, the number of items appearing on a game is limited and the data is relatively easy to determine and modify based on testing. In the early days of computer and video games, one person could be programmer, artist, designer, and sound engineer on a game because the code was small and the graphics and audio were very limited. Of course, these games are relatively simplistic in terms of content and rely either on randomness to vary startup conditions or on precise mastery of the controls by the player to win.

Over time, as game platforms became faster and more powerful, the amount of information that could be handled by the central processing unit (CPU) increased. Graphics became more detailed with larger color palettes, audio assets expanded to include music, sound effects, and voiceovers, and the AI and physics allowed for more realistic movement and actions for objects in the game world. One person could no longer handle all the data required for a game, and development teams expanded. The programming team became tasked not only with writing the many code modules that comprised the game engine but also with creating tools to be used by other teams. Artists were brought in to create the 2D and 3D visuals for the playfields and the beings and objects that occupied them. Specialists in audio were hired to compose the music, create the sound effects and record voice artists. Finally, designers were hired to come up with the game design concepts, document the team's ideas, and generate the charts, tables, and other information that kept the game flowing.

The designer is now a role as important to game development as a director is to movie production. The designer defines how the game will play by describing the various game mechanics in the documentation. The program team then implements these mechanics, and the designer continually tests and revises the values to make the game play the way the team has envisaged. Additionally, the designer sets up the plot elements for the story (assuming there is a story) and describes the characters, locations, and items found in the game world so the art team can build the playfields and models. When necessary, the designer may be forced to rethink the game mechanics if things do not behave in the game world as expected, and the necessary changes must be worked out with the program and art teams and then executed. The designer has the vision for the game, just as a director has the vision for a movie, and it is up to the designer to be the keeper of the flame throughout the long, long production cycle.

There are many books available on game design, but most talk about the production cycle and the responsibilities of the designer during each phase of the cycle. Other books look at story construction or level design. Some expound on theories about making games. There is almost nothing available on how the game designer goes about building the charts and tables that drive the game play. This book is intended to fill that gap. It looks at the most important game mechanics individually and in detail, and explains the process a designer must go through to figure out how each mechanic will work and what assets will have to be created to make it work. There is some discussion of other important topics the designer must know—that is, story and dialogue structure, designing levels and maps, and determining what the interface will look like. But the main focus is on game mechanics—what they are and how they work. As an extra feature, the last chapter of the book is an extended interview with one of the leading game designers, Chris Taylor of Gas Powered Game, who shares his experiences in the industry and gives his insights about the process of designing and building games.

This book is intended for the novice who has very little technical experience but who loves games. There are no map editors or level editors for the reader to learn and no complex code examples to wade through. An adroit reader should be able to create paper prototypes of game mechanics without needing anything but pencil and paper. Think of it as a first step for anyone interested in learning what really goes into designing a complex video game (or board game, for that matter).

The term *data-driven* can apply to the kind of game discussed in this book, because all the numbers and values included in the database are used to resolve game actions. However, *data-driven game architecture* means something different and refers to how the various code modules for graphics, AI, audio, etc., work together in the game engine. To prevent any confusion, the term *data-driven* is not used here.

ACKNOWLEDGMENTS

The author would like to thank the following people for their assistance in gathering images and information for the book. First and foremost, a boatload of thanks to Thomas Skillman, Kendrick Fleck, and Ben Colgan for playing tons of games and getting many wonderful screenshots. Thanks for Chris Taylor of Gas Powered Games for granting an interview plus Bert Bingham, Kellyn Beeck, and Dionne Roselli of Gas Powered Games for their valuable help. The author would also like to thank Jay Wilbur of Epic Games, Todd Howard and Pete Hines of Bethesda Softworks, Amy Yeung of ZeniMax Media, Nao Zook and Jack Niida of NIS America, Mitzi McGilvray of TikGames, Ned Cocker of CCP Games, Eric Walter and Garth Chouteau of PopCap Games, Susana Meza Graham of Paradox Interactive, Mike Wiering of Wiering Software, Mike Sigman of Albion Sword, Ltd., Ahmed Hakeen, Vidar Rapp, and Steve Neeley for helping with the approval process in getting permission to use images from their games and products.

The author would also like to pass on a big thumbs-up to artist Ed Williamson for providing layout sketches and storyboards from the race game they worked on together. Additionally, many thanks to Thomas Wilhite, who provided technical assistance during the screen capture of images in the book.

A special thanks goes out to Dave Eberly who connected the author with A K Peters. And finally and most importantly, many thanks to Sarah Cutler and all the great folks at A K Peters for their help in turning this dream into a reality.

PART I: INTRODUCTION

CHAPTER 1

MAKING GAMES

The video game industry (lumping console, computer, and mobile games into the same category) has grown from a hobby enjoyed by a small cadre of technophiles into a multibillion-dollar form of entertainment that appeals to players across the globe. Games have matured to the point where they now challenge such traditional forms of entertainment as books, movies, recordings, and even television. Never before has there been a form of entertainment where the user gets to interact so directly with the end product, and it is this interactivity that attracts so many players to video games.

Some video games are relatively simple and can be played in just a few minutes. Some are played solitarily while others are played online with many players joining in. Others are much more complex and take days or weeks to complete. There are enough different kinds of video games that everyone can find something to amuse themselves for however long they wish to play.

What is it about video games that makes them so attractive? Depending on the type of game, there are many different payoffs for players. One player may enjoy the physical dexterity required to make a character perform a series of wild actions—jumping over barrels, dodging falling rocks, pulling a gun, and blasting away at the bad guys. Another player may enjoy the mental exercise of solving a puzzle while another fantasizes about being a famous baseball player who empties the bases with a grand-slam home run. Still others may enjoy the challenge of clawing their way to the top by becoming millionaire captains of industry or tycoons. There are many different ways that players can enjoy video games. In all cases, however, the player interacts with the game via controller or keyboard/mouse to move objects across the screen and perform various actions. This interactivity, so unlike traditional forms of passive entertainment, has helped make video games popular worldwide.

Game Play and Game Data

The actions a player performs during a game constitute the game play. Each game genre has its own set of actions, although many games share common actions, such as moving objects around on the screen. Simple games have few actions for the player to perform while complex games can have many actions. In the classic arcade game of *Pong*, for example, the players only have to move a paddle up and down the screen to intercept a moving ball and send it flying back at, and hopefully by, the other player (see Figure 1.1). In a first-person shooter, the primary focuses are on moving a character through the game world and shooting AI-controlled enemies (and sometimes other players in deathmatches). There might be several different kinds of movement—running, walking, jumping, leaning, crouching, and so on. There are also a number of different weapons the player can collect and wield during play.

As games get more complex, the actions involved also get more involved. In a role-playing game, for example, there are many activities for the player to perform—from exploring the world, to engaging in combat, to talking with non-player characters (NPCs), to buying and selling items in stores, to solving puzzles. Some simulation games let players imagine they are flying aircraft or driving racecars while others allow players to build financial empires. In such complex games, there is much for the player to do and many decisions to make. These complex games can be played repeatedly because each ending is different from previous plays thanks to the multiplicity of events happening in the game world.

Simple and Complex Designs

In all cases, whether in simple or complex games, it is the designer who has the responsibility of determining how game play works. In simple games, the designer often works directly with the programmers to decide how events occur in the game—from the speed of the ping pong ball moving across the screen, to how quickly the paddle reacts to a player's movement, to how much force is applied to the ball by the paddle upon contact, and so on. Simple games often rely on randomization to keep from becoming too predictable, and the designer has little control over the element of chance except to specify the probabilities of events occurring.

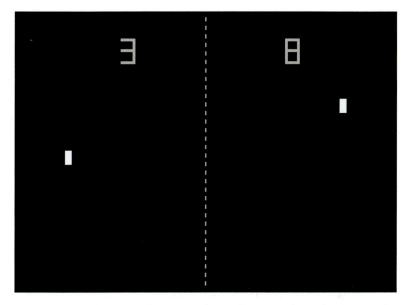

Figure 1.1. *In the game of Pong, similar to the image shown here, game play consists of simply moving a paddle up and down to hit a ball over the center net.*

In more complex games (for example, first-person shooters and real-time strategy games), the designer often needs to come up with considerable information about the game world and what is in it. For example, if there are weapons in the game, the designer has to take into account such things as the rate of fire, damage done, amount of ammunition per reload, and so on. In very complex games (for example, role-playing games and wargames), the amount of information is huge and can take a long time to balance so as to ensure that no unit is too powerful and that no one line of play always succeeds.

In a simple game, there is usually not much information—or data—for the designer to deal with and so everything is hard-coded into the game engine. Making changes to the code to improve play is usually not too difficult. In more complex games, however, where there is much more data, it is best to keep the data separate from the game engine. Doing so allows the designer to tweak the values as needed during testing without requiring that the code be recompiled so the changes are in the game and can be tested. Recompiling code takes time and keeps both programmers and designers idle during the process. Therefore, for more complex games, the data is kept separate in files that designers can access and change without requiring code to be recompiled. Once the game is ready to ship, the final data can be incorporated directly into the game engine code so crafty players can't manipulate it.

Game Data

This book focuses on designing data-heavy games and discusses the different types of data that the designer must create and maintain during production. For designers, the data falls into four major categories: charts and tables, level/map layout, scripts, and dialogue.

- *Charts and tables* refer to the lists of values and other information about objects in the game—for example, weapons, monsters, treasures, production, character generation, and so on. Tables refer specifically to the methods in which the chart data are manipulated to perform game actions—for example, combat resolution, magic attacks, buying/selling items, and so forth.

- *Level/map layout* refers to how the playfields are created in two or three dimensions and how objects are placed on them for the player to interact with.

- *Scripts* refer to the methods by which the game world states are changed, dialogues are structured, and encounters are triggered.

- *Dialogue*, of course, refers to what characters in the game world say, and it also refers to other text strings appearing during play (for example, the description of an item when the player highlights it).

Creating all this data can be a monumental task, and it is incumbent upon the design staff to keep the design documentation updated regularly so that the whole team knows it is working on the same design.

Designers and the Development Process

Depending on the company and the game in production, there might be only one designer who is responsible for creating and maintaining all data. Designing simple games is relatively fast compared to designing a complex game, for there are far fewer game elements to think up, test, and balance. More complex games usually involve a team of designers, with a senior designer overseeing the workload of junior designers and level designers. The senior designer is responsible for the overall design and play of the game, while the junior designers help out with various tasks during development. The level designers know how to use 3D modeling programs like Autodesk's 3ds Max or Maya to create the environments of the game world and also scripting languages to trigger events in the environment.

Designing a video game is certainly not a solitary task. Designers work closely with other team members—programmers, artists, audio engineers, and management—during the whole process. Actually, all team members should be encouraged to come up with ideas to make the design better. A good designer is willing to listen to what other people suggest and select those suggestions that improve game play. There does come a time, however, when changes to the design have to end so that the game can be completed on schedule. But any remaining good ideas can be written down and then incorporated into add-ons or sequels.

Game Development Cycle: Preproduction Phase

Each company has its own method for coming up with a game design and implementing it, but there are generally three phases in game production. The first phase is preproduction, where game ideas are evaluated until one stands out. The idea for a game can come from many places within the company, depending on how the creative process is handled, and if the design involves a license, it is likely that marketing will want to be involved to make sure the design stays within the parameters of what the licensor demands. In many cases, the originator creates a one- or two-page paper called a *pitch paper* and presents it to the design staff and management.

Once a concept has been accepted, a designer might develop it by writing a *game proposal*, a longer document describing the game world and major game play elements. It usually includes a marketing section that points out competing products and explains why the new game will successfully compete in the market. The designer receives feedback from artists and programmers during the process of writing up the game proposal to make sure the final product can be done as presented.

A developer or publisher might evaluate a number of game proposals before deciding on one that everyone thinks will succeed. Once the game idea has received the green light, the designer (perhaps with help from other designers) writes up a *game design document* that describes in detail how the game works and what the game world looks like. At this point, a senior programmer and several sketch artists might assist in the process of creating the final document. By the time the design document is complete, the team should have a very good idea of what they plan to build. The documentation process is particularly useful for complex games that include a lot of data, and its creation allows the designers and other teams to think through what will be involved in turning the idea into a final commercial product.

Some companies do not go through a documentation process and instead use an iterative design process. For example, a developer planning to create a first-person shooter (FPS) game—like *Doom*—might decide to create a prototype of the game rather than spend time documenting his or her ideas. The basic game play of FPS games is pretty well defined, and the main challenge is coming up with new and interesting weapons, enemies, and game worlds. The company might build a number of prototypes to experiment with different fictional genres before settling on one concept to pitch to management or to a publisher. These prototypes are played by focus groups and their feedback helps the designers and management understand which ones are most appealing from a game play and commercial perspective.

Once management approves a game design, either at the end of the documentation process or after agreeing on a prototype, the team starts to assemble and more programmers and artists are added. Before barging ahead with production, however, the teams take time to analyze the design objectives through a technical review.

Technical Review

Another important part in the preproduction process is for other teams to look at the overall design to see what work is expected of them during development. The programming team often creates a *technical design document* in which they analyze the requirements for the game engine and figure out the architecture for making the code modules interact with one another. They also decide what tools they will have to create for various teams working on the project. Likewise, the art team might create their own *art design document* (sometimes called the art bible) in which they not only determine what objects and characters in the game world will look like but also agree on the technical requirements for creating the art assets. Although audio is often worked on later during development, the audio team lead should look at the design document and start creating their own *audio design document*—a list of sound effects, voiceovers, and possible musical themes for the game. Finally, the lead tester (also known as Quality Assurance) should also look at the design document to determine what will need to be tested and then begin writing a *test suite* for checking the product as the components come together.

After all the teams have worked on the project, the team leaders meet with the producer and management to nail down the final production schedule and budget. They determine when new hires should be made and when additional hardware and software is needed. The final schedule is broken down into a series of milestones. The team should also make sure to run the production schedule past marketing so they can point out where working demos and screenshots of the product are required.

The final step in preproduction is often the creation of a working interactive prototype of the game. Not only can it demonstrate to management how the game will play and what the game world will look like, it also lets the design team test some of the mechanics before full production begins. In a very complex game such as a role-playing game, having a prototype of the combat system is a huge help in determining how the values assigned to characters and objects interact. The designers can then tweak the game mechanisms if they detect a problem with the original design. It is far better to make changes as early as possible in the production cycle rather than later when many assets have been created since changes often require extensive modifications to code, art, and audio.

Game Development Cycle: Production Phase

Once the whole production team knows what they want to build and how they plan to create it, they can start work on the real assets that will be used in the game. The artists start building the 2D sprites or 3D models that will be used for characters, objects, and environments (Figure 1.2). The programmers begin writing the code for the game engine. The designers continue refining the data in the game and work with the level builders to determine how the environments will be laid out and what they will contain. As the play elements come together, they are incorporated into

Figure 1.2. *Once sketches for creatures are approved, the models are created in a 3D graphics program; for example, this model of an alligator was created by 3D artist Vidar Rapp. The creature is then rigged, animated, and added to the game.*

the game to be tested and changed as necessary. Based on the feedback they receive, the designers may decide to make significant changes to the design, with the game design document being updated to reflect any changes.

Eventually, the game reaches a point where it can be played from start to finish, even in a very rough form. This point is referred to as the *alpha build*. By this time, the design should be solid with very few changes being needed to the basic design. The teams continue pumping out art and code assets for the final version, and the final audio assets are created and incorporated into the product as well. Meanwhile, testers look for any problems in the game so they can be fixed.

When all assets have been added to the game and the team is down to final polishing and debugging, the game reaches *beta build*. There should be no more design changes at this time and only bug fixes should be allowed. The final product is then shown to the publisher for any final changes they might demand. The final step is when the final version of the game—called the *gold version*—is sent out for manufacturing.

Production is the longest part of game development. It can take several years to complete the code and turn out all the assets that appear in the final product. Many developers and publishers add additional milestones during this phase so they can make sure the game development remains on target. Third-party developers who are independent of the publishers get paid for meeting their milestones, and so there is often a period where everyone has to put in a lot of extra time and effort to get the next build ready—a period known as *crunch* time.

Game Development Cycle: Post-Production Phase

The post-production phase overlaps the later stages of the production phase and involves the marketing and distribution of the final game. The designers may be tasked with writing a first draft of the manual to explain all the controls and features in the game. The final version of the manual is usually written by a professional writer that the marketing departments hires. The marketing department works up a marketing campaign for the product, deciding where to advertise and what additional materials will be needed—e.g., a demo version or strategy guide. Otherwise, the development team is not much involved with the creation of the CD/DVD disks that contain the game, with the package assembly, or with the distribution of the final product to retailers.

The team might be involved with promotional materials after the game ships—for example, web chats and meeting players at trade shows and conventions. The team might also be required to create a downloadable patch if significant bugs slipped into the final shipped version. Even before the final version is released to manufacturing, most of the team is reassigned to other projects. Some might already be at work in preproduction on a new title.

The Designer's Role in Game Development

The senior designer on a game helps define what the team will build. He or she then becomes the keeper of the flame to guarantee that the final product turns out as envisioned and is fun to play. Many mistakenly think that the designer's primary responsibility is coming up with the story for a game, but that is only one part of the job. Many game genres (adventure games, first-person and third-person shooters and, in particular, role-playing games) do demand a central story to link together the parts. Developing a full-length story with interesting characters, settings, enemies, and items is challenging and takes considerable time to work out all the details.

Many game genres, however, have no central story. There are no stories in most sports games, simulation games, puzzle games, or arcade games. If story elements do appear in these types of games, they are only tangential to the central play experience. Nevertheless, there is considerable work for the designer to figure out how all the play elements will hang together as a cohesive whole. It can take just as long to develop the game play elements for a non-story game as it does the central narrative for a huge role-playing game.

Ideating and Pitching Concepts

One of the most important—and enjoyable—tasks for a designer is thinking up an idea for a game and then expanding on it to determine what the player does that is fun. While some designers prefer to come up with their ideas in solitude, many prefer to work with others. Sitting in a bull session with everyone shouting out ideas while the designer steers the discussion and jots down ideas on a whiteboard is exhilarating. Afterwards, the designer writes down notes about the suggestions and then circulates them to the participants for their comments. The interplay of ideas can lead to some interesting and creative suggestions.

The designer then has to take all the ideas and come up with a concrete central concept for the game. Many companies use a process where anyone can come up with the original idea and write it down in a short document, the pitch paper, to present to management and the creative staff. The pitch paper is meant to illustrate the essence of the game and explain why it would be new and fun to play. It should make an indelible impression on the reader and therefore should be written as creatively as possible. It should define the game genre, describe the fictional setting (if necessary), and then talk about one or two of the most exciting aspects of game play. It is intended as a sales tool to get management (especially marketing and sales) interested in producing the title. Ideally, the central concept for the game should be encapsulated in a sentence of 20 words or less in the first paragraph. This sentence is your *high concept* for the game and can be a useful tool for the marketing department to sell the concept of the game.

If management decides an idea is good, they then have a designer flesh it out in more detail in a game proposal. Good game ideas are cheap and many ideas are pitched to management but then tossed aside. For every ten ideas presented, only one or two will be deemed worthy of more work.

Game Proposals

A game proposal elaborates on the pitch concept and describes in some detail the major game play features. It is still a relatively short document and should not go into too much detail on any one feature. The idea is to excite management about how the game will be played and what the game world will be like, and it should show that the concept is worth further development. A designer often works with a sketch artist to come up with ideas for characters, interesting

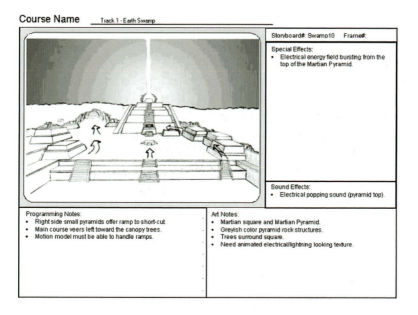

Figure 1.3. *During preproduction, the art staff sometimes creates storyboards to define how action sequences work or to visualize the layout of a level. This storyboard was created by artist Ed Williamson, who worked with the author of this book on a racing game. See Figure 11.4 on page 307 in Chapter 11 for the layout of the proposed racetrack.*

world locations, and objects, but actual in-depth design is not appropriate at this stage. Again, the proposal works as a marketing tool to sell the concept, and one of the most important features is a marketing analysis in which the designer, in conjunction with marketing, demonstrates that the new game will either fill an existing hole in the market or can successfully compete against similar products. In total, the proposal might run about 6–10 pages. If it is too long, management probably won't study it, and if it is too short, it won't cover all the fun elements in sufficient detail.

It takes a designer about a month or two to flesh out a game proposal before showing it to management. Aside from help by concept artists, the designer usually works alone on the document. Sometimes a series of storyboards are helpful tools allowing management and marketing to visualize the game action or the world setting (see Figure 1.3). Asking the company's technical director for advice on the feasibility of the concept is highly recommended.

Again, if management thinks the idea is worth pursuing, they will request the designer expand the concept as a full game design document. However, for every five or six game proposals, only one will likely be given the green light for further development.

Game Design Document

The final step of the design process is the game design document. It can be a very large document since the designer tries to explain in extreme detail how the game play elements interact and what the game world and characters look like. At first, the document can feel highly conjectural because the designer won't know how things actually behave in the world until a prototype is created. Thus, the design document is a "living" thing that grows and evolves over time.

Each company has its own approach to structuring the document. Here is a structure the author has used repeatedly over the years. The idea is to break the piece into sizeable chunks so the rest of the team doesn't have to absorb the whole document at once. They can focus primarily on their areas of interest and then read about other parts of the game if they so wish.

- *Introduction*. Written specifically for management. It starts off explaining the high concept of the game (often drawn directly from the game proposal) and gives an example of play from the game so the reader can visualize what is happening. It also includes the basic information about the game genre, fictional world (if necessary), target platform and audience, and a very rough estimate of budget and schedule. This section should be short, about 4–6 pages maximum.

- *Game Mechanics*. Aimed specifically at the programming team. Each element of game play is discussed in detail, with appropriate charts and tables as necessary. In addition to explaining how everything works—movement, combat, resource management, magic, etc.—it also includes the designer's suggestions for user interfaces for each screen and descriptions of all the control functions. By the end of this section, the programmers should have a very good idea of what is required for the game engine and what they will need to test first to get the design working as imagined.

- *Game Graphics*. Aimed specifically at the art team. The designer tries to include all the materials the artists will have to make—characters, environments, and items. There should be a physical description of each character, the actions the character can perform (referring to the game mechanics section for more detail), and any special visual effects required. The environment and items are also described in detail. Note that the initial ideas for world objects can change during development, but it is important to provide a starting place for the artists and then update the document over time as changes are made and the final art assets are completed. By the end of this section, the art team should have a good idea of what they will have to create.

- *Appendices*. In this section, everything else that hasn't been described is dumped. It is a good place to include audio requirements for the game, plus all the charts, tables, user interface screen schematics, and anything else the designers might come up with. As the game enters development, this section can become the largest one as other elements are added—maps of finished levels, dialogue, flow charts, storyboards, and more.

The game design document goes through two stages during preproduction and development. The first stage is the concept version of the game design document where the elements of the game play and art requirements are specified, as described above. The designer might have to revise the concept document many times until management is satisfied that all details are explained sufficiently. The second stage is the production version (called the "Bible" since it acts as a reference tool for everyone working on the project), which is used to track changes to the original design throughout the Production Phase. This version includes both frequent updates of changes made to the original design and also some materials created during the Production Phase—for example, maps of the final levels, dialogue, scripts created with a scripting language, bug report updates, and even directory listings for all assets in the game. The production version of the game design document can be hundreds of pages long by the time the game is finished. It can prove useful later as an invaluable resource for the team (or for an outside developer) tasked with making add-on modules or a sequel.

Prototyping

With complex games, a designer often needs to experiment with game play elements before settling on those to be used. One way to experiment is to create some simple prototypes, both paper and electronic. A prototype is an abstraction of a game system and gives the designer feedback on how well the system works. For example, the designer of a role-playing game might have an idea for an unusual combat system, and creating a simple paper prototype can be used to test the system and modifying how it works before any other teams get involved. A paper prototype can be used to try out systems for combat resolution, resource management, technology tree evolution, and puzzle solutions. They are also very useful for fleshing out the structure for levels and determining where things will be placed in the playfield. The designer doesn't need to involve other employees working on other projects except to involve them in testing and getting feedback about how well the system works.

As useful as a paper prototype can be, any final design decisions will not likely be made until the game engine is up and running. What looks fine on paper can change radically once assets become available and the engine is working as expected. If possible, a designer should ask for an interactive prototype in electronic form as part of technical review. The prototype can still be very simple, using an existing game engine and art (see Figure 1.4). Once the game appears on the screen, even in a rudimentary form, it can look and feel quite different than what the designer had in mind. The scale of objects might need to change, forcing the designer to rebalance the values used to resolve game actions. If there is going to be a multiplayer

Figure 1.4. *This is an interactive prototype for MEDS Games' first-person shooter Zombie Swarm. The prototype lets the team check the scale of objects on the playfield as well as testing simple game play.*

version of the game, having an electronic version for early testing can prove to be a godsend. By working with a programmer and artist or two, the designer can have a very useful tool to test multiple versions of the game at a minimal cost.

The whole idea of using prototypes is to nail down how things will work before other teams start buildings the final assets for the game. There is nothing worse for artists than to invest a large amount of time in art assets only to find out that they don't look right once they appear in the game. Likewise, programmers hate rewriting code because the designers keep changing their minds. Simple prototypes can help designers determine and balance the values assigned to game objects and guarantee that game mechanics work as described in the documentation.

Asset Creation

Once the whole team is ready to work on the game, the design team either joins in creating the assets or oversees the work of other team members. Depending on the type of game being developed, the tools used to make the assets might be simple enough for designers to use, or they can be so complex that only skilled team members can use them confidently and with ease. Sometimes, companies will build tools like map editors and scripting languages for the designers to use. In this case, the designers can build assets directly and test and balance them while testers send in their suggestions and bug reports. At other times, companies prefer not to spend the time building tools for the designers and rely on commercial products. Most designers, for example, aren't adept with complex 3D modeling applications such as Autodesk's 3ds Max or Maya, and so they would have difficulty building environments with these applications. Instead, the work of creating environments is left to artists who work with the designers to determine the layouts of the levels. The paper prototypes of the levels can help the artists visualize what the designers have in mind and thus make level creation much quicker.

The designers also work with the programming and art teams to make sure that the various game systems work as planned and that the characters move and act as envisioned. The designers massage the data in the charts as necessary, revising values and modifying attributes assigned to objects until the game system is balanced and complete. Meanwhile, they work with artists and programmers on the graphic user interface so that players will understand at a glance all the information presented on each screen, and they also help to solidify the control scheme until it feels intuitively obvious to players.

Testing and Debugging

One of the most important jobs for a designer is continually testing the game to make sure that the values are balanced and that there are no holes in logic or storytelling. As levels are finished, they are given to testers to check over both for play value and for problems in the game elements. The design team constantly has to tweak the values for game objects until they are at a point where both novice and veteran players enjoy the experience. As development winds down, the designers also have to take care that any changes made during later stages of production don't unbalance assets that have been completed earlier.

It is always a good idea to get fresh eyes to look at the product starting at alpha stage and later. There is a temptation to make finished levels more difficult as testers who are overly acquainted with them complain that they aren't hard enough. It is important to get a stream of new players looking at the game in order to evaluate the orchestration of action throughout the whole product.

As the game reaches beta, some of the designers might be pulled off to start work on the next project. The last round of debugging is devoted to fixing problems with the code and the final art, and usually designers are no longer needed at this point (unless there are problems with the database or loose story threads that need to be tied up). The end of a project usually means a well-deserved vacation for the designers, so they can recharge their creative batteries for the next project. Then they begin the process all over again—coming up with ideas, pitching them to management, and documenting game play.

Conclusion

This chapter gives an overview of what designers do during the production cycle to get a game from original concept to final shipped product. Coming up with a central story is only part of the design process, and the real focus should be on creating interesting game play elements. It is vitally important that designers test their assumptions on very complex games by using both paper and simple interactive prototypes. Using a paper prototype is a great help in developing the values and statistics that appear in the initial game design documentation, and the interactive prototype lets the team see what the game looks like on the screen. Once the game is in production, the designers work with artists and programmers to build playfields, filling the game world with interesting places to visit, exciting encounters, and valuable items to take or manipulate. Throughout the development process, the design team tweaks values and attributes and makes changes to game play, and these changes should be included in the game design document on a regular basis. As the team grows larger and new members come on board, it helps to have a source that they can go to for information about the game that is as up-to-date as possible.

The remainder of this book looks more closely at the actual process of designing complex, data-heavy games. In the next chapter the differences between game play and game mechanics are discussed. While being able to spin a good yarn is undoubtedly important, understanding the fundamental elements that make up game play is central to becoming a successful designer.

Exercises

1. Come up with a list of 20 games you've played and enjoyed recently, and determine if they fall into the category of simple or complex games. Make sure you have at least five complex games on your list.

2. Of the complex games from Exercise 1, try to determine what information would go into the database vs. what would be hard-coded by the programming team. Select at least five games from your list.

3. Work up an idea for a complex game you would like to design completely. The game should be a wargame, role-playing game, real-time strategy game or other complex game. Try to summarize the concept of the game and game play in a sentence of 20 words or less—your *high concept* for the game.

4. Once you have your high concept, create a two-page pitch paper using the high concept as the first sentence of the first paragraph. The pitch paper should define the most enjoyable game play elements of the game. Define what the players will do that is fun and makes the game exciting. Do not simply write the story of the game.

5. Do a marketing analysis for your game concept. Check for other games currently on the shelf or about to come out that are in the same genre as yours.

    a. Do some research on the Internet to see how much revenue these types of games have generated.

    b. How popular is the game genre you selected? What makes it so popular?

    c. What would be the best game platforms for it to appear on?

6. Expand your pitch paper into a game proposal of at least 8 pages.

    a. Give a short synopsis of the plot or history in your game (if it has one) or give an explanation of why the topic is exciting.

    b. Then give a summary of the main game play elements without going into too much detail.

    c. Finally, include your marketing analysis.

7. Create the outline for a game design document based on your game concept using the guidelines from this chapter. You will need an introductory section, a section on game mechanics, a section on art requirements, and appendices. Don't worry about filling in the details yet, although you may want to make notes about what you plan to discuss in each section.

8. Think about what you will need to create a simple paper prototype for your game.

   a. Make a list of the materials you will need – for example, hex maps, counters, index cards, play money and the like.

   b. Create an outline of how you plan to make the prototype.

Note the areas where you may need to do some research before you can begin building the prototype.

CHAPTER 2

GAME PLAY AND GAME MECHANICS

In the last chapter there was frequent mention of "game play" and "game mechanics," but there was no definition of what those terms mean. In this chapter, the focus is on the elements that make up game play and how the designer needs to define those elements in detail in the game documentation.

Too often, a novice designer spends more time in design documents on story development rather than on how things will actually work in the game world. How the elements of game play hang together is assumed instead of discussed. So, the novice designer might simply mention in passing that there is a combat system without explaining exactly how it works. This approach leaves the burden of actual design to the programming staff, and the final product may wind up completely different from what the designer had in mind.

On the other hand, experienced designers can get so wrapped up in the minutia of how things work they wind up handcuffing the programming team, who may have some very good ideas on how things should work in the game. An initial game design document that is too detailed can be tiresome to read, and much of its contents is likely to change during production. As work continues on the project, the design document can and should be modified to accommodate changes to actual game play.

Game Play and the "Fun Factor"

When starting work on a game, the most important question the designer should ask is: What will the player do during the game that is "fun"? Obviously, customers buy a game because they feel it will keep them busy and make them happy for a time. There are actions the player performs that are fun, and these are the actions the player wants to do most often. Other actions are not as much fun, but they are necessary as precursors to the fun actions. Some of the "fun" actions in games are:

- Exploring unknown areas.
- Resolving combat situations.
- Finding treasures.
- Building things.
- Destroying things.
- Interacting with characters in the game world.
- Living through a story.
- Solving puzzles.
- Manipulating resources.
- Piloting aircraft.
- Driving fast-moving cars.
- Playing a sport.

The other actions that are less fun are often needed to prepare for a fun action. The player is willing to perform these actions in anticipation that they will lead to later, more interesting, more enjoyable actions. Some of these less interesting actions include:

- Inventory management.
- Buying and selling game objects.
- Bookkeeping.
- Retracing one's steps through previously explored areas.
- Managing a sports team with trades and salary negotiations.
- Reloading a saved game.
- Breaking out the manual to look for an obscure control input.

The designer, of course, wants to maximize the fun factor time and minimize the drudgery for players. It is not possible to make everything fun all the time. Many complex games have a steep learning curve where players have to learn all the interactions in the game and the control scheme for each one. In such cases, it is often best to teach players a few lessons at a time in a tutorial system that extends over several hours of play.

Assigning Percentages to Game Play

When mulling over a design concept, the designer should consider how much time the player will devote to the various play elements. One approach is to assign percentages to the amount of time a player is expected to spend in each section of the game. For example, a typical role-playing game has these play elements:

- Combat.
- Exploration.
- Interacting with non-player characters (NPCs).
- Storytelling.
- Puzzle-solving.
- Inventory management.
- Buying/selling game objects.

At first glance, the designer might decide that combat is the most important element in the game and assign it the highest percentage of play time. It can be difficult to assign values to all the play actions, but here is what the breakdown for a role-playing game (RPG) might look like:

- Exploration—60%.
- Combat—15%.
- Interacting with non-player characters (NPCs)—10%.
- Puzzle-solving—5%.
- Storytelling—5%.
- Inventory management—3%.
- Buying/selling game objects—2%.

It might seem surprising that combat is not higher, but if you study the play elements in an RPG, you will quickly find that most of your time is spent traveling across large areas or exploring cities. If you want to bump up the percentage devoted to combat to 25%, you'll have to reduce the amount of time exploring, get rid of the puzzles, or limit the storytelling. The result could be a "dungeon crawl" (also called a "hack-and-slash") in which there are many more enemies to engage in combat and the maps are typically much smaller in size. Indeed, a designer

Role-playing

Movement
Combat
Character generation
Experience levels
Magic/technology
Character interactions
Inventory management

Wargames

Movement
Combat
Strategy and tactics
Supply
Leadership
Production (reinforcements)

Real-time Strategy

Movement
Combat
Resource management
Production (reinforcements)
Technology

Simulation

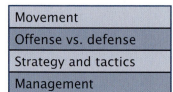

Movement
Combat
Resource management
Production

Sports

Movement
Offense vs. defense
Strategy and tactics
Management

Shooters

Movement
Combat
Puzzles
Resource management

Table 2.1. *Play elements listed by game genre.*

might find that too much combat is bad because it becomes repetitive and predictable.

Because exploration is so important in an RPG (and in other story-based games), it is important to make the world large so monster encounters, treasures, NPC encounters, and urban centers can be sprinkled throughout each world area. There are usually different lands to visit with different environments and therefore different kinds of creatures and beings to bump into. Of course, having very large maps can lead to problems, too, since the player may have to visit each area multiple times. Trekking long distances to revisit places you've already explored gets dull, and so adding a mechanism for quick long-distance travel keeps the game from dragging.

Once the designer is happy with the percentages assigned to game play elements, he or she can structure the game design document to describe the most important elements first and in most detail. The production team will then be able to tell which elements they should focus on first.

Play Elements for Game Genres

Complex games are composed of many different game play elements and it can take time to describe them all in the documentation. The mechanics of each element will be analyzed in more detail in later chapters, but see Table 2.1 for the most important play elements by game genre. For example, in CCP's *Eve Online* role-playing game (see Figure 2.1) the player not only explores planets as a character but can turn into a

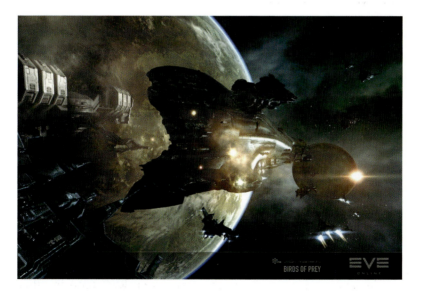

Figure 2.1. *One of the play elements in CCP Games'* Eve Online, *a massively multiplayer online role-playing game found online, is the ability to become a spaceship, in this case a Bird of Prey, and to explore the universe.*

spaceship to explore the galaxy itself so movement would be one of its major game elements.

As you can see, some play elements can be found in several genres. Movement, for example, is found in most games—whether it be moving a token around a game board or marching armies into battles. However, the importance of game elements changes from one game type to another. Movement, for example, might be very complex in a wargame but highly abstracted in a simulation game.

What Is Not Game Play

It is important for designers to understand what is not central to game play. While having a unique look to the game's graphics is important to the commercial success of the product, the graphics are not game play. For a long time, there seemed to be an overwhelming desire among developers and publishers to make the 3D graphics in games look almost photorealistic, particularly as the central processing units and video cards grew ever more powerful. But there is a limitation as to how realistic graphics can be because nature is so chaotic as to be almost impossible to mirror exactly in a game. The blink rate and shifting expressions of 3D characters, the movement of small objects fluttering in the wind, the subtle shading of reflected light are all very expensive to model realistically in a video game. Indeed, there is a hypothesis called the "uncanny valley" in the field of robotics that applies to video game graphics as well. As the graphics for video games becomes more realistic, the empathy of the player for the characters increases, but there is a point where the player gets put off by the mechanical look of the characters. Trying to incorporate all the tics and muscle movements of a talking human face is almost impossible because the game engine still has to deal with physics, AI, and other important functions. No matter how good the graphics of a game look, they are not what constitute game play and keep the player coming back for more.

Storytelling is often not game play. If the player initiates conversations with NPCs in a game, game play is involved as long as there is some actual interaction between the NPCs and player. Long cinematic scenes that give the background of the story but don't require the player to interact is not game play, no matter how compelling the narration. There have been unsuccessful attempts to have completely cinematic games where the player does almost nothing except trigger the next cinema section. Watching a movie is passive, and games are active…interactive. It does little good for the designers to create a massive, highly convoluted plot line for a game—a *War and Peace* for the Wii—when players are likely to forget some of the plot elements and not want to retrigger the long cinematic sequences to fill in the gaps.

Likewise, the audio—music, sounds effects, and voiceovers—in a game isn't game play, although the audio certainly enhances the ambience of the world and provides great feedback. If the game were somehow about making audio—for example, composing music— then game play would be involved. The audio can be a reward for achieving some goal, but it would then force the player to be passive instead of interactive.

The elements mentioned above are vitally important to good games, but they are not what the player *does* that is fun. The designers have to cover the graphics, audio, and story in the game design document, but they also have to talk in detail about the actions the player performs—the game play.

Mechanics of Game Play

Simply describing game play in general does little to help the programming team understand what they will have to do to make it work. If the designer were simply to say in the design document "the player uses different vehicles (car, motorcycle, truck, tank, etc.) to elude the police" without going into any explanation, the programming team might wind up building a racing game instead of a simpler *Grand Theft Auto* driving scheme that the designer had in mind. It is up to the designer to explain in detail how driving is to occur and to suggest screen schematics and control inputs.

In the above example, the designer might better describe driving thusly:

> *The players drives three types of vehicles: light (motorcycles), medium (cars), and heavy (trucks and tanks). Light vehicles are very fast and reach top speed quickly, they can enter tight spaces other vehicles can't enter, they can hold one driver and one passenger, but they are more prone to tipping over and don't offer much protection during combat. Medium vehicles are slower to accelerate but can reach fairly high speeds, they must stick to roads and alleys, they can hold one driver and three passengers, and they offer decent protection if hit. Heavy*

Vehicle Chart

Vehicle Type			
	Light	*Medium*	*Heavy*
Driver	1	1	1
Passengers	1	3	6
Acceleration	Fast	Moderate	Slow
Top Speed	120 mph	90 mph	50 mph
Accident Damage	Heavy	Moderate	Minimal
Surface Movement			
Narrow spaces	Yes	No	No
Alleys	Yes	Yes	No
Roads	Yes	Yes	Yes
Open spaces	No	No	Yes

Table 2.2. *This is what an initial Vehicle Chart might look like, giving information about the number of passengers, the speed, movement restrictions, and the amount of damage from accidents.*

vehicles are slow to accelerate and can't match light and medium vehicles for speed, they must stick to roads, alleys, and open spaces, they can hold one driver and up to six passengers, and they take minimal to no damage from an accident.

Note that in this description, vehicles are grouped together into classes (light, medium, and heavy) and the descriptions of game play use relative values (Table 2.2). The final values won't be determined until there is an interactive prototype available to test the different vehicle types. Note that the information in the paragraph could be made more evident with a chart, which would make the same point with less verbiage. However, some description to point out important features is helpful because an endless sea of charts can become as meaningless as endless text.

In the documentation, the designer would also include schematics for what the player sees when driving the different vehicles and also what control inputs are used to move, steer, and stop the vehicle.

Modeling Reality

Some games, especially simulation games, attempt to model reality instead of a fantasy world. On the one hand, it can be easier to design such a simulation because it isn't necessary to create a fantastic world populated with fabulous creatures and extraordinary technology or magic. On the other hand, trying to create a simulation that feels close to the real world while not overwhelming the player with too much detail presents its own challenge. For example, a real cockpit on an airplane is filled with dials and gauges that are all important in keeping the vehicle airborne and for taking off and landing safely. However, to present all these instruments to players and expect them to absorb their functionality in just a few minutes is unreasonable. So, only a handful of the most important instruments are included in a flight simulation, making it easier for players to grasp the controls and what they must do to fly the plane. If combat is involved, then there are even more controls to worry about since the player must keep the plane from crashing while tracking and attacking the enemy.

Games are abstractions of reality. Even the most realistic game can't include every element of the real world lest the player spend so much time in minutia that the fun elements of play get lost in the overload. Much of game design is about removing the extraneous elements to focus on those that are truly most important and enjoyable. For example, in the board game *Monopoly*, game play is about acquiring properties and developing them, eventually taking over the whole board and driving the other players into bankruptcy. The most important game play is acquiring the deeds for properties and trying to acquire all properties of the same color or type. Building houses and hotels is a secondary play element and is highly abstracted. Charles B. Darrow, inventor of the game, could have included rules for slowly building up the houses floor by floor and then bulldozing the property to convert the residential areas into commercial zones for hotels. But those rules would have slowed the game even more and made it less popular, even though it was closer to reality. He decided to abstract the whole construction aspect of real estate in favor of acquisition and domination.

When working on the initial concept, the designer should flesh it out as much as possible. Using prototypes to test game play helps the designer select which elements to include in the final game and which ones to cut. It is better to over-design early on and trim back features during production than to realize that there is not enough activity in the game and have to add more substance late in production. Making changes late in alpha is not only very expensive, but it can cause problems with assets that have already been built.

The Fudge Factor

Because games don't try to mimic real life accurately, the designer can add in a certain *fudge factor* to make actions in a game more exciting than they would be in life. Characters and vehicles can move and maneuver more quickly than they do in real life. Combat is resolved rapidly without the tedium of drawn-out firefights. Resources appear when needed. The designer can act like a magician to make things happen outside the realm of reality to keep the game moving along and be fun.

For example, a major feature of role-playing games is the growth of the player's abilities over time. The player gets stronger, can move faster, and otherwise becomes more and more superhuman. In real life, continuous exercise will improve a person's body, but there is a limit to how much the person can do. In games, this limitation can be ignored. So, characters become demigods able to carry multiple weapons, tons of ammo, and limitless health potions. As long as players are willing to suspend their disbelief, they will accept the conventions of the game world. If designers were forced to keep within the limits of the real world, the player's inventory would be far emptier and the game would likely be less fun.

The designer has to be careful about using a fudge factor when working with enemy units because players might notice that they are being given help by the computer—for example, a sentry being able to detect the player while his or her back is turned or enemies always finding the fastest path toward the player's units—and therefore they feel the game is cheating. However, the players will probably never notice that the computer is cheating for them too, because they has bought into the abstraction of reality in the game.

Conclusion

When approaching a new game, designers have to think about what players will do during play that is fun and then figure out how those "fun" game actions, or mechanics, will work. It is not enough to simply be vague about game play—for example, saying "the party members can fight with swords and bows as well as magic spells during combat." The designers have to explain the workings of melee combat (with hand weapons), ranged combat (with bows), and magic combat in enough detail so that the programmers can create the code that enables these actions. But the designer should not try to manacle the programmers by being too specific early in the design process until some of the design choices have been tested in prototypes. As the game takes form, the game mechanics become clearer and the documentation should be continuously updated to reflect the latest changes.

In this chapter, the focus was on the elements that make up game play and the underlying mechanics of these play elements. These mechanics will be examined in more detail in later chapters, but for now it's important to understand how math is used in game design. A good designer needs a solid understanding of basic math and logic, because most of the data used in games is mathematical.

Exercises

1. Play at least three different kinds of complex games (for example, role-playing, real-time strategy, first-person shooter and so on) and write up your own list of the "fun" elements in those games.

   a. Were similar fun elements found in different kinds of games (for example, moving or combat).

   b. If there were basic similarities how did they differ from one another genre to the next?

   c. Write up your conclusions in a short document.

2. List all the game play elements for the game you want to design based on the chapter 1 exercises. Come up with initial estimate of percentages of time a player is expected to spend on each game play element.

3. Play at least three complex computer of video games in the same category as the one you plan to design.

   a. Try to time yourself while playing to see how much actual time you spend in each game play mechanic.

        b. Compare these results with the percentages you came up with from Exercise 2.

4. Now list the elements you noticed while playing the three complex games that you think were not central to game play.

        a. How important were these elements to each game?

        b. Could you have played and enjoyed each game without these elements?

5. Write up your own description for a game play mechanic from each of the three complex games you played. The description can be one or two paragraphs per mechanic, but try to capture the essence of each mechanic in your description.

6. Analyze how closely the three complex games you played attempted to model reality. Write up a short description of each game on what game play elements felt "realistic" vs. those elements that were abstracted or completely ignored.

7. Looking at three of the games you played as exercises in this chapter, discuss which ones had the largest "fudge" factors.

        a. How was reality "abstracted" to make the game more fun?

        b. What real-world actions did they leave out completely?

        c. Discuss your findings with others to see what fudge factors they noticed in the games they played.

8. Make notes in your Game Design Document outline about which game play elements you want to feel "realistic" and those you think can be "fudged" to make them more fun.

CHAPTER 3

MATH AND LOGIC IN GAMES

Fortunately, the math used in game design is relatively simple: primarily addition and subtraction with occasional multiplication. The math used by programmers, however, is much more complex and involves calculus, analytic geometry, quaternions, and other advanced subjects. Even though a designer doesn't need to be proficient in advanced math subjects, it does help to have a basic understanding of them in order to converse knowingly with the programming team during production. It is also important to have a good sense of logic, especially Boolean logic, which is used in scripting languages to change conditions on the playfield during play.

Probability and Statistics

One branch of mathematics a designer would be wise to study is probability and statistics. Many game functions involve some kind of random number generation, and a designer should understand the basics of probability—how likely it is that a given result will happen. In some games where multiple random outcomes may result from one game mechanic—for example, determining a critical hit in a role-playing game—understanding the probabilities for possible results is important to successfully balancing the game.

Statistics, which can be used to analyze results after they happen, is also an important design tool for balancing game play. If testing reports that a critical hit against enemies happens multiple times per combat encounter, then the probability for a critical hit is likely to be too high. During the initial design process a designer can use a paper prototype to test some of the more important game mechanics to see if they are within the boundaries he or she imagined. Playing with the numbers early on in the process can save considerable work during testing and debugging.

One drawback in taking a class in probability and statistics is that it usually assumes the student already has a basic understanding of calculus, which is used to find many solutions. However, there are online websites that can offer some basic understanding of probability without getting into too much detail.

Coin Flipping

The simplest probability is the flip of a coin, where there are only two possible results (ignoring the probability of the coin landing on its edge)—heads or tails. There is a 50% chance of either result with a flip. If the coin is flipped twice, there is still a 50% chance that the result will be heads or tails. However, to see how often either two heads or two tails come up, a simple chart can be created with the possible results (see Table 3.1)

There is a 25% chance for any of these results. However, the likelihood of a coin coming up twice either heads or tails is only half that of getting one heads and one tails. That is, there is a 50% chance of tossing a heads and tails and only a 25% chance of tossing either two heads or two tails.

As a coin is flipped more often, it becomes less and less likely to get all heads or all tails. With three flips, there are eight possible results, and there is a two-in-eight chance (25%) to get all heads or all tails, and a 75% chance to get a mixed result. Likewise, with four flips, there are sixteen possible results, and there is a two-in-sixteen chance (12.5%) to get all heads or all tails, and an 87.5% chance to get a mixed result. Each time an extra flip is added, the results are to

First Toss	Second Toss
Heads	Heads
Heads	Tails
Tails	Heads
Tails	Tails

Table 3.1. *Results for two coin flips.*

the next power of two: 1 flip = 2^1 (2 results), 2 flips = 2^2 (2×2 or 4 results), 3 flips = 2^3 ($2 \times 2 \times 2$ or 8 results), 4 flips = 2^4 ($2 \times 2 \times 2 \times 2$ or 16 results), and so on.

When there are only two possible outcomes, the results are relatively easy to figure out in one's head. Most games do not have mechanics based on only two possible outcomes because the mechanics would quickly become boring. You can only engage in a game of flipping a coin for so long before wanting things to become more interesting (e.g., adding gambling as a mechanic).

"Coin Flipping" in Games

Although modern games seldom use Heads-or-Tails to resolve actions because the number of outcomes is so limited, there are games from ancient cultures that did use such an approach. In ancient Egypt, a popular board game called Senet used throwing sticks that were red on one side and white on the other (see Figure 3.1). Each stick had the same probability of outcomes as a coin flip: two. Senet used four or more throwing sticks to generate random results for moving pieces around the game board. Using four sticks at a time

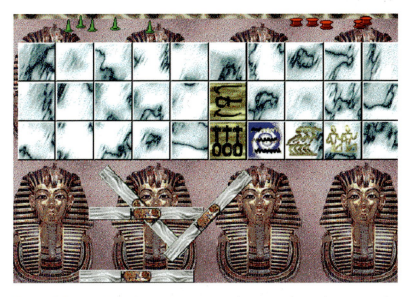

Figure 3.1. *In P. S. Neeley's online version of Senet, a player alternates with a computer throwing the sticks to determine how many spaces a token moves across the board. The four sticks (at the bottom) have all landed with their white sides up.*

allows sixteen possible results, the same as flipping a coin four times. Although the rules for Senet are unknown, it seems likely that one side of a throwing stick (red, for example) meant a piece could move one space while the opposite side meant no movement. Thus, if all four sticks showed the red side, a piece could move four spaces while four sticks showing the white side meant that no movement was allowed that turn.

The probabilities of movement in Senet are thus easy to determine:

- There is a 1-in-16 chance (16.7%) that all sides will show white, meaning no movement that turn.
- The chances for one stick showing red are 4-in-16 or 25%, so a piece can move one space that turn.
- The chances for two sticks showing red are 6-in-16 or 37.5%, so a piece can move two spaces that turn.
- The chances for three sticks showing red are 4-in-16 or 25%, so a piece can move three spaces that turn.
- There is a 1-in-16 chance (16.7%) that all sides will show red, so a piece can move four spaces that turn.

A number of games from India used cowry shells to generate random numbers. When thrown, a shell will land either with its mouth facing up or with its shiny shell showing. This method is the same as using throwing sticks or going with Heads-or-Tails.

It should be mentioned that modern games do use Heads-or-Tails, although not during play. If an American football game ends in a tie at the end of the fourth quarter, a coin is tossed to determine which team will receive the ball in overtime. Coin tosses are also used for a similar purpose in soccer, volleyball, cricket, and other games. In some duels, a coin toss was used to determine which dueler would have the sun to his back. One game where coin flipping is very important is in New Zealand's Big Wednesday lottery game where a player who has drawn six correct numbers must then correctly call heads or tails in a coin toss to determine the size of the final prize.

Randomization in Games

Most games include some kind of randomization to add uncertainty to outcomes. A few games like chess and checkers do not rely on randomization, and winning depends completely on the skills of the players. Such games are said to be *perfect information games* because nothing is hidden from the players who know exactly what can happen from turn to turn. There is no hidden information (for example, cards being dealt face down) and no randomization in such games.

Most video games rely on some randomization, which not only can keep the players guessing about what will happen next but also allows games to be replayed because each playthrough will be different, even though the starting conditions are always the same. Such games are *imperfect information games* because the players cannot predict the outcome of game actions that use randomization. *Tetris* (designed by Alexey Pajitnov) is an example of an imperfect information game because the player doesn't know the order in which the pieces (tetrominoes) will appear at the top of the screen. There are seven pieces in the game, and they appear randomly, forcing the player to figure out quickly where to place them.

Random Number Generators

In the olden days when processing power for computer and video games was very limited, a programmer might create a large chart of random numbers, and the game engine would select a starting number randomly; for example, the computer would use the current millisecond to determine the starting position in the chart. There were problems with this approach, because players might detect patterns of results from the table and thus be able to cheat. Also, the numbers in the chart might not really be random and follow unseen patterns, again allowing players to detect patterns that repeated.

As game platforms grew more powerful, programmers turned to pseudo-random number generators—algorithms that generated long series of random numbers whose values are determined by a fixed value called a *seed*. The problem with this approach is that eventually sequences of numbers start repeating or the algorithm uses too much memory that is needed elsewhere. The algorithms for generating pseudo-random numbers have grown more sophisticated over time, so it becomes less likely that player will start detecting patterns they can react to.

One tool that can prove extremely helpful during game production is a text-capture program that loads the outcomes of the random number generation algorithm into a text file. While the designers could try to analyze the outcomes visually, it would help to have another tool created that searched for patterns in the text files. As long as there are no glaring errors or repeated sequences found, it is unlikely players will notice anything wrong with the game. If problems are detected, the programmers may want to try a different algorithm.

Using Dice for Randomizing

In board games, randomization can take several forms. Players might need to use a spinner to generate a random number or the draw of a card from a deck can make each turn different. The way most commonly associated with board games is to roll a die (or two or more) to generate random numbers, which are then used to determine movement, combat, or other game actions.

Some games use a single six-sided die (referred to in game parlance as d6) to generate a number. In this case, there is a one-in-six chance (16.6%) that any number will be rolled. Using only a single die offers a limited number of results and any result is equally likely.

Most games tend to use two six-sided dice (referred to as 2d6) to get higher numbers and a different probability of results. Unlike

Results for 2d6 Roll

Dice		
Total	Chance	Percentage
2	1-in-36	2.8%
3	2-in-36	5.5%
4	3-in-36	8.3%
5	4-in-36	11.1%
6	5-in-36	13.8%
7	6-in-36	16.7%
8	5-in-36	13.8%
9	4-in-36	11.1%
10	3-in-36	8.3%
11	2-in-36	5.5%
12	1-in-36	2.8%

Table 3.2. *This chart shows the chances and percentages for two six-sided dice rolls.*

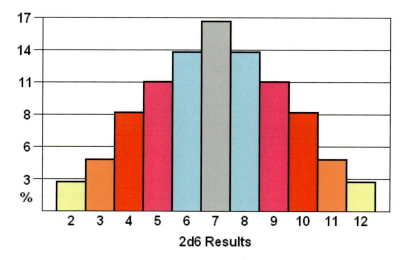

Figure 3.2. *This graph shows the Bell Curve for dice rolls using two six-sided dice.*

a single die, where all results are equal, when rolling two dice, the results can vary greatly. There are 36 possible results for rolling two dice. Note that there is no "1" result since the minimal number of each die is "1" and when added together, they equal "2." Table 3.2 shows the possible percentages of 2d6 dice rolls, and Figure 3.2 shows the results as a visual bell curve.

It is interesting to note that a double result is as likely to occur when a "7" is thrown (16.7% in both cases). Using two dice is popular in games, especially gambling games. The results are weighted towards the middle (results of 6, 7, and 8), and players roll extreme results (2 and 12) rarely. On a board with around 40 spaces, such as the *Monopoly* board, the median results mean that tokens move at a nice pace, with only an occasional burst of speed or minimal movement.

Another Way to Look at Dice Rolls

So far, there are some disadvantages of using six-sided dice in games. Rolling more than one die and adding the numbers together cumulatively means that the lowest result can never be a "1" for two dice, "2" for three dice, "3" for four dice, and so on. Also, most of the outcomes bunch together in the middle of the bell curve; it is impossible to assign equal odds to all dice outcomes. There are other ways to deal with two dice and get more interesting outcomes than a simple bell curve.

Dice Roll Matrix

2nd Die Result

		1	2	3	4	5	6
1st Die Result	1	1	2	3	4	5	6
	2	7	8	9	10	11	12
	3	13	14	15	16	17	18
	4	19	20	21	22	23	24
	5	25	26	27	28	29	30
	6	31	32	33	34	35	36

Table 3.3. *This matrix cross-references the result of two six-sided dice being thrown sequentially.*

One way is to throw the dice and deal with the results sequentially instead of cumulatively. For example, in a game a player has the option to throw two dice (2d6) one at a time. He throws the first die and considers the result before deciding to throw the second die. Maybe using the first die result lets him move his token to a space with a positive result, so he decides to use this result and ignore the second die altogether. Or, if he has to throw the second die, he then moves his token that number of spaces after moving it a first time—in effect, having two movements in the same turn. A similar approach is used in Backgammon, where a player can split the results of the dice roll between two pieces or use the combined result to move one piece.

Another approach is using a matrix for results. In this case, the row corresponding to the first die roll is cross-referenced with the column corresponding to the second die roll. In this case, there are 36 potential outcomes and there is an equal chance of obtaining any result. For example, in Table 3.3, the first roll of a "3" is cross-referenced with the second of "4" to get the result of 16. Matrices are used in some games, particularly for resolving combat in paper wargames (see Chapter 5).

Percentages

In 1980, the first ten-sided die (pentagonal trapezohedron) was introduced to the gaming industry at Gen Con and was quickly adapted for use in many role-playing and some board games. Percentage dice had been used earlier but were mostly 20-sided, requiring players to divide dice results by "2" to get a percentage result of 1–100. The advantage of such a ten-sided die (referred to as d10) was that by rolling two dice in sequential order it was possible to generate 100 numbers. One die was assigned to roll for tens and the other for single digits, giving a range of 1–100 or 00–99 (the latter configuration is more often used in electronic game design). The result of 00 on both dice can stands for either 00 or 100. Two ten-sided dice are referred to as percentile dice.

The advantages to using percentile dice in games are twofold. First, every number has an equal chance of being rolled, unlike the bell curve result of rolling 2d6. Second, the designer can assign varying ranges to results instead of having a one-to-one relation with a number rolled and a corresponding game action. For example, if the designer wants one game action to occur most frequently, he or she can assign a range of 1–50 for that action. Less frequent actions can then be assigned smaller increments down to a single die roll result, which would make that result very rare (1-in-100 or 1% chance). Thus, a percentile combat table for a role-playing game might looks something like Table 3.4.

Sample Combat Table

2d10		%
Number	Combat Result	Chance
1–5	Miss (no damage)	5%
6–15	Glancing attack (75% damage inflicted)	10%
16–65	Normal attack (100% damage)	50%
66–80	Heavy attack (125% damage)	15%
81–95	Very heavy blow (150% damage)	15%
96–100	Critical hit (roll on Critical Hit Table)	5%

Table 3.4. *This simple Combat Table is weighted so that most attacks result in a standard amount of damage being inflicted on the target (depending on how damage is calculated).*

Sports Games

Most games don't use three ten-sided dice since there is seldom a need to have a result of 1–1000. However, sports games—especially baseball—often express percentages to three places. A batter with an earned run average (ERA) of .346 is a respectable slugger. In a board or video game, the determination if the batter hits a thrown ball can be determined by dice roll. While a six-sided die could be used to resolve a swing, the results would eventually wind up looking very similar. For a slugger with a .346 ERA, a roll of 1 or 2 on a six-sided die would mean a hit since the probability of these results is 33.3%, which is fairly close to the ERA. A batter with a poor ERA of around .170 would get a hit on a roll of 1 only. Very few batters have an ERA anywhere near .500 so almost no one would be eligible to get a hit on a roll of 1, 2, or 3. Most of the hit results would come on results of 1 or 2 only, not allowing much differentiation among batters in the game.

Using only a single ten-sided die would mean the batter hits on a result of 1–3 and misses on any other result. While the results are slightly more varied than those using a single six-sided die, better batters are still cheated. Switching to percentile dice allows a much greater range of outcomes, since a batter with a .346 ERA gets a hit on a result of 1–34 (or 1–35 if the desire is for more hits in the game). There is much more separation between good and bad hitters using this method.

To use the batter's true ERA requires three ten-sided dice, which is much closer to the real world. For a baseball game trying to mimic real baseball as closely as possible, using three ten-sided dice to resolve a bat swing makes sense. (The real stats for players are owned by Major League Baseball and can only be used if one gets a license.)

Percentages in Video Games

While using results of 1–100 is very practical and easy to understand in board and paper role-playing games, it does not have to be used in video games. Unlike a paper RPG where the DungeonMaster directs the play and resolves conflicts among players, in video games the resolution of game actions is handled by the game logic. Any range of randomized possibilities can be handled equally well, so the designer is free to use whatever range best suits each game action. An advantage of creating a paper prototype of the game before coding begins is that the designer can test various probability ranges for game actions and make as many changes as necessary before settling on the most workable ranges.

If it feels more comfortable working with probability ranges of 1–100, the designer certainly can do so. When the programming team creates the algorithms that resolve the action, they can either keep the designer's desired ranges or change them as necessary to simplify the code.

There are two other dangers to keep in mind when setting up percentages for game actions. The first is to limit the number of possibilities per game action. If the designer has 20 different possible outcomes for a game action, the player can't predict with any accuracy what the likely outcome is going to be. Some randomness in results makes for an interesting game while too much randomness leads to player frustration. The second is to make sure that the values assigned to probabilities are meaningful during play. If the probability is 51% that something will happen and 49% that it won't, then the player will see the result as 50–50. On the other hand, skewing the results such that if the probability is 70% the event happens and 30% it doesn't might result in it happening more often than the designer wishes. Testing the game mechanics in prototype form allows the designer to settle on good initial values; as the game is implemented in code, the values might need to be tweaked, but hopefully not enough to cause problems or shipping delays.

Keeping the Math Simple

Many complex games use numbers of some kind to present important information to players—for example, how many experience points are needed to get to the next level in an RPG. In most cases, the numbers should be relatively low and easy to comprehend at a glance. If the numbers presented to the players get up into the thousands or millions, it takes time for players to parse them to figure out what is happening and what to do next. It is also difficult for the player to process too many numbers at once, so having a whole interface screen filled with many different number fields can look more like an Excel spreadsheet than a screen from a game. Likewise, as more video RPGs move to real-time combat action (instead of turn-based), it can be confusing for the player to see a slew of numbers fly around the screen as attacks are resolved.

If the numbers appear on secondary screens that aren't used much during play, then they can be large since the player has plenty of time to determine how many tens or hundreds of thousands of experience points are needed to reach the next level. Likewise, huge amounts of cash might accumulate over time in simulation or role-playing games, and it can be useful to have the amount appear when buying and selling items, checking one's current status, or performing other actions that involve the cash. As long as the huge numbers don't pop up during combat or puzzle-solving, the player won't be distracted by trying to comprehend how much of a game object he or she possesses.

There is a trend in many games to cut back on numbers the player has to deal with and replace them with other visual clues. An icon near the character that grows progressively redder as the player takes more damage in combat can replace the slew of numbers flying across the screen as each attack is resolved. Likewise, meters and thermometers are often used to show how many Hit Points or mana (the mystical material that powers magic) a character has left. A countdown timer can be used to show how much time remains until an action happens (for example, how long a poisoned player has left to live or when a new combat unit is scheduled to appear). However, it can be just as dangerous to use too many icons to reflect game action resolution because it still takes time for the player to remember what each icon stands for. In the midst of a battle against a horde of enemies, trying to pick out each icon and remember what it means can lead to player overload.

Defining Play through Algorithms

According to Wiktionary.com, an algorithm is a "precise step-by-step plan for a computational procedure that begins with an input value and yields an output value in a finite number of steps." When describing game play, a designer should approach the description with this definition in mind. Each action in the game should be defined by an algorithm—a step-by-step procedure for resolving each action. The algorithm description does not have to be a mathematical formula, but it should give the programmers sufficient information to figure out how to code the procedure.

Sometimes the algorithm can be very short—for example, for a turn-based game where units have movement points, the algorithm for describing a movement action could be: "When a unit enters an allowable space, the movement point cost for entering the space is subtracted from the unit's remaining movement point total. If the unit does not have enough movement points, it cannot enter the space and an alert message is played to warn the player. Otherwise, the unit moves into the space." Notice that there are some things that need to be described in detail to provide more information about the conditions of the algorithm. In the example just mentioned, the designer would want to explain what an "allowable space" means— i.e., that it is a space a unit can enter as opposed to a space containing impassable terrain.

At other times, an algorithm can get fairly complex and have a number of different steps—for example, the combat resolution in a role-playing game. It helps to break down the procedure step by step and include an example to help the programmers understand the process.

Logic and Scripting Languages

As important as it is for a designer to have a good grasp of common logic so as to be able to think through the ramifications of design decisions, it is equally important to understand the basics of Boolean logic and conditional statements that are used, in one form or another, in scripting languages. There are two definitions for scripting languages as far as game design is concerned. The first is a special proprietary coding language created by a game developer and used by level designers to trigger events during play—for example, enemy encounters, changes in dialogue with NPCs, and controlling NPC behavior and movement. This language is sometimes tied in directly to the level or the map editor so designers can enable events as they build the levels. The second definition is a special commercial coding language, like PERL, JavaScript, Lua, or Python, which is used to control something in a software application. Some game developers use a commercial scripting language like Lua or Python in the level editor while others create their own languages.

The trouble with trying to use scripting languages is that they can be very much like standard C/C++ code and therefore difficult for someone who isn't a programmer to use. Game developers try to make their proprietary scripting languages easier for non-programmers, meaning the design team and the general public. Many companies allow players to play around with the tools that were used to build the game and to create new levels that can be shared with

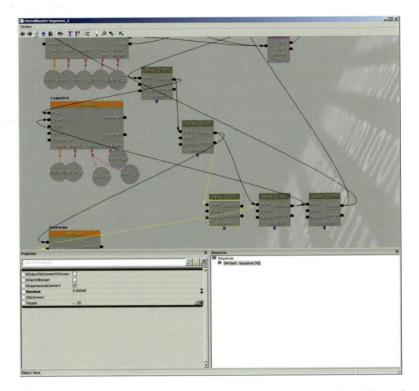

Figure 3.3. *UnrealKismet is a visual scripting system used in Epic Games' Unreal Engine that allows designers to make links between conditions and resulting actions with connecting lines.*

friends (known as *modding*). Including a user-friendly scripting language can greatly extend the shelf life of a game and even lead to commercial add-ons that are built by players and sold by the game company.

The scripting language has to be interpreted by the game engine code before anything happens. It's as though the designer is writing a script in French, a language in which he or she is fluent, and handing the script to a printer to be issued in an English edition. The printer has to translate the French into English and then make sure the final interpretation agrees with what the original author wanted. Both the author and printer have to agree to follow certain conventions (for example, sentence structure). Once the agreement has been worked out, the author can scribble away on new text while the printer churns out final editions of erudite English documents. This arrangement requires some lag time while the script is being interpreted, but it does allow each craftsman to work at his or her own speed independent from one another.

Likewise, designers can use a scripting language (see Figure 3.3) once it has been designed and coded by the programming team. As long as the designer stays within established guidelines, the language should allow him or her to create and change the events in the game without having to ask the programmers to recompile the main engine code. Scripts run slower than the original code because they have to be interpreted, but modern computers and consoles have so much processing power that there are seldom any noticeable slowdowns during play.

Conditional Statements

There are certain logical processes that most proprietary scripting languages employ. A designer should be familiar with these processes since they are vital to making things change during the game. Some of these processes come directly from programming, but they aren't difficult to understand and use. Conditional statements are often used to check the current game state to see if anything needs to change. For example, if a condition was originally set to "false" but is now "true," a change is made (and vice versa). Otherwise, as long as the statement remains "false," the existing condition continues. These statements are called "if-then" constructs (also "if-then-else"). In code, a construct might look like this:

```
If (QUEST_OF_STONE_SWORD = ACTIVE)
    Then   (SHOW_TEXT "You are currently
    seeking the Stone Sword.")
```

In this case, the script checks to see if the Stone Sword item has been found, and if it hasn't been found yet, then the appropriate text appears on the screen.

The same construct could be extended to cover more circumstances:

```
If (QUEST_OF_STONE_SWORD = ACTIVE)
    Then   (SHOW_TEXT "You are currently
    seeking the Stone Sword.")
```

```
Else
If (QUEST_OF_STONE_SWORD = COMPLETE)
    Then  (SHOW_TEXT "You found the Stone
          Sword.")
```

In this case, ACTIVE and COMPLETE are variables that are checked by the code. If the variable is set to ACTIVE, then the first message appears, and when the sword is found, the variable is changed to COMPLETE and the second message appears. The construct could be extended to include many other variables, although in this case the game code always uses whichever variable is currently set.

This is a simple example of how scripts work in a game. The scripts can be relatively simple or quite complex, depending on the needs of the designers. Some scripts are written in pseudo-code or in Lua or another commercial scripting language, while others, such as Epic Game's UnrealKismet, have more user-friendly graphic interfaces. Teaching oneself to use a proprietary scripting language is a good way for a newcomer to gain the skills needed for an entry-level position in a game company. Many games come with a level editor that also includes a proprietary scripting system.

Boolean Operators

It is possible to have multiple checks for the status of a conditional statement, thus allowing a designer to deal with more complex situations. For example, in the example above, there were just two variables to check to see if the Stone Sword quest was active. The scripting language could include logical connectives (or Boolean operators), which can then determine the status of multiple variables before acting. The most common operators are AND, OR, and NOT. The AND operator demands that all variables about a condition are "true" before an action takes place. The OR operator checks if at least one variable about a condition is "true," and NOT checks to see that no variable is "true." The operators can be combined to check on many variables before taking an action, and if none of the conditions are true, it defaults to the ELSE action.

For example, in the previous example, if there are two conditions needed to initial the Stone Sword quest (in this case, talking to two NPCs), the construct might look like this:

```
If ( (NPC1_STONE_SWORD_QUEST_CHAT = 1)    AND
        (NPC2_STONE_SWORD_QUEST_CHAT = 1))
     Then (QUEST_OF_STONE_SWORD = ACTIVE)
```

The code checks to see that the variables for the text that initiates the Stone Sword quest have been set to "1" (meaning the player has talked to the two characters about the quest). Note that both of the statements in parentheses are placed within a second parenthesis that includes the Boolean operator AND. If both variables have been set, then the quest is active and the characters' dialogue now changes from initiating the quest to asking if the quest has been completed. If the design requires the player to talk to either of two characters to start the quest, then logic for activating the quest would be:

```
If ( (NPC1_STONE_SWORD_QUEST_CHAT = 1)    OR
        (NPC2_STONE_SWORD_QUEST_CHAT = 1))
     Then (QUEST_OF_STONE_SWORD = ACTIVE)
```

The simple replacement of the AND with OR in the second example completely changes how the quest is initiated. These simple Boolean operators are very powerful and can be used to create some very interesting situations in games. A designer should understand the basics of Boolean logic because it is used in scripting languages to initiate quests, pay rewards to the player, change NPC dialogue options, and so on.

It should be mentioned that many proprietary scripting languages mask the Boolean operations with graphic shortcuts to make it easier for designers to work out the logic of how things happen on the playfield. For example, in Figure 3.4(a), there are two conditional boxes with arrows that link to an action box, and as long as there is no link between the boxes, the game engine interprets this as an OR operation, where the action will happen if either condition is true. In Figure 3.4(b), the two conditional boxes are connected by a line between them and an arrow links to the action box. In this case, the connecting line acts like an AND statement so that both conditions must be true before the action occurs.

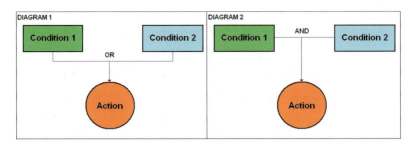

Figure 3.4. *(a) Diagram 1 shows an OR statement where if either condition be "true," the action happens. (b) Diagram 2 shows an AND statement where both conditions must be true for the action to happen.*

Conclusion

The math used during game play is usually quite simple, although the math used in the code can be very complex. Players don't want to be distracted by having to deal with lots of numbers during play because their minds have to shift away from controlling a character's actions to remembering what the numbers mean. Many games are shying away from numbers to show amounts graphically through icons like thermometers and gauges. So, while designers don't necessarily need advanced math classes to design games, they should have a basic understand of what kinds of math are used by the game engine so as to be able to talk to the program team intelligently.

On the other hand, designers should have a good comprehension of the basics of Boolean logic if they wish to employ a company's proprietary scripting language while working on levels. Scripts allow designers to change the conditions of the game world as players perform actions, and so understanding the basics of Boolean logic is important to learning any scripting language. Otherwise, designers would have to work with the programmers to enable the changes they have in mind as the game progresses, which not only slows down the development process but can also lead to unintended or mistaken effects that can take considerable time and effort to correct. Boolean logic is a fundamental tool for designers.

Exercises

1. Figure out the percentages for heads and tails when flipping three coins and then four coins. Do they also form Bell curves?

2. Make six throw sticks from Popsicle sticks or tongue depressors, coloring one side to be able to tell them apart. (You can break a single stick into thirds to achieve the same effect.) What are the percentages for each side when throwing five or six sticks?

3. Try playing a board game that uses six-sided dice (e.g., Hasbro's Monopoly) with the throw sticks. If the game requires "doubles," consider a result when all sticks show the same color as a double.

    a. Use four sticks for a while, then move to five sticks and finally to six sticks.

    b. What are the difference between playing the game with dice and with sticks?

    c. Did adding more sticks speed up the game play?

    d. Write a short essay outlining your findings on playing the game with sticks vs. playing with dice.

4. Start collecting dice with different number of faces. Try to get at least two of each type. In particular, make sure you have at least two ten-sided dice.

    a. Now play the same board game from Exercise 3 with different pairs of the same dice type (that is, two four-sided dice, two ten-sided dice, etc).

    b. Make sure that you play with the dice total being cumulative (for example, using two ten-sided dice would give your results from 2 to 20).

    c. Compare playing the game with throw sticks vs. playing with different types of dice.

5. Create Throw Tables for a board game, using two ten-sided dice to generate *percentage* outcomes (that is, results of 1–99 or 2–100).

    a. The first Throw Table should have all results being of equal value.

b. The next Throw Table should be weighted so that certain dice results happen more often than others.

c. The last Throw Table should be a matrix of some kind. Note that for the matrix, you might want to combine numeric results with possible game play mechanics (for example, "Lose 1 turn," "Move 2 spaces and throw again," "Move back 3 spaces," and so on).

d. Play the game from Exercise 3 using the different Throw Tables and determine which table made the game most enjoyable to play.

6. Consider the token you move around the game board as a player in a professional sport you enjoy.

a. Look up the statistics for players in the sport and then create a "trading card" for your token with three or four statistics as percentages.

b. Tie each statistic to some game mechanic. For example, if you are using Baseball as the model, you could give your token a hitting average of .349 to determine its ability to move in a turn. Its runs-batted-in (RBI) statistic might determine the percentage of money you get for buying or selling items or collecting money from the bank.

c. Try playing the board game using the "trading cards" you've developed for the tokens.

d. Did the "trading cards" add to your enjoyment while playing the game?

7. Look at the rules to the board game and see if you can express them as "if-then" statements. For example, you might say "*if* you land on the "X" space, *then* you collect $25." See if you can express the rules using the "if-else if-then" structure as well.

8. Now see if you can express the rules of the board game using Boolean operators with the "if-else if-then" logic structure. For example, "*if* you land on the "X" space *OR* the "Y" space, *then* you collect $25" or "*if* you land on the "X" space *AND* you have the yellow token, *then* you collect $50 instead of $25." Try to create a half dozen game rules using this approach, even if they don't relate directly to the board game you've been playing.

Part II: INSIDE GAME MECHANICS

CHAPTER 4

ON MOVEMENT

Most games have some kind of movement. Movement deals with the physical displacement of game objects in a two- or three-dimension world. In board games, movement is usually restricted to special spaces on a flat surface, and the player generates a random number through dice rolls or other mechanics to move a token from space to space around the board. For such games, it is important to keep players within established boundaries; otherwise, the game dissolves into anarchy. Imagine a Monopoly player deciding to take a "short-cut" because the dice roll would otherwise cause his token to land on the "Go to Jail" space. The other players would be up in arms because he broke the rules of the game.

In video games, movement is also very much restricted. The game engine has restrictions to keep players from moving a character, unit, or token wherever they want. Video games often reflect the real world when determining how movement is restricted, so a car can't move through a lake, projectiles don't shoot around corners, or a character can't scale a building with his bare hands. At other times, players have to learn on their own where not to move—for example, discovering that walking into molten lava is deadly or strolling through a cloud of putrid-looking gas is poisonous.

In the documentation, the designer defines how movement works and what restrictions are involved. Any special actions that characters or other game objects are expected to perform should be worked out in detail with the art and programming teams before incorporating them into the design document. The initial concept may have to change when the game is implemented, but it's better to start off with as full a description of how movement works as possible so that both the programmers and artists know what assets they will have to build and how those objects will interact with the game environment.

Scale

One aspect that determines how movement works in a video game is the scale of the game world and objects appearing in it. Scale refers to the size of objects on the screen and how they relate proportionately to one another. Sometimes the scale is abstract, as in puzzle games where a *Tetris*-like grid and pieces could be any size. More often, the scale is relatively realistic, where game units (characters, vehicles, etc.) are proportional to the landscape, as in first-person shooters. However, the scale is sometimes distorted for play purposes, so that oversized objects move around on the playfield and are as tall, if not taller, than the landscape features. For example, in a wargame like *Sid Meier's Civilization*, a single solider or tank might tower above the surrounding terrain and represent a much larger military unit. This distortion helps the player locate the unit on the map and to control its actions when moving and attacking.

Large and Small Objects

When coming up with a game, the designer should have at least an initial idea for its scale. It's not necessary to worry about how many pixels tall and wide game objects will be, but it is important to know whether objects on the screen will be large or small. Large objects take up a lot of space on the screen and can obscure objects behind them. In a first-person shooter game, the viewpoint is through the eyes of a character moving through the playfield, so objects are fairly large near the character and smaller at a distance. If the game camera were perched on the shoulder of the character, much of the playfield would be blocked by the body, making it harder to detect enemies and items at a distance. Perspective is very important in this kind of game. The artwork for objects in the playfield is much more detailed because they will be seen up close by players, so texturing is very important.

Small objects are useful if there are multiple objects on the playfield for the player to interact with or if it is important for the player to take in a large part of the playfield at one time. However, objects can be hard to detect if the playfield is cluttered with objects. In a simulation game like *SimCity*, the buildings are small and there are usually no people to be seen because they would be the size of a few pixels, therefore lacking any detail. The player needs to be able to move around the city quickly to decide what to build next, and so the scale of objects is quite small so more real estate fits on the screen.

Many games use a medium-size scale where the main objects are large enough to be clearly distinguished during play but don't obscure the terrain features or other important game objects. These games typically show objects from a third-person point of view (as opposed to the first-person view of a shooter game), looking over the shoulder of units or top-down at them. The objects are sometimes proportional to the terrain features and sometimes they are oversized.

Graphical Interface Requirements

In addition to the size of units on the screen, the designer also has to be aware of what the graphical interface requirements will be. If the game has lots of controls appearing on the screen, the sizes of objects on the screen will have to reduced to allow room for the interface artwork. In BioWare's role-playing game *Baldur's Gate*, there are many different interface icons appearing on the screen and they are gathered in groupings around the outer edge of the screen, framing the playfield area and objects on it. The objects on the playfield are relatively small and sometimes difficult to detect. Making interface elements transparent so the playfield can be seen behind them allows for larger units. For example, in Valve's *Half-Life 2* the interface displays are transparent and so the player can see what is happening behind them on the playfield.

Whatever scale is selected, it should be consistent throughout the game. It can be distracting to suddenly change the scale on the player without warning. Having different scales for different interface screens is fine, but changing the scale of objects on the playfield breaks the player's immersion in the game.

Military Scales

Wargames have a slightly different sense of scale, based on what part of a battle the game is trying to simulate. Obviously, the larger the battle, the more reduced the map has to be to cover the entire battlefield and still be manageable. There are three basic scales for wargames: tactical, operational, and strategic.

These scales are useful when talking about games that include combat, including role-playing games, strategy games, wargames, real-time strategy games, and some simulations (for example, combat flight games and tank games). It should be noted that real-time strategy games are at a tactical level, not a strategic level, since the player is dealing with individuals or small military units. It should also be mentioned that the term "strategy games" is used by many people to refer to games that have a military theme, no matter what their actual scale.

Tactical (Skirmish) Scale

At this level, the focus is on individual soldiers or small units (squads or platoons), and so the game usually covers only a small portion of a battle. A mission might cover a few hours to a few days of real time. The player controls a handful of playing pieces and has to worry about keeping them supplied and healed. The units are usually proportional to the terrain features, and the player gets a sense of the danger of moving across a landscape where enemies are hiding and waiting to attack. This scale is perfect for first-person shooter games with a military theme, such as Electronic Arts' *Medal of Honor,* Red Storm Entertainment's *Red Storm Rising*, and the US Army's *America's Army*. Many real-time strategy games like Westwood Studios' *Command & Conquer* and Blizzard Entertainment's *Warcraft* series are at this scale as well. Also, most air combat games like Ubisoft's *Blazing Angels: Squadrons of WWII* and Wild Hair Entertainment's *Air Battles: Sky Defenders* fall into this category.

Operational Scale

The scale is used to recreate whole battles at the regiment to battalion level. The size of the battlefield determines the scale of the playfield map, and smaller terrain features are ignored while large features like rivers, forests, and roads affect the movement rate of units across the map. Other factors affecting play are the weather, logistics, and command control. The units are representational and oversized, so one tank on the map could stand for a whole tank platoon. These games are often turn-based, and a typical game turn lasts from a single day to a week with the whole battle lasting a few weeks to months in real time. One drawback to games of this size is that it is difficult for the player to view the whole map at a glance, and the player might have to scroll around repeatedly to see everything or zoom out, thereby losing a sense of the units' locations in relation to enemy units. This scale seems to have limited appeal to video game players because there are few examples, but *Sid Meier's Gettysburg!* and *Sid Meier's Antietam!* are two relatively recent examples.

Figure 4.1. *Paradox Interactive's* Victoria II *is set at a strategic level and covers not only warfare on a worldwide scale but also political diplomacy, technological innovation, and economics.*

Strategic (Grand Strategic) Scale

This scale is used to recreate war on a large scale, covering whole nations, continents, and even the entire world (or many worlds in science fiction-based games). The playfield map is often broken down into theaters of operation. In this case, only the largest features (oceans, land masses, mountain chains) affect unit movement. This type of game often includes production as a major component of conflict and the ability of countries or alliances to engage in combat for a lengthy period. These games are often turn-based, and a typical game turn lasts from several days to a week to a month or longer, with the whole battle lasting many months or years in real time. Some video games at this scale include MicroProse's *Sid Meier's Civilization,* Paradox Interactive's *Victoria II* (Figure 4.1), and even Hasbro Interactive's *RISK: The Game of Global Domination.*

Regulating Movement in Wargames

It is important in military games and some simulations that movement across the playfield be regulated, especially in turn-based games. There are several approaches to regulating movement, either by using a system that imposes a grid over the playfield or by severely restricting where units can move. In either case, the restrictions can sometimes feel arbitrary to players even though they are necessary to maintain a sense of realism of where and how quickly units can and cannot move across a battlefield.

The designer should talk to the programmers about what approach will work best in the game being designed. In games where only one unit is moving at a time and there are no significant obstacles to dodge, a straight line between two points might be best. If terrain features do have an effect on movement, then another approach might work better. Creating a simple electronic prototype during technical review is one way to test which approach will be best before committing the program team to create a version that needs to be changed later.

Hex Maps

In most paper wargames, a hexagonal grid overlays the map of the battlefield, and units move from one hex into an adjacent hex one at a time until their movement allowance for the turn is used up. The battlefield map is enlarged or reduced to fit a standard printed hexagonal sheet (with hexes being about a half-inch to three-quarters inch from side to side). Of course, the hexes for an electronic version

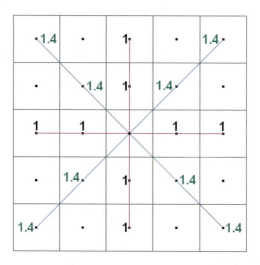

Figure 4.2. *Using a square grid for movement allows units to move more quickly across the map on the diagonal than in a horizontal or vertical direction, assuming the unit expends one movement point for entering a square.*

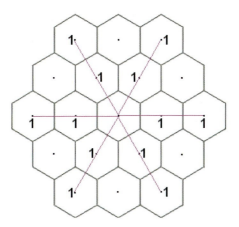

Figure 4.3. *Using a hexagonal grid allows for the same movement rate from space to space in all directions.*

of a wargame can be any size as long as they allow standardized movement for all units in the game.

The terrain on the hexagonal map is sometimes altered slightly to shoehorn it inside the grid. Roads normally run through hexes as opposed to along hex sides to help regulate the movement of units. Rivers and streams, on the other hand, are usually along the hex borders because they either block movement from one hex to the next across the feature or there is an extra movement cost required to cross. Major terrain features, such as lakes, mountains, forests, and the like, are also modified slightly as necessary to keep them within hexes. While forcing terrain features to conform to a hex grid skews the real battlefield layout, it standardizes movement and combat effects caused by the terrain. The idea is that each hex has a single movement cost to enter based on the dominant terrain in the hex, and some hex sides cost additional movement points to cross.

Hexagons are used instead of squares because the movement rate between adjacent hexes is always the same value, as opposed to a square grid where moving horizontally and vertically into adjacent squares uses the same value, but moving into a diagonal square (along the hypotenuse) is a greater value (see Figure 4.2). As a result, units on a square grid can move more quickly along the diagonal than horizontally or vertically. The game could force units to move orthogonally only (into adjacent horizontal or vertical spaces), but then the rate of movement is slowed. Using a hexagonal grid fixes this problem (see Figure 4.3).

Video wargames sometimes hide the hexagonal grid to make the landscape look more realistic while still using one to regulate the movement of units. As a result, it can look odd to see a unit moving along what should be a straight road jiggle up and down or side to side as it moves from one invisible hex to the next. The movement can be smoothed by the game engine to remove the worst jiggling. In many cases, a hexagonal grid doesn't even need to be shown to players.

Splines and Waypoints

Sometimes units are programmed to move along invisible strips called splines, especially in games requiring movement along curved surfaces in two or three dimensions. The spline acts like a rail to direct and limit the movement of a unit through curves. The unit is can be given some elasticity during movement, as though a unit is bound to the spline by a rubber band, so it can avoid other units or obstacles in its path. For example, splines are often used to control the movement of enemy cars in race games. Unlike hex movement, units moving along splines go at a constant rate unless acted on by external forces (for example, gravity), and the splines wind around impediments that would normally slow movement on a hex grid.

Another way to have units move is to use waypoints, which are invisible points on the map. The AI path-finding routine determines the best path for getting from one waypoint to another and moves an active unit accordingly. In a real-time strategy game, for example, the player might click on a unit to activate it and then click on a point on the map where the unit is to move. The AI code then determines the best route between the unit's current position (waypoint) and the spot that was selected. The path-finding AI often uses an invisible square or hexagonal grid superimposed over the playfield to count the shortest path from one point to another, and terrain features on the map can block the pathway, forcing the AI to choose another path around obstacles.

Zones of Control

In a battle, units of one side often are tasked with getting to a certain distant point on the battlefield, forcing them to come into contact with the enemy. In real combat, units do not simply move through small gaps between enemy units like water through a sieve because

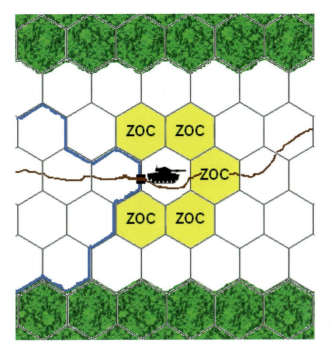

Figure 4.4. *This unit exerts a Zone of Control into the adjacent shaded hexes, but not across a river hexside. An opposing unit is forced to stop the first time it enters an enemy Zone of Control.*

they would come under decimating fire from the enemy if they tried. Instead, the opposing units form up lines and try to punch their way through a weak point or swing around the opponent's flank. In paper wargames, most units exert what is called a zone of control (ZOC) into the hexes surrounding the unit (see Figure 4.4). When an enemy unit moves into an adjacent hex, it has to stop its movement so combat can be resolved. In the next turn, the unit can continued moving forward but must again stop if the new hex is in an enemy's zone of control. Thus, units can move slowly past the enemy, but at a cost of time and material.

Zones of control are sometimes used in real-time strategy games to prevent units from blasting their way past enemy units. The players do not have to be told about the zones of control since there is nothing they can do to change them, but they might notice that their units slow down once they come in direct contact with enemy units. This concept can also be used in tactical role-playing games where units are activated one at a time to move across the playfield. If the game reveals all possible spaces a unit can move to when it is selected, then zones of control can be used to restrict the movement of that unit by not including spaces behind the enemy units. Thus, a unit is forced to move adjacent to the enemy and possibly engage in combat.

Game Statistics for Movement

The designer determines the rate at which units move across the playfield. In a typical board game, movement is controlled by dice roll (or other randomization method), and during each turn the players generate new movement rates for their tokens. Normally, tokens move one space per dice result unless they move into a space having special effects (for example, a shortcut, a "go to jail" space, or a "lose a turn" space). Describing movement in such games is very straightforward.

In more complex games, however, players often control more than one unit and these units might each have different speeds at which they move across the playfield. For example, a vehicle moves much more quickly in a given amount of time than a character on

Movement Chart

Terrain	Unit Type		
	Infantry	Cavalry	Artillery
Road	1	½	1
Open	2	1	2
Light Woods	3	2	4
Forest	4	NA	NA
Ford	+2	+1	NA
River	NA	NA	NA
Town	1	1	1
Uphill	+1	0	+2
Downhill	0	-1	-1

Table 4.1. *This is a simple Movement Chart that might appear in a Civil War or Napoleonic Era wargame. Note that "NA" means "not applicable," signifying that the unit cannot enter that space.*

foot. Unit speed is also affected by terrain features on the playfield. Some terrain is impossible to enter and other terrain slows the pace of a unit crossing it. As an example, a walking soldier unit normally moving at a pace of five feet per second on open ground might have its movement rate cut in half when slogging through a swamp or trying to cross a stream. Other features block movement completely—for example, a building wall, chasm, mountainside, or deep river. As part of the design process, the designer has to figure out what types of units the player will control and what features on the playfield will affect movement. This information should be included in the design documentation and can best be presented as a Movement Chart (Table 4.1). Some typical terms used in creating this chart for a turn-based wargame include *Movement Rate* (the speed at which a unit moves through different terrain types) and *Movement Point Allowance* (the number of points allotted to a unit to spend in a turn as it moves across the map).

Action Points

Another approach used in many games is the concept of Action Points, where movement and combat actions are combined into one value. Each unit is given an Action Point total for a turn, and the unit expends these points by moving and engaging in the combat. If the unit runs out of Action Points for a turn, it can no longer act. The player can spend these points as desired, so a unit might move first and then engage in combat, engage in combat first and then move, or move a bit, engage in combat, and if it survives and still has points left, continue moving after combat. When using this approach, it's a good idea to visually show the player how much farther the unit can move in a turn as it performs actions and also to let the player cancel a selected movement path if the unit runs low on points before reaching a desired location.

Terrain Features

Early in the design process, the designer works with the art and programming teams to determine the pace at which units travel across the playfield, tweaking values as necessary until the movement looks and feels right. For some games, such as first-person shooters, the pace is pretty standard, and characters move as they would in the real world (barring unusual environments such as zero-G). At other

Terrain Effects Chart				
Symbol	Terrain	Combat Effect	LOS	Other Effects
	Open	No effect	Open	None
	Forest	Defender receives *two* column shift	Blocks	Line of Supply extends only into first forest hex
	Railroad	No effect	Open	Line of Supply extends through all linked hexes
	River	No combat allowed across river hexsides	Open	No Line of Supply across river hexsides
	Bridge	Attacks allowed only across bridges	Open	Line of Supply can be traced across bridge
	Town	Defender receives *one* column shift	Blocks	Line of Supply source
	City	Defender receives *two* column shift	Blocks	Line of Supply source
	Set-up	Other terrain in hex determines effects	None	None

Table 4.2. *This Movement Chart provides information about how the terrain types affect the movement rates of different combat units.*

times, the pace isn't really known until either an interactive proto-type is made or the game engine is far enough along to allow objects to move across the screen at runtime speed. The designer should study other games in the genre to see how they deal with the pace of units and then make whatever modifications are required for the revised game design.

It is important as the design firms up to take into account all the terrain types and possible features the player will encounter during the game. Breaking terrain types and features into classes helps the whole team understand the behavior of units on the map under various conditions. For example, an *open* terrain type might include roads, paths, fields, grasslands, rocky plains, and other similar flat and featureless ground, and units moving across this terrain type might spend one Movement Point per space. Likewise, there might be *blocking* terrain including light woods, heavy brush, mud, icy rocks, and other broken ground, and units would have to spend two or more Movement Points to enter each such space. Depending on the scale of the game and the terrain on the playfield, the blocking terrain could be typed in several ways, for example, *light* and *heavy*, with light having the effects just describe while heavy means units are slogging through tricky terrain with many obstacles (swamps, dense forest, steep slopes, etc.). Finally, there can be terrain that is *impassable* to one or more unit types, meaning units simply cannot enter those spaces.

Another approach is to assign movement point penalties for crossing certain kinds of terrain. For example, to cross a creek or ditch might require infantry units to spend an extra Movement Point; these special penalties should also be listed in the Movement Chart and discussed in the game documentation. Note that the terrain can also impact how combat is resolved (see Chapter 5), so it is sometimes better to create a Terrain Effects Chart that shows how terrain affects both movement and combat (see Table 4.2).

Strategic Movement Map (World Map)

Sometimes units or characters have to cross long distances between points of interest, and the designer has to come up with a method for allowing fast movement over great distances. One method is to use a separate interface screen for such strategic movement. It could be a world map, where the player simply clicks on a location to have the unit/character move to that place. However, immediate displacement of a unit/character across vast distances can be off-putting to players and shatter their immersion. Therefore, designers try to come up with some method to account for long-distance travel.

For modern era games, long-distance travel can be handled by trains, aircraft, sea craft, or even spaceships. Usually, there are terminals in cities or other major urban areas, and the resulting movement across the strategic map includes an animation of the unit's trip along a rail line, air route, sea lane, or between planets. For classical fantasy games set in a medieval setting, long distance travel can be more problematic to represent because the fastest mode of travel might only be horses. Some games simply ignore this limitation and use magical transporters, dragons, or other exotic modes of travel. Many Japanese role-playing games, for example, freely mix fantasy and science fiction elements together so that dragons coexist with spaceships. As a result, strategic travel can take many bizarre forms. Whatever method of strategic travel is selected, it should fit into the overall fictional or historical setting of the game world and not seem incongruous.

When working out the design, the designer should consider whether some form of strategic movement is needed. If, for example, the design requires that players travel over long distances repeatedly, essentially returning to the same territories again and again, a form of strategic transportation is very useful. The designer can restrict movement on the strategic map by showing only those locations the player has so far explored, although it might seem odd that the method of transport (for example, a railroad) has to add connections based on the player's actions. At other times, travel on the strategic map might be unlimited, and allow the player to travel all over the world at any time. The difficulty with this approach is that if there are a lot of NPCs in the world, the designers have to create dialog text for all of them throughout the whole game.

Line-of-Sight and Other Strategic Map Functions

The strategic map can serve other functions in addition to speeding up movement. It might show where resources or other points of interest are located so the player doesn't have to grope around blindly to find them (see Figure 4.5). It can also show interesting locations players have not yet visited and point them in the correct direction. Depending on the game, there can be several levels of strategic maps with each one at a different size and showing different objects of interest for the player. Also, a given strategic map might have a number of interface buttons that act as filters to reveal certain objects on the playfield (different resources, enemy troops, terrain types, etc.).

A strategic map can also be used to show the location of enemy units. In real-time strategy games, enemy units are seen on the strategic movement map while they are in the line-of-sight of friendly units, and when they move out of sight, they disappear from the strategic map. *Line-of-sight* is the distance a unit can see before near and distant objects like hills and greenery block the view and interfere with detection of enemy units. Depending on the scale of the game, line-of-sight can either be blocked by terrain features or not.

Figure 4.5. *On the world map in Bethesda Softworks' The Elder Scrolls IV: Oblivion, the world map shows important locations as the player encounters them.*

In wargames, the objective is a realistic creation of a battle, and terrain features that block line-of-sight also affect the ability of units to fire at unseen nearby enemy units.

To show the line-of-sight of units, the tactical map around friendly units might be brightly lit, and the terrain can be seen along with enemy units. The corresponding viewable area on the strategic map is also lit as well. As friendly units move, the areas no longer within line-of-sight gray out and enemy units in those areas disappear from both the tactical and strategic maps. The inability to detect enemy units is part of the *fog of war*, a term referring to the ambiguity involved in combat where the enemy's movement and intents can only be guessed at until direct contact occurs.

Movement Rates

In a game where accuracy is desired, such as a wargame or simulation game, the designer often has to do research on the subject before determining the rate at which objects move across the screen. Depending on the conflict presented in a wargame, infantry units might move relatively slowly if they travel on foot but much faster if they have transports. Tanks and other vehicles move at a much faster rate than marching infantry, so the designer has to take into account the disparity in movement rates when working on the movement rate for units. In addition, the current condition of the battlefield and its affects on terrain can affect the movement rate. For example, if the designer is working on a simulation of the Eastern Front in the Soviet Union during World War II, the movement rate for tanks can vary greatly based on the weather. During the summer and winter when the ground is dry or frozen, tanks can move relatively quickly, but they get bogged down during spring rains as the frozen ground melts. Infantry, on the other hand, move pretty much at the same rate year round because they don't get badly mired down by the mud. The designer has to do considerable research on the conditions of the battlefield to create a realistic game.

Movement rate for a real-time strategy game is different because the scale is tactical. Vehicles might still move more quickly than foot soldiers, but the designer can ignore the effects of weather and terrain if favor of making the game more action-oriented. Even though slogging through thick mud is a fact of life in real wars, it doesn't have to be in other games that don't strive for verisimilitude. Thus, movement in a role-playing game can be sped up and distances can be compressed to keep the action moving.

To determine the best movement rate for nonrealistic games, consider how long it should take for the player to move from one major location to another in real time. Random encounters can be used to break up long treks. For example, if the player has to spend more than ten minutes or so crossing the map, then there should be plenty of encounters and lots of items for the player to find. It is also possible to change the environment—for example, moving from open plains into a wooded area—but players are less interested in eye candy than in playing the game, meaning they want to do something and not just watch the scenery pass by.

Revealing Movement Paths

One way to help the player know exactly how far a unit can move in a turn-based game is to use an invisible hexagonal grid that becomes visible when the player selects a unit. The visible area shows the spaces where the unit can move. If the game allows a combina-

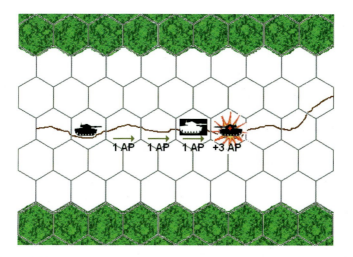

Figure 4.6. *The tank starts off with eight Action Points and spends three to move adjacent to an enemy unit and another three to attack it (six Action Points in total).*

tion of movement and combat, the visible area can be reduced as the unit performs actions.

As shown in Figure 4.6, if a tank unit has an Action Point total of eight, it can move eight spaces along a road (one space per movement point) and only four spaces across an open field, but it can't

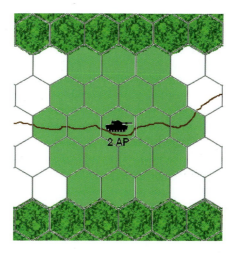

Figure 4.7. *After combat is resolved, the tank still has two Action Points remaining and can move to the shaded spaces on the map. Each space costs one point.*

enter the forest spaces. Assume the tank moves three spaces down the road and then attacks an enemy infantry unit (assume that combat uses up two action points, which are used for movement and/or combat). The second graphic (Figure 4.7) shows the remaining spaces the tank can move into. This form of visual feedback greatly helps players understand the capabilities of their units and speeds up game play considerably.

Gridding Out the Movement

Creating a paper version of the playfield is very useful and can help determine the initial desired movement rate of units. Using a hexagonal grid allows equal movement rates in all directions and prevents the problem of moving more quickly along the diagonal. Start by setting up the two points the character will move between. How much real-world time should the player spend moving between those two points? If the wish is to keep the time to 15 minutes (forgetting encounters or other distractions), then the designer can experiment with different movement rates. Assuming a character can move from one space to another in four seconds of real time, then the map will require 225 spaces between the two points (60 seconds per minute divided by four seconds per space equals 15 spaces per minute; 15 spaces per minute times 15 minutes equals 225 spaces). Creating a map of this size helps the designer figure out how many random and set-piece encounters to include during the trek between points. When playing out the game at this scale, the designer might realize that the movement rate is too slow, that the distance between the points is too great, or that the encounter rate is too great or too infrequent.

Once an initial movement rate has been selected, it should be tested in an interactive prototype. The designer works with an artist to create a sprite or a simple 3D model of the desired size and then works with a programmer to create an extendable grid to test how fast things happen at the scale of the initially selected movement rate. Translating the game into an electronic medium might cause the designer to change his or her mind about the movement rate for units. One can never be one hundred percent sure of what the scale of things will be until objects at the preferred scale start moving around in runtime on the screen.

If necessary, use another game as a model where the movement is similar to that which is desired. The game doesn't have to be in the same genre, but the scale of objects on the playfield should be the same. It is a simple process to measure how long it takes to move across the screen and determine distances between major locations as well as frequency of encounters. It helps to note when strategic movement becomes available to cut down on travel times.

Movement Algorithm

Depending on the complexity of a game, the algorithm needed to explain how movement works can be either simple or complex. If there are no terrain effects, the algorithm could follow these steps:

Step 1. Generate a random number to determine the movement for the turn.

Step 2. The player must move his token around the board a number of spaces equal to the random result.

Step 3. Check the space where the player's token lands to determine if there is any other result:

- If there is nothing in the space, then proceed to Bartering.

- If there is a message in the space, its effects are applied immediately to the player unless it refers to gaining or losing a turn (see the "Message Effects" section for more details).

For more complex games, the algorithm would have to take into account such factors as terrain effects, zones of control, supply status, and the like. When defining the algorithm, the designers should work with the programming staff to determine the order in which any additional factors are applied.

Random Encounters

In some games—RPGs in particular—random encounters happen where the player is forced into combat situations with enemies that did not appear on the strategic or tactical map. These encounters are determined randomly and often help players gain experience, gold, and other items. Their locations and timing are determined on a random basis, meaning that players always have to be prepared for combat. There are usually set-piece encounters as well, where players either are forced to resolve combat because the scripting language has triggered the event or they see enemies on the map and can choose to bypass them or engage them in combat.

While random encounters are useful to keep players alert while moving across the map, they can become tiresome. Having to pause to resolve a random encounter can be annoying, especially if the player has a high-level character and is wading through an area populated by low-level enemies. As a result, players will opt to flee such encounters instead of engaging in battle to speed things up. Some games (for example, Square Enix's *Final Fantasy XIII*) have dropped random encounters completely in favor of set-piece encounters where the player can see enemies moving around the screen and then choose to fight or ignore them. A drawback to this approach is that players can sometimes sneak into areas they shouldn't yet visit if they can escape these set-piece encounters, so the designer often has to add additional preventatives to keep players from jumping too far ahead in the story.

The designer determines the frequency in which random encounters occur and then set up the Encounter Tables for the different locations in the game. Ideally, the designer should be able to adjust the frequency of encounters manually in each area so that the programmers aren't required to recompile the code each time a change is required. The frequency rate should be fairly low, especially if players are required to move through the area often during the game. Raising the frequency rate leads to more encounters but can be irritating. The final frequency rates are decided after extensive playtesting and player feedback.

Encounter Tables

If the game includes random encounters, the designers have to create Encounter Tables for the different areas of the game. The enemy entities are not all grouped together everywhere on the game map. Instead, certain enemies are found in some locations and not in others. The environment of the map often determines what kinds of entities the player will encounter. In some games, a randomization check is made each time the character moves a certain distance on the game map, and if it does not pass the check, an encounter occurs. The game then switches to the combat display where fighting is resolved. The player might never be aware that creatures are lurking nearby until an encounter is triggered.

In more recent games, the enemies often appear on the map, either as a generic "enemy" image or as the model of the entity itself. Gust's *Mana Khemia: Alchemists of Al-Revis* used the first approach

Simple Encounter Table

Dice Result	Enemy Type
1–20	Level 1 wolf
21–40	Level 1 dodo bird
41–60	Level 1 rogue bandit
61–70	Level 2 wolf
71–80	Level 2 dodo bird
81–90	Level 3 rogue bandit
91–100	Special encounters

Table 4.3. *This Simple Encounter Table uses percentile dice results to determine what type of enemy the player will fight in the encounter. Note that for results of 91–100 a special encounter occurs and that is resolved by rolling on a different table.*

where enemies appeared as red or blue blobs depending on if they were a challenge or very weak but not identifying exactly which creatures the blobs represented. Square Enix's *Final Fantasy XIII*, on the other hand, uses the latter approach, so the player see the real monsters roaming around the playfield and can decide to attack them to gain experience or, if supplies are low, to try to avoid combat by sneaking around it.

Using a Random Encounter Table (see Table 4.3) allows more variety in the encounters. In addition to the enemies appearing in the encounter, the designer can also assign experience points and gold (or other currency) to each enemy type. It is possible to assign items that will be made available to the player after a successful encounter to each enemy type, but dropped items are often determined by a Treasure Table (see Chapter 7 for more details).

Depending on the game platform and the type of RPG, an Encounter Table can be very detailed or relatively generic. If the game platform has restrictions as to the number of enemy types that can appear in any area (based on restrictions to the amount of artwork that can be held in memory), the Encounter Table is often relatively simple. In a game where the game platform can support more enemy types (for example, many 2D dungeon crawls as opposed to 3D MMO and standard RPGs), the Encounter Tables can be more detailed and include more monster types.

FRP Random Encounter Table
Map Used: Forest Prime Evil

No. Appearing

Die Result	Singular Name	Plural Name	Minum	Random	Locatn	Flee Minum	Ex. Pts Value	Gold Value	Loot %
1	Dire Wolf	Dire Wolves	1	2	Front Row	35	35	15	20
2	Dire Wolf	Dire Wolves	2	2	Front Row	35	35	15	20
3	Dire Wolf	Dire Wolves	3	2	Back Row	30	35	15	20
4	Boar	Boars	1	1	Front Row	30	45	20	15
5	Boar	Boars	2	1	Front Row	30	45	20	15
6	Boar	Boars	2	2	Back Row	25	45	20	15
7	Bear	Bears	1	0	Front Row	10	90	100	10
8	Bear	Bears	1	1	Back Row	10	90	100	10
9	Rogue Thief	Rogue Thieves	1	1	Back Row	30	100	90	30
10	Rogue Thief	Rogue Thieves	1	2	Back Row	30	100	90	30
11	Rogue Thief	Rogue Thieves	2	1	Back Row	30	100	90	30
12	Rogue Knight	Rogue Knights	1	1	Front Row	5	150	180	20
13	Rogue Knight	Rogue Knights	1	1	Front Row	5	150	180	20
14	Rogue Knight	Rogue Knights	1	2	Front Row	5	150	180	20
15	Rogue Wizard	Rogue Wizards	1	1	Back Row	15	160	300	25
16	Rogue Wizard	Rogue Wizards	2	0	Back Row	15	160	300	25
17	Death Wolf	Death Wolves	2	3	Front Row	0	350	120	10
18	Death Wolf	Death Wolves	4	3	Front Row	0	350	120	10
19	Were-Boar	Were-Boar	2	2	Front Row	0	420	240	5
20	Hippobearamus	Hippobearami	1	2	Front Row	0	600	300	5
21	Archer Prince	Archer Princes	2	2	Back Row	0	350	500	0
22	Woodland Queen	Woodland Queen	1	0	Back Row	0	1200	800	0
23	Forest King	Forest King	1	0	Back Row	0	1800	1200	0

Table 4.4. *This Random Encounter Table could be used in a computer role-playing game. It contains much more information about each creature and allows for multiple copies of each enemy.*

The Encounter Table above (Table 4.4) has more information because it is meant to be used in a fantasy role-playing game. Assume that the combat interface screen allows characters and enemies to occupy two rows, and units in the back row can use only ranged weapons and magic spells while units in the front row can use any weapon. The information appearing on this Encounter Table includes the following data fields:

- *Map Used.* Indicates which map in the game this table is used for.

- *Die Result.* This is a random number generated to identify which group of enemies takes part in the fight. Note that the first 17 rows of the table are used to resolve random encounters while the last seven are used for special encounters triggered by the scripting language. These last seven enemies never appear in random encounters.

- *Name.* A text string for the enemy (sometimes a second entry is needed as well for plural spellings—e.g., "wolf" and "wolves" and "thief" and "thieves"). The name also acts as an identity number pointing to the enemy chart where its statistics are located (see Chapter 6).

- *Number Appearing.* There are two columns used. The first column indicates the minimum number of enemies of that type appear in the encounter. The second column ("Random") indicates the maximum additional enemies that appear based on a random die roll of a range of 0–2. A result of 0 on this table means no extra enemies of that type appear while other results mean one or two extra enemies appear.

- *Location.* Depending on how combat works, the enemies might need to be placed on a battle display. By using a numbered grid overlay, each enemy type can be assigned to a space on the grid where it will appear. This column indicates the preferred starting row for that enemy group, either the front row where an enemy can directly attack characters or the back where they prefer to use magic, ranged combat, or simply wait until a space in the front row becomes available. If a selected row is already filled, then enemy is automatically moved to the other row.

- *Flee Minimum.* This value is used to determine if the enemy will flee at the start of a combat round. A low value means the enemy is unlikely to flee while a higher value means it is more likely to take off. Note that the seven special encounter enemies have a result of 0 for this value, indicating they will not flee from battle. Having this value on the Encounter Table means that the same creature can be given different flee values in different areas of the game world. For example, a wolf might have a very low flee value if attacking in the forest but a higher value if attacking on open ground. Note that this value could also appear in the Entity Attributes Chart, but only one value should be used in the game.

- *Experience Points.* This value indicates the number of experience points the player receives for defeating each enemy of the indicated type. This information could otherwise appear on the enemy chart rather than here. Having the experience point rewards appear on the Encounter Table allows the designers to change the value over time and in different locations.

- *Loot.* Amount of gold (or other currency) given to the player at the end of the battle for each enemy of the indicated type. This information could also appear on the Entity Attribute Chart rather than here (see Chapter 6). Putting this information on the Encounter Table allows the cash payoff for defeating an enemy to be tied to the current area of the game world.

It should be mentioned that this Encounter Table assumes that there will be one enemy type generated for each member of a party. Thus, a larger party of player-controlled characters encounters more enemies. It is possible to set up the table so that multiple groups and their locations on the combat display can be defined per row so that only one random result needs to be generated.

This approach uses some randomization to determine the number of enemies appearing in an encounter. The entries on the table could be of any length, as long as they consistent from one table to the next. Also, it assumes that the total number of different entities encountered will be generated randomly, which could result in some odd situations where an encounter includes both characters like thieves and creatures like bears. Another approach to creating Encounter Tables is shown on the opposite page (Table 4.5). In this version the location and type of entity in the encounter is determined by a single random generation result. The combat display in this case has three spaces in the front row numbered 1–3 and one space in the back row. (Entries for special encounters have been removed.)

Additional information might be added to the Encounter Table based on the desired effects of encounters. For example, instead of giving a set amount of gold per enemy, the amount could be determined randomly just like for the number of enemies of a type. For example, one row might include the minimum amount of gold per enemy type (e.g., two gold pieces per level 1 wolf) and then a second row has the randomization range appears. The random result is added to the base amount to determine the final gold count per enemy type. (e.g., "0–2" means that zero, one, or two extra gold pieces is added to the base amount of two, for a final result of 2–4 pieces of gold per enemy).

Encounter Table
Map Used: Forest Prime Evil

Die Result	Group 1	Num Front 2	Group 2	Num Front 1	Group 3	Num Front 3	Group 4	Num Back
1	Dire Wolf	2	NA	0	NA	0	NA	0
2	Dire Wolf	2	Dire Wolf	1	NA	0	NA	0
3	Dire Wolf	1	Boar	1	Dire Wolf	2	NA	0
4	Dire Wolf	1	Boar	1	Boar	1	Bear	1
5	Boar	1	Boar	1	NA	0	NA	0
6	Boar	2	Dire Wolf	1	Dire Wolf	1	NA	0
7	Boar	2	Bear	1	Dire Wolf	2	NA	1
8	Boar	2	Dire Wolf	2	Bear	1	Bear	1
9	Bear	1	Dire Wolf	1	NA	0	NA	0
10	Bear	1	Boar	1	Dire Wolf	1	NA	0
11	Bear	2	Boar	2	Boar	1	NA	0
12	Bear	2	Dire Wolf	2	Boar	2	Bear	1
13	Rogue Thief	1	Rogue Knight	1	Rogue Knight	1	NA	0
14	Rogue Thief	1	Rogue Knight	2	Rogue Wizard	1	NA	0
15	Rogue Thief	1	Rogue Knight	2	Rogue Knight	2	NA	0
16	Rogue Thief	1	Rogue Knight	1	Rogue Knight	1	Rogue Wizard	1
17	Rogue Knight	2	Rogue Knight	1	Rogue Knight	1	NA	0
18	Rogue Knight	2	Rogue Thief	1	Rogue Thief	1	NA	2
19	Rogue Knight	2	Rogue Thief	1	Rogue Wizard	1	Rogue Wizard	1
20	Rogue Knight	2	Rogue Knight	2	Rogue Knight	2	Rogue Wizard	1
21	Rogue Wizard	1	Rogue Knight	1	Rogue Knight	1	NA	0
22	Rogue Wizard	1	Rogue Knight	2	Rogue Knight	2	NA	0
23	Rogue Wizard	1	Rogue Knight	1	Rogue Thief	2	NA	0
24	Rogue Wizard	1	Rogue Thief	2	Rogue Knight	2	Rogue Thief	1

Table 4.5. *In this version of an Encounter Table, all possible combinations of enemy entities are listed individually by the position where they appear on the combat interface screen.*

Items on the Map

Many games have items that are visible on the playfield. There are a number of decisions the designer must make about how such items are presented and how they are removed. In many games, there are chests scattered about for players to open and collect weaponry, gold, and other useful items. In other games, resources (wood, metal, ammo, etc.) are scattered across the map as well.

In most cases, the items can be selected either by using a game control or moving into a space with them. Another screen or window might pop up, showing what the player has just discovered and allowing the player to move items into an inventory. The player can choose which items to keep and then discard the rest. Another approach is to have items automatically be added to the inventory as soon as player contacts them, and this approach is particularly useful for games where resources have to be gathered to build objects. A third approach, used frequently in real-time strategy games, is to have "gatherer" units be assigned to harvesting resources so the player doesn't have to do all the tedious work by alone.

The designer has to determine how items will be handled early in production. If the player enters a space with ammunition, for example, does all the ammo automatically go into the player's inventory with any excess being discarded? Or does only enough ammo get picked up to fill the player's current inventory, leaving some behind on the playfield to be picked up later? Depending on the ferocity of combat, it can be a great help to be able to leave some ammo available in reserve for later use. Extensive testing helps designers make the final decision about how items on the playfield are handled.

Conclusion

In many action games, movement is just about the most important game element, with the player having to learn to jump from platform to platform and dodge enemies and other obstacles. Most complex data-rich games, on the other hand, have simpler movement mechanics since they are less frenetic. The player enjoys exploring the game world and finding enemies to combat and items to acquire at a more leisurely pace. However, in both simple and complex games, the designer has to figure out how characters and objects will move across the screen.

Determining movement rates in turn-based games is relatively simple if the objective is to mimic reality closely. The real-world pace of humans and vehicles can easily be determined and translated into game pieces moving across the screen, and then it becomes a straightforward process to determine equivalent rates for enemies and other game objects. In addition to movement across the main playfield, the designer also has to think about how strategic movement will be used in a large game world and also how often encounters occur and what enemies will appear. Simple paper and interactive prototypes are helpful in estimating initial values for movement and numbers of encounters before the final values are determined through testing.

Exercises

1. Research several game sites on the Internet and find at least 5 games (they do not have to be wargames) that show the playfield at tactical, operational and grand strategic scales. Do not use any of the games mentioned in this chapter.

   a. Note the size of the objects on the playfield – people, machines, terrain features and the like.

   b. Write up a short essay on the advantages and disadvantages of showing game objects at the different scales and explain what scale you plan to have for your game.

2. Either create a simple hex grid in an art program or find one on the Internet. (You can also draw one and scan it into a computer.)

   a. Create a hex grid in outline form that is 18 hexes wide by 12 hexes high (see Figure 4.8 below), making it transparent so you can superimpose it on another image and still see the outlines of the hexes.

   b. Find an overhead view of a map on the Internet, either a battlefield from some war or a city layout, and position the hex grid over the map.

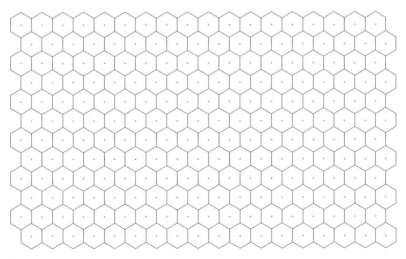

Figure 4.8: *Create a hex map that looks like this for Exercise 2.*

  c. If you were to use the map in a game, what changes would you have to make to the map so it conforms to the hex grid?

  d. What terrain features need to be changed most to fit them inside the hexes?

3. Do some research on the Internet to see if you can find the average movement rate of soldiers on the battlefield in wars of different ages.

  a. Try to find information about movement of units on the battlefield during these eras:

   i. The Napoleonic Wars (1775–1815)

   ii. The American Civil War (1850–1870)

   iii. World War II (1930–1950)

   iv. The Gulf Strike War (1990 to the present).

  b. Select one battle from each of these eras and research how effectively each side moved its troops during the fighting.

   i. If possible, try to find the movement rates for infantry, cavalry (or motorized cavalry), artillery, and (for the last two eras) tanks for each of these battles.

   ii. How did the terrain on the battlefield and the weather affect movement of units?

  c. Write up your findings on one of these battles.

4. Consider the movement of objects in the game you're designing.

  a. Here are some of the factors to keep in mind while determining how objects will move:

   i. Do you need to keep accurate track of movement of units as they move across the playfield or can you "fudge" some movement values?

   ii. How does terrain and weather affect the game mechanics (for example, in movement and combat)?

     iii. Do you think movement of units would be better regulated by using a square grid or hex grid?

  b. Make notes for the chapter in your game design document where you discuss the movement mechanics in your game.

5. Create a paper prototype of one map or playfield in your game. The first version can be rough as you figure out what terrain features to include on your map and what to exclude. You may need to create a number of prototypes until you find the scale that is most appropriate.

  a. Create a simple Terrain Effects Chart for you map to help you remember the initial values you select.

  b. Consider the scale you've selected for you game. How much distance do the units cover moving from hex to hex (or square to square)?

  c. Create some pieces to represent units in your game from paper or thin cardboard, and try moving them around on the map to see how fast they move in relation to one another.

6. Create a Random Encounter Table either for the game you're designing or for a simple action game.

  a. What information do you consider most important for the table?

  b. How do you plan to generate the randomized result when using the table (e.g. by using six-sided or ten-sided dice or some other method)?

  c. Do you want the encounter results from your table to have an equal chance of happening, or do you want to "weight" some results so that they happen more often than others?

7. Make a list of all the objects that appear on the map/playfield in your game.

  a. Group those objects that are controlled directly by the player from all the other objects the player either encounters or picks up during play.

b. How numerous do you want the various objects on the playfield to be? Should some objects appear more frequently than others?

c. Create representations of these objects (in paper or cardboard) that are found and/or encountered on the playfield and experiment with their placement on the paper prototype you've created. Try to visualize what players will see as they move through the game world at the scale you want.

d. Write up a brief essay on how you plan to handle object placement in your game.

8. Write up a first draft of the chapter about movement for your game design document. You can break the chapter into separate sections covering scale, time, terrain features, objects on the playfield, encounters, and so on. Remember that this information is likely to change as you develop the other game mechanics, so don't spend too much time trying to finalize the final text at this point.

CHAPTER 5

ON COMBAT

Many games focus on the clash of characters or nations in conflict, which is resolved through battle. Combat can either be central to game play as in RPG, RTS, and wargames, or it can be nonexistent as in sports and many simulation games. If a game features combat, the player directly control characters or units during the fight as in RPGs and wargames or simply direct units towards the battle as in RTS games. In either case, the designer has to decide how combat is resolved and what factors will affect the sides involved during the fighting.

The designer has to spell out in detail how combat is to be resolved. The method selected has to be consistent and interesting enough to keep the player involved for hours on end. During the design process, the designer comes up with the algorithm or formula for how a combat situation is resolved, and there can sometimes be several forms of combat to discuss—for example, in a fantasy role-playing game where magic combat is often resolved differently than weapon combat. Testing these algorithms in both paper and interactive prototype forms ensures they will work as planned once implemented in code.

How combat is resolved differs for each type of game, and so this chapter examines combat by game genre. In data-rich games discussed in this book, the combat systems are usually more complex and require considerable calculation, whereas games that have abstract combat can get by with much simpler calculations. However, even games requiring a lot of calculations employ fairly simple math.

Rock-Paper-Scissors

One approach to creating balanced units or weapons in a game can be seen in the simple children's game of rock-paper-scissors. Two players count one-two-three and then show an open hand (paper), a

Figure 5.1. *Ensemble Studios'* Age of Empires II: The Age of Kings *is set in the Middle Ages when cavalry, archery, and infantry were the primary military units.*

clenched hand (rock), or the first two fingers sticking out (scissors). Winning the game is simple because paper covers rock, rock breaks scissors, and scissors cuts paper. If both players pick the same option, the game is a draw. There is a 33.3% chance of selecting an option, and all three options are therefore equally viable. There is no clear-cut advantage in choosing one option over the others. The options in the game are balanced.

In games with combat, the designer has to come up with a similar approach when designing weaponry and unit abilities. If one unit or character has an overwhelming capability to destroy all others, then players will naturally gravitate towards it, resulting in an unbalanced game. In a combat game with a medieval theme such as Ensemble Studios' *Age of Empires II* (Figure 5.1), for example, there might be three classes of units—knights, infantry, and archers. The knights move fast and are heavily armored, and therefore they do well against infantry that can only attack when the enemy is close. Archers, on the other hand, can fire at the knights at a distance and retreat before the enemy gets close enough to engage in hand fighting. Infantry is slower than the knights and less well-armored, but they are strong enough to attack archers and to take a certain amount of damage before breaking.

In modern wargames, armored units are equivalent to knights, and they have heavy armor and strong attack ability. Modern infantry units are still relatively slow but they are needed to hold ground that tanks can't. Artillery acts like archers and allows a player to attack units at a distance, but it is very weak if attacked. There are other factors involved in modern combat—for example, air and sea power, supply lines, command and communications, and electronic and chemical/nuclear warfare—that muddy the picture, but in general a well-balanced national army does not rely on one branch only and strives to have equal capability across all branches.

Whatever the period and whatever the game genre, the designer has to make sure that there is some kind of balance in the game. It is fine to give a side a major advantage of some kind—for example, a super-tank that moves fast, is well-armored, and has devastating firepower—but there should be a limiting factor that offsets the advantages—for example, a long production cycle or limited resources to build the unit. It can be devastating to the whole development team to be near beta and suddenly discover that one or two units destroy game balance. Many games unfortunately ship with such glaring errors, so if at all possible, the production teams tries to keep the game balanced from start to finish before releasing it to manufacturing.

Turn-Based vs. Real-Time Combat

Most action video games use real-time combat where both sides move units and attack at the same time. The action is more intense in such games because players never know when someone will pop up to attack and so they have to be continuously on guard. Usually, players control only a single character or unit in these games, so they can move across the playfield looking for enemies, items, and goals. There is little time to plan long-range strategy because the pressure on the player is constant. Most first- and third-person shooters, arcade, and dungeon-crawl role-playing games are real-time, and more standard role-playing games are moving to this mode.

Complex data-based games often require that the player control multiple characters or units, and therefore a turn-based combat system is used. There are two approaches to turn-based combat. Either one side moves and performs attacks with all its units first before the other side has the opportunity to do the same, or players alternate activating units one at a time to move and attack. In games where players needs to think about their actions and plan things out ahead of time, turn-based combat works well. There are drawbacks to this system—for example, being forced to commit all one's units without knowing how the enemy will react or sometimes winning a battle only because one side gets to act first. Wargames as well as many strategy and simulation games usually employ a turn-based combat system. While older role-playing games have traditionally used turn-based systems, the trend is now towards real-time action. Tactical RPGs, which are like mini-wargames, typically retain the turn-base method of combat.

One difficulty in creating paper prototypes to test the combat system is the difficulty of mimicking real-time combat. Turn-based combat is easy to model on paper, but real-time combat is more problematic. The easiest approach is to break down real time into a series of mini-turns lasting a few seconds. It is still difficult to remember to move all units on the battlefield and begin various attacks unless players are willing to use lots of information markers (paper or cardboard) to note changes to ongoing actions. An interactive prototype works much better to test a real-time combat system, although even this prototype is not perfect. While the initial values for movement and combat can be estimated using an interactive prototype, the real values won't be nailed down until the designers can test they game at the correct scale at runtime.

Combat Attributes (Statistics)

Attributes (also called statistics) are quantitative properties assigned to units to give uniformity when resolving game actions. As mentioned in Chapter 4, units are assigned movement rates to quantify the ability of each unit when moving, allowing units with high movement rates to move a greater distance in a given length of time. Likewise, combat attributes are assigned to units to help resolve combat actions. Some simple action games use only a few attributes for combat while other games that try to simulate real life require more attributes. A game combining ground, air, and naval combat, for example, usually requires numerous attributes because the units involved have many different real-world capabilities.

The most common attributes used to resolve combat include:

- *Attack Value.* The strength of a unit when attacking. The value is determined by the offensive capability of the unit and the weaponry it uses.

- *Defense Value.* The ability of a unit to withstand an attack. The value is determined by the defensive capability of the unit and how well it is armored or can deflect damage.

- *Hit Points.* The total amount of damage a unit can withstand before being rendered incapable of participating in combat. A powerful unit like a tank normally has many more Hit Points than a weak unit like infantry.

These attributes are used, in one way or another, in a formula—or algorithm—to determine the outcome of an attack. For example, the algorithm might be:

Determine Successful Attack Number

Step 1. Attack Value – Defense Value = Hit Point Modifier.

- If the result is 0 or less (meaning the defender is stronger than the attacker), nothing happens and the combat ends.

- If the result is 1 or more, the defending unit takes damage so proceed to Step 2.

Determine Damage to Defending Unit

Step 2. Current Hit Point Total – Hit Point Modifier = New Hit Point Total.

- The unit's current Hit Point Total is reduced by the number determined in Step 1.

- If the unit's new Hit Point Total is 0 or less, the unit is incapacitated or destroyed.

In turn-based games, a defending unit can be removed from play without being able to inflict damage on the attacking unit because it has been destroyed before the owning player has a chance to re-act. In real-time games, however, the defending unit is allowed to counterattack, possibly inflicting some damage on the attacking unit as well. If necessary, the designer should experiment with real-time and turn-based combat in prototype form before settling on one approach.

Note that the values attributed to units in a game are often called "statistics," which can be confusing because there are two different meanings to the term. On the one hand, statistics can refer to numerical values assigned to players in sports games—for example, ERA (earned run average) and RBI (runs batted in) in baseball. These statistics or "stats" help the public compare one player with another to determine who is the better pitcher or batter. The other meaning of statistics is the branch of mathematics concerned with collecting and analyzing numerical data, as in probabilities and statistics. Unless otherwise indicated, statistics in this book refers to various classes of data assigned to units in a game and are referred to as attributes.

Combat in Role-Playing Games

One of the more complex approaches to combat in games can be found in role-playing games. Video RPGs descended from paper RPGs such as TSR Hobbies' *Dungeons & Dragons* and Steve Jackson Games' *GURPS (Generic Universal Role-Playing System)*. There are several kinds of electronic RPGs, each with its own form of combat:

- *Tactical RPGs* are like turn-based mini-wargames where the player moves a number of units around a gridded playfield and has them attack enemy units. Because these games are more like traditional wargames, they are discussed in more detail later in the chapter in "Combat in Wargames."

- *Dungeon-crawl RPGs* are action-based and are usually in real time, with the player controlling a character or party that moves through a multi-level playfield and engages in short battles with the many enemies running around the environment. Combats are usually short with only a few options available to the player. The idea is to kill as many enemies and gather as much treasure as possible. Some popular dungeon-crawl RPGs include Blizzard Entertainment's *Diablo* series, Atari's *Gauntlet* series and Ascaron's *Sacred 2: Fallen Angel*.

- *Traditional RPGs* are modeled on paper RPGs and therefore offer more options to the player. In addition to attacking with weapons and magic, players can choose to use items in their inventory, just defend against attack, or try to flee. The combats take much longer since the enemies are more sophisticated in their choice of options as well. There are many popular RPGs including BioWare's *Baldur's Gate* series and Square Enix's *Final*

Fantasy series. Many of the massively multiplayer online RPGs (MMORPG) like Sony Online's *EverQuest* and Blizzard's *World of Warcraft* use complex combat systems as well. Some of the most popular modern RPGs like Bethesda Softworks' *The Elder Scrolls IV: Oblivion* and *Fallout 3* use combat that is action-based and feel more like a first-person shooter than a traditional RPG.

In RPGs there are usually three kinds of attacks available to the player: melee, ranged, and magic/technology. Melee combat involves hand-to-hand fighting where opposing units are adjacent to one another and the weapons are knives, swords, axes, clubs, and the like. Both opponents are subject to damage during such attacks, and so stronger units generally are assigned to melee combat. Ranged combat involves the attack staying at some distant and using a long-range weapon like a gun, bow, javelin, or missile launcher to inflict damage on the opponent. Generally, the damage depends on the projectile being fired and can range from light for knife strikes to very heavy for missile blasts. Normally, only the defender is damaged in the attack (unless it too is capable of attacking long-range). Magic/technology combat involves the use of mystical forces or exotic science and involves the attackers casting a spell, using a magic item, or employing some exotic alien technology that seems like magic. Such combat can take place near an enemy or at a range. Magic/technology combat is handled slightly differently from physical melee and ranged attacks (see below).

Available Actions during RPG Combat

Whether playing a turn-based or real-time RPG, the player usually can select an action for a character to perform in the upcoming combat. Sometimes the player selects all actions for the characters in a party before they are resolved, and sometimes the actions are selected in an ongoing manner with the player continually assigning new actions. Typical actions found in an RPG include:

- *Attacking.* The player attacks with the weapon currently being wielded, and the combat is resolved as described below. This action is always an offensive action.

- *Using Magic/Technology.* The player selects a magic spell or psychic or other quasi-supernatural ability known to the character. The action can be either offensive if it is used to attack enemies, defensive if it is used to protect the character and/or party, or modifying if it is used primarily to change the current condition of a character or enemy (for example, healing or removing poison). This form of combat is discussed in detail below, while different kinds of magic and technology are discussed in Chapter 8.

- *Using an Item.* The player can either select an object from a character's inventory (e.g., a potion, scroll, or other item) or can swap out a weapon or piece of armor from the inventory to the character. An item can sometimes be used to attack, defend, or modify something. See Chapter 7 for more about items.

- *Fleeing.* This option allows the character and/or party the chance to flee the current combat. Usually the outcome is determined by randomization, and if the player succeeds, the combat ends. Otherwise, the combat continues until one side or the other is incapacitated or the player succeeds in fleeing.

- *Defending.* The player selects this option to put a character into a defensive stance. The character only defends and does not attack. The amount of damage inflicted during the attack is often less because of the defensive stance. This option is only occasionally used, but it does come in handy when trying to get more experience points for a low-level character. In some games, this option is also used to restore a small amount of mana.

The designer might decide to add other options as well based on the overall complexity of the game. If the characters have skills as well as abilities, there might be a "Use Skills" option available. There might also be a "Steal" option that allows a character to try to steal something from an opponent. The designer should be thoughtful about how many actions to include in the game, since it is best if they all fit on one menu in a small window (particularly in real-time games) so that the player can see what is happening on the playfield. Some options require one or more additional menus, and it can be painful to wade through a number of menus to find the right spell or item, especially if the action is real-time.

Combat Attributes in RPGs

RPG combat is usually based on the attributes assigned to a character (see Chapter 6 for more about attributes). The attributes are expressed as values that grow over time as characters win combats and resolve quests. Depending on how the game system is set up, combat resolution involves several of these attributes. The attributes most often associated with combat are:

- *Strength* (Body, Brawn, Might, etc.). The physical muscle the character has that determines what kind of weapon he or she can carry and how much energy is inflicted with each physical blow. It is used to determine the Attack Value in combat.

- *Constitution* (Stamina, Endurance, Vitality, etc.). The ability to withstand attack and the overall health of the character. It also helps define how well the character can resist various debilitating attacks (for example, poison). It is used to determine the Defense Value in combat.

- *Size* (Health). The character's overall mass and physical dimensions, which influence its total number of Hit Points.

- *Dexterity* (Agility, Speed, Reflex, etc.). This ability defines how quickly the character can act and react. It can be used to figure out the attack order during combat and also as a defense against magic attack.

- *Luck* (Karma, Fate, Chance, etc.). This ability sometimes can have an effect on combat if the system includes a step allowing a character to avoid an attack.

RPG Combat Algorithms

There are any number of approaches to creating a combat algorithm for a role-playing game. In a paper RPG, players have to understand the rules for resolving combat lest the game dissolve into bickering, and the rules for combat resolution differ from one game system to another. In electronic RPGs, players don't have to appreciate the intricacies of how combat is resolved, but they do have to understand their options during combat and feel that each attack is being resolved directly without cheating.

To resolve combat, the algorithm should clearly outline a step-by-step process for completing the action. The design staff needs to work with the programming team to help them understand what is to happen in each step, and then the code has to be tested vigorously to make certain that everything is working according to plan. Here are the main steps needed to resolve a combat algorithm:

- Determine the type of combat action being performed, either using a weapon or using magic/technology.
- The order in which attacks will be resolved.
- How Attack Values are determined.
- How Defense Values are determined.
- How an attack is resolved by randomization.

The remainder of this section deals with resolving combat with a weapon. Magic/Technology combat is discussed in more detail later on.

Determining the Order of Attacks

In many RPGs, especially turned-based games, the order in which attacks take place is very important. The process can be rather simple—checking an attribute (for example, Dexterity) to see which unit has the highest value and then going in order until all units have acted. Other processes are more complex, involving a formula to determine who has the "initiative" in a round. For example,

$$1/4 \times \text{Attribute}_{Constitution} + 3/4 \text{ Attribute}_{Dexterity} = \text{Initiative Value.}$$

In real-time games, the matter gets a bit muddier because units are performing actions constantly, and the player would be upset if he or she could perform some action and then have to wait a long time for all the other units to act before being able to perform another action. One method around this problem is to allow units to perform actions after a limited amount of "reload" time. Square Enix used the Active Time Battle (ATB) system starting in *Final Fantasy IV* (1991) where the player selects an order in real time. As soon as the order is finished, the player can then input the next one no matter what the other characters and enemies in the combat are doing.

If the player controls only one character, giving orders in real time is not a problem. However, if the player has to control a party of players and issue orders to each of them, the situation can get almost too frantic. There are usually a number of orders available to the character, so deciding which one everyone in the party is to use is time consuming—and therefore can lead to the incapacitation of an ally in the party. One way around this problem is to have time stop when the player selects a character and then restart once an order has been issued.

Determining the Attack Value

Depending on how combat is modeled, the attack value (AV) in a combat has to be determined. It could be one of the values listed above (usually Strength) or it could involve a formula of some kind. For example,

$$3/4 \times \text{Attribute}_{\text{Strength}} + 1/3 \times \text{Attribute}_{\text{Size}} = \text{Attack Value (AV)}.$$

Note that as these attributes increase as the player levels up, the overall attack value increases too. This value is often referred to as the *base value* because it is frequently modified for a variety of reasons. It can be used to determine the Attack Value if the player attacks with bare hands instead of a weapon.

Another approach is to use the attack value of the weapons (see Chapter 7 on Items for more details) instead of the character's attributes. In this case, the abilities might act like modifiers to the weapon's attack value. For example,

$$\text{Sword}_{\text{Attack Value}} + 1/3 \times \text{Attribute}_{\text{Strength}} = \text{Base AV}.$$

Once the base attack value is determined, then any modifiers are applied to it to improve or weaken the attack. These modifiers can come from the weapon being wielded (for example, a "+1 Sword of Doom"), other magic equipment worn by the character (amulet, ring, etc.), and any magical spells/technology cast upon the character. Modifiers are usually cumulative and can be both positive and negative. For example, a character might be carrying the +1 Sword of Doom and a ring that increases the character's Strength attribute, but the character has been poisoned, which weakens him (for example, -1 to Strength).

The formula for determining the modified Attack Value for the combat thus becomes

$$\text{Base AV} + \text{Positive Modifiers} - \text{Negative Modifiers} = \text{Modified AV}.$$

If the designer wishes, this modified attack value can be used to determine the results of the combat. A randomized result can then be generated using the Combat Table, and the result from the table is the damage inflicted on the enemy. There are times, however, when the designer might wish to fine tune the weapon combat to take into account the type of enemy being attacked and the armor and defensive magic spells affecting it.

Determining the Defense Value

Using too simple a formula to determine the amount of damage inflicted on an enemy can lead to odd results. For example, if the player is fighting an unarmored goblin with a short sword, and the combat result winds up with six Hit Points of damage being inflicted on the goblin in each attack, it might seem odd if a similar amount of damage is inflicted against a heavily armored rhinoceros. The player would expect the rhino's skin to absorb some and possible all of the damage. To account for variability in an opponent's defenses, the designer might include a defense value in the combat resolution algorithm.

As with determining the attack value, the designer can use the enemy's attributes to define the base defense value (DV). For example,

$$1/4 \text{ Attribute}_{Constitution} + 1/6 \text{ Attribute}_{Size} = \text{Base DV.}$$

This base value can either be used as is or be modified by other factors, such as the enemy's armor, magic equipment, and magic spells. The formula to determine the modified defense value would be

Base DV + Positive Modifiers – Negative Modifiers = Modified DV.

Combining the two formulas together results in a final attack value:

Modified AV – Modified DV = Final AV.

Example of a Combat Algorithm

Now that the basic formulas for figuring out how character and item attributes and modifiers work, the designer can set about defining the algorithm for how combat will be resolved. The algorithm is a step-by-step process explaining how combat takes place. In this example, the algorithm first checks to see if the cumulative Attack Value is greater than the cumulative Defense Value, and if so, uses a Combat Table to determine how much damage is inflicted on the defender. The algorithm might look something like this:

Determine Attack Type

Step 1. Determine the kind of attack to resolve.

- If magic combat, use magic combat resolution (see below).
- If ranged combat, use weapon combat resolution and apply results only to the target.
- If melee combat, use weapon combat resolution, apply results to the target, and then repeat to apply damage to the attacker.

Determine Modified Attack Value

Step 2. Use the attacker's Attack Value based on its current attribute level.

Step 3. Find the attacker's base Attack Value.

- $Weapon_{Attack Value} + Attributes_{Attack Value} = Base AV$.

Step 4. Find the attacker's modified Attack Value.

- Base AV + Positive Modifiers – Negative Modifiers = Modified AV.

Determine Modified Defense Value

Step 5. Use the defender's Base Defense Value based on its attribute level.

- $Attribute_{Attack Value} = Base AV$.

Step 6. Fine the defender's modified Defense Value.

- Base DV + Positive Modifiers – Negative Modifiers = Modified DV.

Determine Final Attack Value

Step 7. Find the Final Attack Value.

- Modified AV – Modified DV = Final AV.

Determine If Attack Succeeds

Step 8. If Final AV = 0 (or less), end combat resolution.

- Show "Attack misses" message.

Step 9. If Final AV >= 1, continue resolving the combat.

- Go to Step 10.

Resolve Attack

Step 10. Generate a random result using the Combat Table.

Step 11. Determine the amount of damage to the target.

- If the result is 0, do nothing and end the combat.
- If the result is 1+ but not within the Critical Hit Range (see below), then go to Step 14 and apply damage to the target.
- If the result is within the Critical Hit Range, go to Step 12 and use the Critical Hit Table to determine the total damage to the enemy.

Resolve Critical Hit

Step 12. Generate a random result on the Critical Hit Table.

Step 13. Multiply the original amount of damage from the Combat Table by the multiplier result on the Critical Hit Table and go to Step 14.

Apply Damage to Target

Step 14. Subtract the final damage amount from the target's current Hit Point total.

- If the target still has Hit Points, end the combat.
- If the target has no more Hit Points, remove it and play its death animation.

Note that this example can be changed based on the designer's concepts for how fighting should work in the game. In a simple dungeon-crawl RPG, there might be no Combat Table involved and any damage is applied directly to the enemy's Hit Point total. Usually, to keep things moving, an enemy is killed in a blow or two, so an elaborate combat resolution is not needed. In a full-blown computer or video RPG, though, combat can usually last for several turns, with the confrontation against the main villain taking a considerable amount of time, effort, and resources. However the combat resolution algorithm is defined, it should be consistent throughout the game, so the player doesn't feel the game is cheating by suddenly switching to an unfamiliar attack method.

Combat Table

If the result of each attack is always the same during the course of battle, the player might grow suspicious of how combat is resolved or try to use the system against itself to minimize damage. It is highly unlikely that in real life the same attack would always cause the same amount of damage, because as the combatants move around while

Combat Table (Weighted)

2d10 Result	Effects	Damage Modifier
1–2	Miss	NA
3–10	Near miss	-2
11–30	Normal hit	0
31–50	Normal hit	+1
51–60	Normal hit	+3
61–70	Hard hit	+6
71–80	Hard hit	+10
81–90	Hard hit	+15
91–95	Very hard hit	+25
96–100	Critical hit	**

** = Roll on Critical Hit Table and use
that modified damage result.

Table 5.1. On this Combat Table, the results are weighted towards the center so that most damage occurs in this range. Compare this table with Table 5.3 and note that they both include a Damage Modifier column.

engaged, blows can be dodged or dampened by armor. As a result, the designer might decide to use a Combat Table to come up with various results for each attack. The advantage of using such a table is that the designer can weight the results so that some are more likely to occur than others because their probabilities are greater (see Table 5.1). It is possible to create any number of Combat Tables based on how the algorithm for combat is structured.

The results on the table can be a value that is subtracted from the enemy's Hit Point total. Or the value can be increased or decreased based on other factors that affect the combat (for example, if the player is poisoned, there might be a -5 die roll modifier applied to the final 2d10 die roll). Many games use a traditional 2d10 randomization system allowing for 100 possible outcomes, but electronic RPGs can use any range to determine results.

Workarounds for Limited Results on a Combat Table

There is a problem with just using the given results from random die rolls on such a table. The system has to work for the whole game, from beginning enemies with few Hit Points to the major villain at the end who has a ton of points. If the maximum result on Combat Table is 50, for example, it could take a long, long time to kill off a very strong enemy with many Hit Points. Likewise, it might seem odd to get a result of 50 against a level 1 wolf very early in the game when the player is still weak and has poor equipment.

There are several approaches to solve this problem. One idea is to use the player's current weapon to determine the amount of damage inflicted on a target. For example, if the player has a Short Sword with an attack value of "2," that number could be used directly to determine the damage against the target (in effect the Combat Table is not used). As the player finds more powerful weapons, they do increasing amounts of damage to enemies. Modifiers for spells and magical equipment can also be used to improve or weaken attacks.

Another approach is to limit the range of results on the Combat Table based on where the player currently is in the overall story. For example, if it is early in the game, only the first five entries in Table 5.2 are used. As the player increases in experience levels, new entries on the table are made available, allowing for greater damage results, while lower entries are ignored. Thus, over time, the player inflicts much greater damage as higher experience levels than at lower levels.

RPG Combat Chart

2D10 Result	Base Damg	Char Level	2D10 Result	Base Damg	Char Level	2D10 Result	Base Damg	Char Level	2D10 Result	Base Damg	Char Level	2D10 Result	Base Damg	Char Level
1	3	1	21	22	3–4	41	62	5–6	61	103	5–7	81	164	7–8
2	4	1	22	24	3–4	42	64	5–6	62	106	5–7	82	168	7–9
3	5	1	23	26	3–4	43	66	5–6	63	109	5–7	83	172	7–9
4	6	1	24	28	3–4	44	68	5–6	64	112	5–7	84	176	7–9
5	7	1	25	30	3–4	45	70	3–4	65	115	6–7	85	180	7–9
6	8	1–2	26	32	3–5	46	72	5–6	66	118	6–7	86	184	7–9
7	9	1–2	27	34	3–5	47	74	5–6	67	121	6–7	87	188	7–9
8	10	1–2	28	36	3–5	48	76	5–6	68	124	6–7	88	192	7–9
9	11	2	29	38	3–5	49	78	5–6	69	127	6–7	89	196	7–9
10	12	2	30	40	3–5	50	80	5–6	70	130	6–8	90	200	8–9
11	13	2	31	42	4–5	51	82	5–6	71	133	6–8	91	205	8–9
12	14	2–3	32	44	4–5	52	84	5–6	72	136	6–8	92	210	8–9
13	15	2–3	33	46	4–5	53	86	5–6	73	139	6–8	93	215	8–9
14	16	2–3	34	48	4–5	54	88	5–6	74	142	6–8	94	220	8–9
15	17	2–3	35	50	4–5	55	90	5–6	75	145	6–8	95*	230	8+
16	18	3	36	52	4–5	56	92	5–7	76	148	6–8	96*	240	8+
17	19	3	37	54	4–6	57	94	5–7	77	151	6–8	97*	260	8+
18	20	3	38	56	4–6	58	96	5–7	78	154	7–8	98*	280	8+
19	21	3–4	39	58	4–6	59	98	5–7	79	157	7–8	99*	310	8+
20	22	3–4	40	60	4–6	60	100	5–7	80	160	7–8	00*	350	8+

*=Critical hit. Roll on Critical Hit Table to get final result.

Table 5.2. *The damage on this Combat Table is based on the player's current Experience Level, and as the level increases so does the damage.*

The results on a Combat Table do not always have to be hard numbers, either. Instead, the results could be percentages that modify some value that is used to define damage (see Table 5.3). For example, in the following Combat Table, the percentages are applied to the player's current weapon, with fractions being rounded up. Thus, if the player has a Long Sword with a damage value of 6 and rolls a 5,

Combat Table (Percentages)

2d10 Result	Effects	Damage Modifier
1–2	Miss	NA
3–10	Near miss	.9%
11–30	Normal hit	0
31–50	Normal hit	1.05%
51–70	Normal hit	1.10%
71–85	Hard hit	1.15%
86–95	Hard hit	1.20%
96–100	Critical hit	**

** = Roll on Critical Hit Table and use that modified damage result.

Table 5.3. *In this Combat Table, damage results are given as percentages based on the player's current weapon, so damage increases as a weapon gets more powerful.*

the value of 6 is multiplied by the result of 25% and the final damage to the enemy is 2 (6 × .25 = 1.5, with fractions rounded up to 2).

Critical Hit Table

There is nothing more exciting than hitting an enemy so adeptly with a weapon that it inflicts grievous injury. To reflect this idea of doing excess damage, many games include a Critical Hit Table of one kind or another. Depending on how the combat system works, a critical hit often occurs if the random die roll falls within a certain small range (for example, "97–100" on a 2d10 Combat Table). In this case, the normal result of combat is greatly increased, usually by some multiplier. Another random roll is made on a Critical Hit Table (see Table 5.4) and the result on this table modifies the original damage. For example, in the Critical Hit Table below, a random result of "26" means the final result is doubled, so whatever the original damage was supposed to be, that result is multiplied by two before being applied to the enemy's Hit Point total.

Magic/Technology Combat

The main difference between magic/technology and weapon combat is that the defender has only limited defense against such an attack. (Technology is used in science-fiction RPGs for mystic and psychic

Critical Hit Table

Random %	Text	Damage Effect	Extra Effect or Target
1–30	Nasty hit	1.25 × Damage	NA
31–45	Vicious blow	1.50 × Damage	NA
46–60	Wicked strike	1.75 × Damage	NA
61–70	Grievous wound	2.00 × Damage	NA
71–80	Devastating injury	2.25 × Damage	NA
81–90	Monstrous hit	2.50 × Damage	Stunned 1 turn
91–93	Formidable strike	2.75 × Damage	Stunned 1 turn
94–96	Dire injury	3.00 × Damage	Stunned 2 turns
97–98	Suppurating wound	4.00 × Damage	Unconscious
99–00	Life-threatening damage	5.00 × Damage	Unconscious

Table 5.4. *This is an example of a Critical Hit Table. The text column could appear directly on the screen. The Damage Effect is a multiple applied to the final damage of the attack, which is determined by the combat algorithm.*

abilities that mimic magic, and for ease of reference this section will refer to all such attacks as "magic.") The magic attack can be handled like weapon combat, as described in the previous section, but often the resolution process is simplified. Most magic attacks follow this kind of procedure:

Determine Magic Attack Type

Step 1. Check the magic spell that was selected.

- If the magic is a scroll or enchanted item, proceed to Step 2. There is no reduction to the attacker's mana level.

- If the attacker has enough mana to cast the spell, reduce the attacker's mana level by the amount and proceed to Step 2.

- If the attacker does not have enough mana to cast the spell, the combat ends and show the text message "You do not have enough mana to cast the spell."

Determine Enemy Type

Step 2. Check the enemy type to see if it is a possible target for the spell:

- If the target can be damaged by the magic, proceed to Step 3.

- If the target can't be damaged by the magic, resolve the rest of the attack but show the text message "This spell has no effect on ____."

Resolve Saving Die Roll

Step 3. Determine if the defender dodges the spell by generating a random result and checking the target's Dexterity value.

- Determine if any modifiers currently apply to the defender's Dexterity value. If so, use the modified Dexterity value.

- If the result is greater than the Dexterity value, the magic attack misses, the combat ends, and show the text message "The spell missed its target."

- If the result is equal to or less than the Dexterity value, proceed to Step 4.

Resolve Magic Attack

Step 4. Subtract the magic spell's Attack Value from the target's current Hit Point total.

- If the target still has Hit Points, end the combat.
- If the target has no more Hit Points, remove it and play its death animation.

Step 3 is referred to as a "Saving Die Roll" in traditional paper RPGs, and gives the target a chance to dodge the magic spell. Depending on how the design works, the die roll can be made against a single attribute (Dexterity in the example given) or against a combination of attributes that give a modified save value:

$$3/4 \text{ Attribute}_{\text{Dexterity}} + 1/4 \text{ Attribute}_{\text{Luck}} - 1/10 \text{ Attribute}_{\text{Size}} = \text{Save Value}.$$

Another approach is to set the save value individually for each creature, so that the designer can influence how likely it is that the character or enemy can dodge the magic attack. However the designer approaches this mechanic, he or she needs to make sure that it works, so testing it early on in prototype form is vital.

Fleeing Combat

If a fleeing option is available during combat, the player can attempt to get out of the current situation, which can be useful if a character is close to dying. In some games where the player controls a party, a flee attempt sometimes causes the whole party to run away and sometimes only the character making the attempt. It can be annoying to have to make repeated flee attempts to extricate the whole party from combat, and this option should be used only if there is a good reason for forcing the player to make repeated attempts. In any case, the results of a flee attempt should be consistent throughout the game.

Once the player decides to flee, the game generates a random result and checks some attribute to see if fleeing succeeds. Sometimes the ability to flee is based on a character's attributes or combination of attributes. "Modifiers" might apply positively or negatively to the flee value for such things as a spell being cast on the character or any magic equipment being worn that affects the flee value. For example,

$$\tfrac{3}{4}\,\text{Attribute}_{\text{Dexterity}} + \tfrac{1}{2}\,\text{Attribute}_{\text{Luck}} +/-\,\text{Modifiers} = \text{Maximum Flee Value}.$$

In some cases, however, the designer wants to make sure that the player cannot flee a battle, especially against major villains or in battles where the player is trying to get some quest item. One approach is to assign the flee value to the enemy involved in the combat, with very tough enemies having very low flee values and major villains having a flee value of 0. To alert the player that a combat cannot be fled, the flee option can be grayed out so the player can't select it.

To encourage the player to take on all battles, the designer might decide to include a punishment for a successful flee attempt. The punishment can take the form of a fine or levy ("You lose ____ amount of gold.") or removing an item from the player's inventory ("You drop your +1 Magic Sword as you scurry ignominiously away from the fight."). However, if players have to battle low-level enemies repeatedly as they move through previously explored areas, fleeing becomes a time saver. Punishment for fleeing a combat should be thoroughly tested before the final decision is made on how harsh it will be.

Combat in Wargames

Perhaps the most complex form of game combat is found in wargames, which trace their roots to paper military simulations published by Avalon Hill, SPI (Simulations Publications, Inc.), and other companies during the 1970s to the 1980s. Trying to model a battle requires many game mechanics and so these paper games usually featured a number of charts and tables used to resolve actions. There are fewer companies publishing paper wargames nowadays, but there are a few, including Avalanche Press and Critical Hit.

There is also a branch of board games that are simpler than traditional wargames but with much more depth than children's games. They often emphasize strategy over luck, are more abstract than wargames but less abstract than Go or Chess, and focus more on economics than warfare. They are referred to as German-style games, and the best-known is *The Settlers of Catan* (Kosmos), first published in 1995 and brought to America by Mayfair Games. These games are a good introduction to wargames, without the same complexity and learning curve.

There are several kinds of wargames, each with its own form of combat:

- *Tactical Role-Playing Games.* These games feel a bit like a combination of chess and tabletop miniatures games (in which the player controls a small number of military units that are moved around on a large playfield to match the scale of the units). These games are turn-based so as to allow the player to experiment with different tactics as units approach the enemy to engage in combat. Sometimes the action is resolved on a unit-by-unit basis and at other times the player assigns movement and attack orders to all units and then each combat is resolved at the end of the player's turn. There is often a story driving the action, and the main characters rise in overall ability and get better weapons as the game progresses as in standard role-playing games. Some popular tactical RPGs include Square's *Final Fantasy Tactics* and Atlus' *Disgaea 2:Cursed Memories* (Figure 5.2).

- *Real-Time Strategy (RTS) Games.* These games focus not only on military action but also on gathering the resources needed to create new war materials and units. The player spends part of the time dealing with resource gathering and building and part of the time sending troops into battle. The battle systems for these games are relatively simple since the action is in real time and the player has multiple chores to attend to at any given moment. Some popular RTS games include Westwood Studios' *Command & Conquer* series, Ensemble Studios' *Age of Empires* series, and Blizzard's *WarCraft* (not to be confused with *World of Warcraft* which is a MMORPG) and *StarCraft* series.

- *Traditional Wargames.* These games try to recreate real battles and wars in miniature on paper maps or on the computer. The emphasis is primarily on leading armies and less about resource management and manufacturing. Because players have to control many units, the games are almost always turn-based, although there have been some attempts to create games using simultaneous movement (for example, SPI's science-fiction game *Starforce: Alpha Centauri*), albeit with limited success. Because of the complexities of modern warfare that includes land, air, and naval units, these games tend to be very complex. They also use

Figure 5.2. *Nichon Ichi Software's* Disgaea 2: Cursed Memories *is a tactical-role playing game that focuses on turn-based combat using a grid to regulate the movement of units.*

many charts and tables to resolve game actions, so the learning curve for such games can be formidable. Fortunately, computers make these games much more transparent because the charts and tables are hidden from players. Some computer games that fall into this category are Sid Meier's *Civilization* series, The Creative Assembly's *Medieval II: Total War*, and Breakaway Games' *Waterloo: Napoleon's Last Battle*. This genre has declined in popularity over time as real-time strategy games gained favor.

- *Combat Vehicle Simulations.* There are many real-time vehicle simulator games that contain combat. Whether it be as an RAF fighting the Luftwaffe during World War II or a tank commander in an M1 tank against Warsaw Pact forces, the focus of these games is driving or piloting a vehicle while engaging in combat. Sometimes the game is relatively simple, much like an arcade game, while others are simulations that try to give players a full sense of what it's like to be inside the vehicle during combat. Some of the best games in this genre include LucasArts *Their Finest Hour: The Battle of Britain*, MicroProse's *M1 Tank Platoon*, and for the science-fiction fan ORIGIN System's *Wing Commander* series.

- *Military-Themed First-Person Shooter (FPS) Games.* Recently, there has been an upswing in interest in military-themed games, due in part to the conflicts in Iraq and Afghanistan. Several FPS series have gained popularity in depicting World War II and even modern combat through the eyes of individual soldiers or squads in battle. These games are, of course, in real time, and their focus is more on action than recreating historical events realistically. Some popular games in this genre include Dreamworks Interactive's *Medal of Honor* series, Activision's *Call of Duty* series, and Red Storm Entertainment's *Tom Clancy's Rainbow Six* series.

Interest in wargames in the United States tends to increase when real wars are happening, and they give gamers a sense of what it feels like to be involved in combat, although in the comfort of one's home instead of in the trenches. Real-time games currently dominate the market because they are easier to learn and can be played on computers. Complex military simulations are of interest to a more mature audience and, because of the many options available to players, are played primarily on computers. Unfortunately, it is difficult to grasp both the details and the full scope of a battle on a computer screen at the same time. The computer can either show a part of the battle in enough detail for the player to decide how to move units or show the whole battle on the full screen with insufficient detail or ability to examine and manipulate units. One way to get around this limitation is to let the player scroll in to see the units on the battlefield and then scroll out to view the whole theater.

Attributes in Wargames

In addition to movement rates, attack and defense values, and Hit Points, the units in wargames can have many more attributes as well, depending on the type of unit, its weapons and movement capabilities, the era being recreated, and the scale of the game. Until the 20th century, the main land units in armies were infantry, cavalry, and artillery, and each unit had its own special limitations as to movement and attack ability. Warships were also available but they were primarily responsible for moving units from one place to another and keeping them supplied; they also attacked one another with artillery and occasionally bombed enemy forts and land units. During the 20th century, new kinds of units were added to the mix, with airplanes dominating the skies, submarines hiding below the ocean surface, satellites for instant worldwide communications, and nuclear and biological weapons that could inflict mass destruction not only on armies but on civilians as well.

Designing a modern era operational- or strategic-level wargame can be daunting because units have so many abilities. Nowadays, a

Figure 5.3. *Eagle Dynamics'* Lock On: Flaming Cliffs 2 *is a simulation about modern air combat featuring air-to-air and air-to-ground combat.*

properly armed infantry unit not only has the ability to attack other infantry but can also take out tanks and aircraft if armed with anti-tank and surface-to-air missiles. It is not surprising then that most modern games are at the tactical level, focusing on individual vehicles or soldiers. For example, Eagle Dynamics' *Lock On: Flaming Cliffs 2* (Figure 5.3) is a computer game that focuses on different forms of combat by modern aircraft.

Here are some of the additional attributes for military units, based on the scale of the battle in the game. Note that units in these games can have additional attributes as well.

Tactical Level

- *Weight Level.* The amount of materials (weapons, armor, ammo, etc.) a unit can carry.

- *Ammo Capacity.* The amount of ammo for each weapon type the unit is carrying.

- *Reload Time.* How long it takes to reload a weapon. Very powerful weapons generally have a longer reload time.

- *Blast Radius.* The distance the damage from an exploding projectile or bomb reaches and inflicts damage. The damage is worst at center of the blast and then diminishes as distance increases.

- *Line-of-Sight (LOS).* The ability of a unit to see a target and attack it with a ranged weapon. LOS is blocked by terrain features between the attacker and target that are opaque or are higher than the attacker.

- *Indirect Line-of-Sight.* The ability of a unit to fire at a target it can't see. Some mortars and other projectile weapons can lob projectiles at the position of an unseen enemy, attempting to cause damage by the blast.

Operational Level

- *Weapon Range.* The distance a projectile can be fired by a ranged-weapon. In tactical games, this attribute is used for hand-thrown weapons like knives and hand axes since many ranged weapons can fire a projectile great distances.

- *Supply Lines.* The distance between a unit and a supply base. Units rely on bases for food, ammo, and gasoline.

- *Command Radius.* How far a leader can be from the units he or she commands and still effectively give them orders.

- *Leadership Ability.* The rating of a leader in terms of command ability and overall competence as a military leader.

- *Morale.* The nerve of a military unit when under fire. A unit new to combat may break and rout when first fired upon (called "seeing the elephant" from Roman times).

- *Reinforcements Rate.* How quickly and effectively reinforcements can reach the front line of battle to shore up a weak spot or assist in a breakthrough.

- *Zone of Control (ZOC).* The area immediately around a ground unit where its weaponry and other support affect enemy movement, preventing them from sneaking through small holes in a line or being unable to retreat in good order.

- *Line of Communication.* Similar to a line of supply, the line of communication is a clear linking area between a unit and the central command center (e.g., the national capital). It is important for receiving orders from the top commanders as well as supplies.

- *Production Times.* How long it takes a side to turn out new units or come up with new forms of weaponry. As new materials are created, they are shipped to various fronts by air, land, and sea.

- *Carpet Bombing.* The capability of massed bombers to drop explosives over a large area and destroy or damage the enemy's transportation and production.

- *Corps/Army Headquarters (HQ).* The central command center that controls the movement of many units before, during, and after battle. Battlefield commanders need a link to HQ to coordinate their attacks.

- *Early Warning System.* The linking of satellite and radar information to detect and intercept enemy missile attacks.

- *Electronic Countermeasures.* An attempt to disrupt the enemy's communications or neutralize a weapon attack with static, an electromagnetic pulse (EMP), or other methods.

- *Fallout Zone.* The distance that nuclear radiation or debilitating chemicals are carried by the prevailing winds.

Combat in Turn-Based Wargames

Because the pace is slower and more deliberate, combat in turn-based games can be more complex. In paper wargames, there are many different ways to resolve combat, each involving its own form of resolution. There are methods for resolving:

- Air-to-air combat between airplanes.

- Air-to-surface combat for bombing runs on ground and naval targets.

- Surface-to-air combat for ground and naval units trying to shoot down aircraft.

- Indirect fire combat for mortars and naval units trying to damage unseen ground units.
- Direct fire combat between ground and naval units.

In many cases, there are appropriate attack and defense values for each type of combat that can vary from one type of attack to another and from one combat unit to another. For example, an infantry unit can have a good defense value against direct fire attacks from other ground units but almost no defense against attacks by aircraft and indirect fire. The designer has to research the battle being simulated to see what weapons were involved, how much damage the weapons caused, and what types of combat occurred and which were most effective against various targets. Then the designer can create an appropriate sequence of play and combat resolution table for each type of attack.

Sequence of Play in Wargames

In most turn-based games there is a strict sequence of play (SOP) in which one side performs actions in a certain order before opponents perform their actions. The actions are grouped together in phases, which in turn can be divided into steps or pulses or whatever units

---

***Up the Revolution!* Sequence of Play**

Preparation Phase:

1. *Game-Turn Advancement*: Move the Game Turn marker one space ahead on the Game Turn Track.

2. *Supply*: Check the supply status of all units on the map. Place an "Out of Supply" marker on units that cannot trace a line of supply.

Rebel Player Phase:

1. *Move Units*: The Rebel player can move some, all, or none of his military units.

2. *Combat*: The Rebel player can attack any and all Loyalist units to which they are adjacent, resolving each combat one hex at a time.

Loyalist Player Phase:

1. *Move Units*: The Loyalist player can move any and all Army units on the map.

2. *Combat*: The Loyalist player can attack any and all Guerrilla or Insurgent units to which they are adjacent, resolving each combat one hex at a time.

Figure 5.4. *This is an example of what a simple Sequence of Play (SOP) look like. There are three phases: a preparation phase where bookkeeping occurs and two player phases where they move units and engage in combat.*

the design requires. The number of phases depends on the scale of the battle and the capabilities of the units involved in the fight. For example, in a game of modern warfare, motorized units can move much more quickly than foot soldiers, so the SOP might include an initial movement phase, a combat phase, and then a second movement phase for motorized units plus infantry that did not move in the first movement phase. Figure 5.4 is an SOP for a fairly simple game that has a bookkeeping phase and then a phase for each player. Figure 5.5, on the other hand, shows an SOP where there more activities for players to keep track of in addition to moving their units and engaging in combat.

Generally, most games use an SOP where one player moves all his units into position and resolves combat between units within range of the enemy. In multiplayer games, each player in turn has the chance to complete all movement and combat before another player acts. Such an approach can be unfair, however, because it lets several players gang up against one player and deplete his units before he or she has a chance to act. One way around this problem is to use real-time or simultaneous actions, breaking down the overall turn into a series of pulses where each player performs an action with one unit per pulse. The problem with this approach is that it becomes difficult to coordinate all of one's units for a concentrated attack because the enemy has a chance to react constantly to each threat as it presents itself. To get around this problem, many games use "fog of war" where the action of enemy units can't be seen unless they are within the line of sight of a friendly unit.

If a game is complex and the player has to keep track of many units, using a turn-based system is probably a better approach. It becomes a matter of working out a sequence of play that is fair for all players. It might be useful to use an initiative rating of some kind or to alternate who goes first in a turn to prevent any player from gaining too much of an advantage by being able to act first. Testing such a system in paper prototype is fairly easy and should help point out any design issues that need to be resolved early in the production process.

One approach to making the sequence more interesting is to use a fluid sequence of play in which the phases (usually movement and combat) are selected randomly during the turn. Because players never know exactly when one of their phases might appear, they have to be prepared for all eventualities. For example, a planned attack on the enemy's flank might dissolve if at the end of one turn the

Up the Revolution! Sequence of Play

Preparation Phase:

1. *Game-Turn Advancement*: Move the Game Turn marker one space ahead on the Game Turn Track.

2. *Supply*: Check the supply status of all units on the map. Place an "Out of Supply" marker on units that cannot trace a line of supply.

3. *Uprising Determination*: Each hex containing an Unrest marker is checked to see if the disturbance turns into a full-fledged uprising. Roll a die for each hex and check the Uprising Table to determine whether the area revolts, becomes peaceful, or remains in unrest for the rest of the turn.

    Step 1: If the result is Revolt, remove the Unrest marker from the hex and place an Insurgent counter there. The Rebel player gains control of the hex.

    Step 2: If the result is Peace Restored, remove the Unrest marker from the hex. The Loyalist Rebel player regains control of the hex.

    Step 3: If the result if Unrest Continues, leave the Unrest marker in the hex. Neither player controls the hex for this turn.

Rebel Player Phase:

1. *Move Units*: The Rebel player can move some, all, or none of his military units.

    Step 1: All Insurgent units are moved first.

    Step 2: All Guerrilla units are moved second.

2. *Combat*: The Rebel player can attack any and all Loyalist units to which they are adjacent, resolving each combat one hex at a time.

3. *Enlistment*: The Rebel player can attempt to upgrade Insurgent units on the map to Guerrilla units. Roll the die for each Insurgent and check the Rebel Enlistment Table.

4. *Reinforcement*: Any Guerrilla units scheduled to appear this turn are moved from the Reinforcement Track onto the map at a Rebel-controlled depot or airport.

Loyalist Player Phase:

1. *Move Units*: The Loyalist player can move any and all Army units on the map.

2. *Combat*: The Loyalist player can attack any and all Guerrilla or Insurgent units to which they are adjacent, resolving each combat one hex at a time.

3. *Appeasement*: The Loyalist player rolls the die and consults the Appeasement Table to determine how many Rebel units are persuaded to change sides.

4. *Reinforcement*: Any Army units scheduled to appear this turn are moved from the Reinforcement Track onto the map at a Rebel-controlled depot or airport.

Bookkeeping Phase:

1. *Victory Determination*: At the end of turn 20, both players add up their Victory Points based on cities and resources they control to determine which side wins.

2. *Disband Insurgent Units*: The Rebel player rolls a die for each Insurgent unit on the map to determine if it disbands or not. Check the Disband Insurgent Units Table to determine results.

3. *Appeasement Point Determination*: The Loyalist player rolls a die to earn Appeasement Points.

    Step 1: The Loyalist player can try to gain more Appeasement Points for the next turn by taxing cities under his control. Roll a die for each attempt and check the Taxation Table to determine if the result gives an Appeasement Point or results in unrest, placing an Unrest marker in each affected city hex.

    Step 2: For each successful taxation, the Loyalist player moves the Appeasement Point marker one space up the Appeasement Points Track.

4. *Marker Removal*: All markers are removed from units on the map in preparation for the next game turn.

Figure 5.5. *This is an example of a more complicated SOP. Note that some phases are broken down into steps to help players perform actions in an orderly manner.*

enemy player gets to move and attack with his or her units and then in the next turn gets to move and attack again before the flanking player can do anything. Such an approach shows how important it is to keep reserve troops aside for any contingency.

Combat Result Table (CRT)

Traditional paper wargames normally use a Combat Results Table for resolving most ground combat. The table determines which side of the battle is the winner and how much attrition each side suffers. The first version of this CRT was created by Charles S. Roberts in 1952 for the first commercial wargame *Tactics*. By 1958, Charles had revised the game as *Tactics II* and started the Avalon Hill Game Company in Baltimore, MD. Roberts did considerable research on the subject and came to the conclusion that an attacking force three times the strength of the defending force is very likely to be the winner in a fight, and his CRT reflects this finding.

When using a CRT, the player first determines which column to use, based on the ratio of the attacker's combined attack strength to the defender's combined defense strength in that particular attack. A die is rolled (usually a six-sided die) and the player checks the result on the appropriate column to determine the outcome of the attack. Results of the attack can result in units being depleted, being entirely destroyed, or having to retreat. For example, if three units, each with an Attack Value of 2, are attacking a single unit with a Defense Value of 3, the combined Attack Value is 6 (2+2+2=6); thus, the "2-to1" column would be used. It is not the number of units attacking that determines the column but the combined Attack Value of the units engaged. See Table 5.5 for an example of a standard CRT.

The CRT has been altered over time but the same basic principle holds: a strong attacking force can almost always push back or deplete a weaker force. Of course, there are situations where this principle doesn't quite work out. If the attacker has to struggle with some terrain feature while attacking, the defender might not be as badly hurt. For example, if a cavalry unit is attacking an infantry unit across a stream, its formation can be disrupted while crossing the water and therefore it doesn't have the same punch as if it were attacking in closed formation over open ground.

There are several ways to reflect how much terrain can affect a combat. For a minor problem—say, an infantry unit moving through scrub brush—the designer can include a die roll modifier

Combat Results Table

Die Roll	1-4	1-3	1-2	1-1	2-1	3-1	4-1	5-1	6-1
–1	AE	AE	AE	AE	3r/–	2/–	2/–	1/–	1/–
0	AE	AE	AE	3r/–	2/–	2/–	1/–	1/–	–/1
1	AE	AE	3r/–	2/–	2/–	1/–	1/–	–/1	–/1
2	AE	3r/–	3r/–	2/–	1/–	1/–	–/1	–/1	–/2r
3	3r/–	3r/–	2/–	1/–	1/–	–/1	–/1	–/2r	DE
4	3r/–	2/–	2/–	1/–	–/1	–/1	–/2r	DE	DE
5	2/–	2/–	1/–	–/1	–/1	–/2r	DE	DE	DE
6	2/–	1/–	1/–	–/1	–/2r	DE	DE	DE	DE
7	1/–	1/–	–/1	–/2r	DE	DE	DE	DE	DE
8+	1/–	–/1	–/1	DE	DE	DE	DE	DE	DE

Use the "–1" row for die results of less than –1 and the "8+" row for die results greater than 8.

Use the "1-4" column for column shifts less than 1-4 and the "6-1" column for column shifts greater than 6-1.

Table 5.5. *This is an example of a typical Combat Results Table used in paper wargames. "AE" means all the attacker's units are eliminated, "DE" means the defender's units are eliminated, the number equaling the number of hits applied to either the attacker (left of the slash) or defender (right of the slash). An "r" indicates that side's units involved in the combat must retreat one space.*

that increases the likelihood of a poorer combat result and thus reduces the damage inflicted on the defender. For example, the attacker might have a +1 modifier to a d6 die roll so that the possible results are only rows 2–5 on the CRT (a roll of "6" with the +1 modifier would still be treated as "6").

If the terrain presents more of a problem—for example, a cavalry unit charging up a steep embankment—the modifier can be even harsher. In this case, the design might call for a "one column shift to the left" when resolving the combat. Thus, a "3-to-1" attack is resolved using the "2-to-1" column. Die roll and column modifiers can be used to improve and worsen individual attacks based on the terrain features of the battlefield. Some battles are well known for the effect that terrain had on movement and combat—for example, the Battle of the Bulge in World War II that was fought in the dense Ardennes Forest. The designer who wants to recreate a battle as realistically as possible has to study to the battle to see what effects the terrain (and leadership) had on the different units involved.

In electronic wargames, the player doesn't always understand the subtleties of terrain modifiers since the manual seldom goes into the reasons for why things were designed as they were. The algorithm and randomization involved in combat resolution are handled by the game engine and so the whole process is transparent to the player. While a traditional CRT is useful for handling the complexities of combat, it might wind up confusing a player who is more interested in action than in careful consideration of strategy and tactics.

In addition to a table to resolve ground combat, the designer might also have to come up with tables to resolve artillery fire (both direct and indirect), air fights between planes, air-to-ground attacks (similar to artillery), naval combat, nuclear attacks, and other forms of combat. For paper games, the rules and combat results for each table have to be explained in enough detail for players to get through a game without requiring a rules umpire to clear up confusions. In computer games, the game engine handles all the combat resolutions, and the player might not even be aware that air-to-ground combat is resolved differently from naval bombardments unless the designers include that information in the manual or on a website.

Combat in Real-Time Strategy Games

In a real-time strategy game, players have many units to control and a number of different actions to deal with—from gathering resources to erecting and improving buildings to recruiting and improving units and then sending them into combat. In such a system the combat can be relatively simple since the player is constantly sending new units into battle and trying to hold new ground. The designer can ignore terrain effects on combat, although terrain still has an effect on movement. Thus, the algorithm for combat can be relatively simple. For example:

Determine Target

Step 1. Determine which enemy unit is closest within the Attack Range of the attacking unit.

- If there are no units within the Attack Range, no combat occurs.
- If there is only one target within the Attack Range, attack it.
- If there are several targets at an equally close range, select one by random die roll.

Resolve Combat

Step 2. Subtract the target's Defense Value from the attacker's Attack Value.

- If the result is 0 or less, the target does not take damage and combat ends.

- If the result is 1 or more, go to Step 3.

Apply Damage to Target

Step 3. Reduce the target's Hit Point Total by the value derived in Step 2.

- If the target's remaining Hit Point Total is 1 or more, end the attack.

- If the target's remaining Hit Point Total is 0 or less, remove target from map and show its death explosion.

If the designer wishes to add randomization to the combat outcome, another step could be added between Steps 1 and 2 in this example algorithm to determine if the attacking unit hits the defending unit. The additional step could take into account the distance between the units, with a negative modifier being applied to the randomizer range based on how far the units are apart when the attack occurs. For example, if the attacking unit is given an Attack Range attribute with a maximum range of 300 meters (based on the relative size of units in the game) and it moves close enough to fire at an enemy, a -5 modifier is applied to the randomization roll because of the extreme range, making it unlikely that the attacker will inflict damage at that range. Each time the unit moves 50 meters closer to the unit, the negative modifier decreases until at a distance of 0–15 meters, no modifier is applied.

Because combat is simple, the units involved usually have relatively low combat values and Hit Point totals. Armored vehicles generally have more Hit Points than infantry and unarmored vehicles. It is a good idea to use the concept of rock-paper-scissors (see page 87) to make sure each unit has some weakness or shortcoming so that the player is encouraged to build a balanced army. It is possible to work out the basics of combat in a paper prototype, but because the game is in real time and there is so much information to track, it is better to use a simple interactive prototype to nail down the attribute values for units at an early stage of development.

AI Design for Wargames

In paper games, players either engage in combat with each other using the provided charts and tables to regulate movement and combat resolution or, in RPGs, they control their characters in combat while the Gamemaster controls the movement and attacks of enemies. In video and computer games, the game's AI module controls the enemies. The primary functions are path-finding to determine how units move across the board, goal selection to determine the tactics enemy units will use to achieve their strategic objectives, and combat resolution to select which player units to attack and what form of attack to use. Obviously, in electronic games, the AI module is created by a programming team assigned to this task, but it is important for the design team to work closely with the programmers so that everyone clearly understands why certain choices have to be made. The designers can outline in the design document their ideas for how enemy AI should work, but they shouldn't try to determine the code structure for the AI themselves because the programmers can draw upon many libraries of existing code when creating the AI.

Some commercial game engines give designers some control over AI decisions; for example, a game engine can determine the conditions that cause a sentry to notice the approach of players. The conditions for AI in these engines are usually hard-coded, and designers cannot go in directly and change the actual code for the AI. In this case, if the designers need changes made to the AI routines, they have to work with the programming team responsible for that code to get the changes implemented correctly. Of course, making such changes requires extensive testing to determine that the original AI code was not accidentally modified as well.

A major task for the designers throughout the development process is to keep track of the behavior of AI-controlled entities so that they behave the way they expected to. The designers might want to ask the AI programmers to create a tool that creates a text file of how moves and attacks are resolved by AI-controlled units to ensure that the unit attributes and modifiers are being correctly applied during the process. It is also important to make sure that players feel the computer is playing "fair." The programmers are often tempted to use "fudges" to allow the AI respond more quickly to situations, but players should never feel that the computer is "cheating."

Conclusion

Creating a combat system for a game is a lot of work and requires considerable testing and revision. The original idea might not work out as planned, even though it worked well in prototype form. Balancing the attribute values for units is also a daunting task and requires considerable feedback from new players as well as from those who have played the game a while to guarantee that the values are balanced and that no unit has been given an overwhelming advantage.

Despite the workload, it is still a lot of fun to dream up a new approach to handling combat in a game and yet make everything obvious enough for players to grasp within a few minutes of play. While external tutorials are sometimes helpful when players get stuck, the designer should plan to give players step-by-step, hands-on demonstrations of major game systems early in the game. Players only have to know how to perform actions in the game, not the reasons why the designers decided to have the combat system work the way it does.

Exercises

1. Do more research on the Internet to find some discussion about the combat effectiveness of military units in different eras. In particular, use the four the battles you selected from different eras in Exercise 3 of Chapter 4.

    a. While doing your research, keep the following factors in mind:

        i. Which side was more effective during the battle and why?

        ii. What factors most affected the soldiers during combat? Consider the weather as well as leadership, training and how well they were armed and supplied.

        iii. Was there any marked change in effectiveness as the battle progressed?

    b. Write a short essay about one of these battles. In your opinion, which side was more effective during combat? Give several reasons as to why you think one side was better than the other.

2. If your game has combat as a game mechanic, start a list of all the attributes you think will be involved in resolving combat.

    a. Do different units require different attributes (for example, do air units behave differently from ground troops when attacking)?

    b. Start making notes on how the combat might be resolved using these attributes.

    c. If your game does not include combat as a game mechanic, select one of the four battles you've researched and assign attributes to the different units so you can create a mechanic for resolving combat.

3. Create a paper prototype as necessary to test the attributes you selected in Exercise 2.

    a. Write down the algorithm or formula showing how the attributes are used in combat. If any modifiers affect the combat, include them in the algorithm.

    b. Based on your research and testing so far, do you think the same algorithm could be used to solve every form of combat in your game? Or would different units require different approaches to combat resolution (e.g., air attacks vs. ground attacks)?

    c. Assign values to the attributes used in combat resolution. The values can be relative (e.g., devastating, very strong, moderate, weak, and so on).

    d. Test your combat algorithm with the paper prototype and make changes to the relative attribute values as necessary.

4. Create two combat systems for a role-playing game: one simple with few attributes per entity and only three or four actions, and the other with more attributes and additional actions. The actions can include weapon attack, defending, casting magic, using items, fleeing, stealing, and any others you think are appropriate.

a. Create the algorithms for resolving each of these actions during combat. Keep the combat turn-based instead of real-time.

b. Have testers use your algorithms in a combat situation, going step by step through each possible action. Revise the algorithms as necessary to make them as straightforward and logical as possible.

c. If the algorithms can be used in the game you're designing, add them to the game design document in the appropriate chapters that discuss the mechanics of combat resolution.

5. Create at least three different Combat Tables for a role-playing game.

a. Use different combinations of dice with different numbers of faces (for example, using a six-sided die and a ten-side die rolled both sequentially and cumulatively.)

b. Test the Combat Tables in your paper prototype.

c. Write up an analysis of how well your Combat Tables worked compared to simple 2d dice rolls and 2d10 percentage dice rolls.

6. Create a playfield for a *tactical* role-playing game using a square grid.

a. Make the playfield about 12 × 12 squares in size.

i. Devise an interesting setting for the playfield— e.g., castle, ice cave, forest, etc.

ii. Draw up a list of terrain features that could appear on the playfield.

iii. Print out a copy of the square grid and color it in with pencils and pens to show these terrain features.

b. Make a Terrain Effects Chart for the playfield.

i. Now place some markers on the playfield to represent units you control and enemies you have to defeat.

ii. Assign movement rates and attack ranges to the units based on the weapons they carry. For example, a unit might have 4 movement points per turn, expending 1 point per open space. Likewise, an infantry unit with a sword can only attack adjacent squares, while an archer can shoot up to three squares in any direction as long as no terrain feature blocks its line of site.

    iii. Now, move the units around the playfield, paying attention to how terrain affects their movement and combat ability. If necessary, use a straight ruler to determine if any terrain features block the line of fire between units.

7. Create a Combat Results Table (CRT) for the tactical RPG game you created in Exercise 6.

    a. Assign numeric attack and defense values and Hit Points to the units so you can determine the attacker-to-defender ratio during combat.

    b. Your CRT should be a matrix with at least six columns.

        i. The number of rows on the CRT can be determined by the dice combination you select.

        ii. Some of the results on the table can include the attacker/defender retreating, hit points loss to the attacker's/defender's unit, and the attacker/defender unit being destroyed.

    c. After you test your first draft of the CRT, try adding in modifiers and column shifts for such factors as terrain features occupied by the attack and/or defender, proximity to a leader unit, and using magic to attack.

8. If your game includes combat, write up a first draft describing how it work for your game design document. If your game includes several types of combat (for example, weapon and magic combat), make sure to describe each system in detail.

CHAPTER 6

ON CHARACTERS AND MONSTERS

In most board games, such as *Sorry* and *Monopoly*, players move their tokens around the board after rolling the dice. The tokens don't have any special attributes associated with them, except that their current movement rate equals the result of the rolled dice. There are occasionally other pieces involved that do have special attributes when placed on the board—for example, the houses and hotels in *Monopoly* and the triangular prisms in the original version *Risk* that stand for ten armies (in the 1993 edition, infantry pieces represented individual armies, cavalry pieces represented five armies, and artillery pieces represented ten armies). There is not much information about the playing pieces and tokens that the player must remember in these simple games.

In more complex games, the units and characters controlled by players can have a whole gamut of attributes with different values. As discussed in the previous chapters, there are attributes associated with movement and combat. Defining the attributes of units and characters early on in the design process is vital because if new attributes have to be added late in production, the game values can become unbalanced and there might not be enough testing time to catch these imbalances. Also, in complicated games, the testers need saved games at certain points to be able to go in and test changes and fixes. If new fields are added to the save game files, the old versions can become useless, requiring testers to create a whole new series of saved games.

Creating Player Characters

Traditional paper RPGs employ an extensive process for generating characters. Players roll various dice combinations to generate attributes and they also make other choices as to the character's race, guild (or career choice), faction, and philosophical disposition (evil, good, or neutral). Once players are satisfied with their characters, play commences. It can take several hours to generate a character via this method.

Some of the early computer RPGs, such as Sir Tech's *Wizardry* and Richard Garriott's *Ultima* games, used the same process to generate characters, forcing players to go through a long process of assigning values to attributes before starting play. The same process is still observed in massively multiplayer online RPGs like Blizzard Entertainment's *World of Warcraft*, and the many different variants in attributes and visual appearances allow players to create unique characters (although there are bound to be overlaps in choices except for character names).

In other games, there are fewer variants for the player to select from, and in some cases, character attribute values are already pre-generated. The player might be given a few points to assign to attributes, but the characters fall within a very narrow range of attribute values. There are several reasons to restrict character generation this way. One is that players don't often replay a game once they've finished it, so offering a vast number of possibilities is wasteful. Also, it is much easier to thoroughly test a limited number of attribute combinations, rather than making sure no one character type dominates all others.

Basic RPG Character Attributes

Some character attributes were defined in the last chapter. They include:

- *Strength* (Body, Brawn, Might, etc.). The character's physical musculature.

- *Constitution* (Stamina, Endurance, Vitality, etc.). The character's overall health and the ability to withstand attacks.

- *Size* (Health). The character's overall mass and physical dimensions.

- *Dexterity* (Agility, Speed, Reflex, etc.). The character's ability to act and react quickly.

- *Luck* (Karma, Fate, Chance, etc.). The likelihood of the character dodging adverse events or happily chancing on something good.

There are several other attributes that are found in paper RPGs that make their way into electronic games as well:

FRP Character Generation Chart															
Initial Attributes by Race															
Human								**Dwarf**							
							Ex								Ex
Guild	Str	End	Dex	Agl	Int	HP	Pts	Str	End	Dex	Agl	Int	HP	Pts
Warrior	15	12	6	7	5	30	4	18	15	5	4	6	35	3
Paladin	15	10	7	7	9	27	4	16	14	7	6	10	32	3
Archer	12	9	10	10	10	25	4	13	11	9	10	11	30	3
Rogue	10	9	12	12	12	21	4	11	10	8	9	11	25	3
Priest	12	11	9	8	13	25	4	11	12	8	10	14	27	3
Mage	9	8	12	15	16	20	4	10	10	9	13	16	24	3
Elf								**Halfling**							
							Ex								Ex
Guild	Str	End	Dex	Agl	Int	HP	Pts	Str	End	Dex	Agl	Int	HP	Pts
Warrior	13	11	8	9	9	28	4	12	14	9	9	8	27	2
Paladin	12	10	9	10	10	26	4	11	13	12	10	9	24	2
Archer	12	10	11	12	10	26	4	10	11	10	12	8	21	2
Rogue	10	9	12	12	11	23	4	11	12	12	12	10	20	2
Priest	9	10	10	12	12	24	4	11	13	9	10	12	21	2
Mage	9	10	14	16	14	22	4	10	12	12	15	15	18	2

Key:

Strength = Attack and carry	Agility = Save from magic
Endurance = Defense and recovery	Intelligence = Ability to learn
Dexterity = Initiative speed	Hit Points

Table 6.1. *This is a sample Character Generation Chart that could be used in a fantasy role-playing game. It shows the starting attribute values for various combinations of races and guilds.*

- *Mana.* The amount of the character current mana, the magic substance used to cast magic spells.

- *Wisdom* (Knowledge, Intelligence, Power, etc.). The overall smarts a character has that affects its ability to learn and manipulate magic. Sometimes this attribute is split in two with one meaning the character's ability to learn things and the other meaning the character's ability to use magic.

- *Charisma* (Physicality, Beauty, etc.). The character's physical appearance and the likelihood that others will find the character attractive or repulsive.

The beginning values for all attributes are low at the start of play, and they increase over time as the character succeeds in winning battles and resolving quests. Each time a player goes up an experience level (see Table 6.1), the character's attributes improve.

RPG Races

Initial attribute values are also affected by a character's *race*, with some races being very strong but dim while others are very intelligent but weak. There is usually some compensating factor that gives balance to all races. Thus, an elf might be relatively weak in hand-to-hand fighting compared to other races but is devastating with ranged weapons like bows and is able to wield powerful magic more readily.

Creating fantasy characters is far easier since most players are familiar with the archetypes found in J.R.R. Tolkien's epic adventure *The Lord of the Rings* as well as from German folktales, European mythologies, and the works of the Brothers Grimm. Creating science-fiction races and classes, on the other hand, is more challenging since everything has to be created from whole cloth. The popularity of the *Star Wars* and *Star Trek* series has helped define some science-fiction archetypes—for example, the stoic and strong Vulcan and the noble and mystic Jedi knight.

The attribute values are usually found in Character Generation Charts (see the examples below). As is apparent, the initial values are higher in some attributes than others because of race as well as class (see the following list). All initial attribute values are low to begin with, however, and rise over time, and it is up to the designers to make sure that characters are also balanced against creatures and enemies they meet throughout the game. If a very weak character can't defeat a low-level monster, the player can get frustrated and stop playing that character even though later on the character gains all sorts of great spells or technology or weaponry.

The primary races found in most fantasy RPGs include:

- *Humans.* Relatively strong and intelligent so they are good in all kinds of combat and have adequate magic ability. They are often used as the median in RPGs. They usually get along with most other races.

- *Elves.* Tall and thin but can be strong and intelligent. Prefer ranged combat with bows and are exceptional with magic. There are multiple variations to the basic elf character (dark elves, night elves, battle elves, etc.). They often do not get along with dwarves. Very aloof and often found in forests.

- *Dwarves.* Relatively short and stocky so usually very strong although not always intelligent. Very good at melee combat and relatively poor at magic. They often do not get along with elves. Rather short-tempered. Known to be excellent miners.

Other races have been created or adapted to appear in fantasy RPGs as well:

- *Halflings* (Hobbits). Very small and very resilient humanoids. Less adept at heavy hand weapons but adequate with bows. Decent magic users. Friendly towards most other races. (Note that the term "hobbit" is seldom used because it is copyright property of the J.R.R. Tolkien estate.)

- *Gnomes*. Somewhat smaller than their dwarven kin; they are also more agile. Often seen as excellent tinkers and repairmen. Better with small hand weapons and bows. Decent magic users. Sometimes treated as dark creatures who try to trick other races.

- *Changelings*. Originally the offspring of a fairy or other magical creature that was switched soon after birth with a human baby, this character is more often seen as a shape-shifter that can assume many different animal forms including other races. A strong magic user with very strong attack powers when in human form. Not very strong when in human form. Often acts in a mysterious manner.

- *Giants*. Very large humanoid beings who tower over other races. Exceptionally strong but usually not very intelligent. Limited magic power. Primarily wields heavy clubs. Giants appear in mythologies around the world and have many different powers.

- *Faery* (Fairie). In European myths, these folk are magical and are often very tiny. However, they can appear as human-sized beings who, while frail, are very strong and excellent magic users. They are seen as distant relatives of the elves. They are credited with the ability to fly using their gossamer wings.

- *Kobolds*. Forest spirits about the size of a human child but with tremendous magical powers. Sometimes viewed as dark creatures filled with hate towards other races. Often mischievous and fond of nasty tricks.

- *Goblins*. Often associated with gnomes, goblins are small with exaggerated features that make them ugly to other races. They are more associated with magic than with combat. In some cases, they are seen as beneficial and helpful to other races.

- *Ogres*. Large and cruel creatures that are better at magic than giants but not as mighty. Not as mean as trolls or orcs, but not friendly either. They are sometimes condemned for eating human flesh. Can skillfully wield swords, maces, and other punishing melee weapons.

- *Trolls.* Smaller than ogres but usually taller than humans. They are powerfully built and can wield most weapons with ease. They are magic users who focus on evil magic.

- *Orcs.* Look like malformed humans. Very powerful and particularly nasty. Warmongers who charge headlong into fights without looking. Decent with most weapons and aren't very good with magic. Often prefer to dwell in caves and other dank, dark places.

Note that some of these races also serve as enemies. It all depends on the world created by the designers and how the races interact with one another (see Chapter 10 for more details). If unusual races are selected as playable by a player—for example, an ogre—their artwork should make them look sympathetic rather than simply horrific. It is easier for players to identify more closely with an ogre that looks like Shrek from the movies rather than some misshapen lump with fangs and a menacing expression. Of course, if the game allows players to mix-and-match the facial appearance of their characters, there can be a wide variety of face types—both nice and fierce—to select from.

Occasionally, vampires, werewolves, zombies, ghosts, mummies, and other horrific creatures appear in fantasy RPGs as well, but usually as enemies unless the game's genre is horror. There is a branch of fantasy that deals with horror, and several RPG systems have been based on H.P. Lovecraft's Cthulhu mythos and Bram Stoker's *Dracula,* among others.

Science-fiction RPGs also use race to define character types, with humans being the most common race and a whole panoply of alien races available to choose from. Some of the alien races include androids and cyborgs, intelligent plants and protoplasmic creatures, mutations, and star-traveling species of all shapes, sizes, and composition. As with fantasy races, the designers have to make sure that the races' attributes are balanced. They can have advantages based on size and intelligence, but they need offsetting disadvantages to keep any one race from being too popular (see Figure 6.1). The races in a science-fiction game usually rely on technology instead of magic, although psychic powers are often disguised as magic under an assumed name. One difficulty with creating a science-fiction RPG is to create the futuristic technologies for each race and not wind

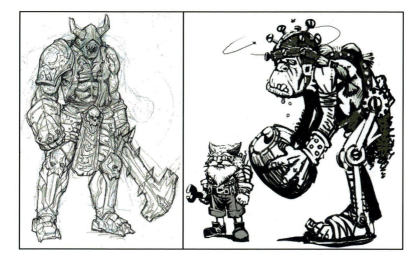

Figure 6.1. *In these character sketches created by artists at Gas Powered Games, the creature on the left is Ork-ish and threatening because of its massive sword and skull insignia on its belt. The characters on the right look friendly; the smaller character seems to have some mechanical ability because he holds a wrench, while the large creature on the right, despite its fearsome size, is not menacing. The characters to the right are comical while the creature to the left is definitely dangerous.*

up borrowing too much from any well-known author or cinematic tradition.

The world in which the game takes place also helps define the character types. In many science-fiction RPGs space travel is a central motif, and characters rocket from one world to another to have adventures. Other popular settings for science-fiction RPGs include post-holocaust worlds where mutants rule, comic universes where superheroes and supervillains battle one another, and the secretive world of secret agents like James Bond with their high-tech gadgets.

RPG Classes

Another factor that affects initial attribute values is the *class* (or career or guild) the character belongs to. The class choice defines how much specialized training a character receives or the innate knowledge he or she is born with. Some classes are more physical than others. For example, wizards tend to be weaker than knights, because they concentrate on developing magic skills over physical prowess.

While classes add more variability to character creation, they can also lead to problems when balancing the game because races, classes, and items must all work together and be balanced. It does no good, for example, to create a hobbit wizard that is great with magic but who can only wield small knives against fierce monsters. In an encounter with a magic-resistant enemy, the hobbit will be toast.

Some of the better-known classes in fantasy RPGs from strongest to weakest include:

- *Barbarian* (Warrior). Extremely strong and skilled with most weapons, excelling in melee weapons. Relatively weak in intelligence and limited in magic. Sometimes referred to as a tank unit because it is strong offensively and defensively.

- *Knight* (Paladin). Strong and also skilled in most weapons, preferring melee weapons. Average intelligence and able to use many magic spells.

- *Ranger* (Scout). Relatively strong and best with ranged weapons. Above-average intelligence and therefore adept with some magic, mostly nature-oriented magic.

- *Cleric* (Healer). Fairly strong and best with clubs and staffs. Very intelligent and adept at a wide range of magic, although primarily specializing in healing and curing.

- *Thief* (Rogue). Limited strength and best with knives and some ranged weapons. Highly intelligent and adept with many kinds of magic. Also particularly expert at pickpocketing, picking locks and other forms of petty thievery.

- *Wizard* (Mage, Sorcerer). Relatively weak and usually armed with staffs that are used more for casting magic than fighting. Very intelligent and an expert in a wide range of magic, particularly magic used during combat.

There are also other classes that can be found in fantasy RPGs. They are not usually as flexible as the primary classes, but they do add variety.

- *Tinker.* A normal person who is very skilled with mechanical objects, both building them and repairing them.

- *Necromancer.* A wizard who specializes in dark magic, particularly raising and controlling the dead.

- *Ninja.* Highly skilled assassin who knows martial arts and uses exotic weaponry (death stars, katana, blowguns, etc.). Can be adept with some magic as well, such as invisibility and shape-shifting.

- *Beastmaster.* A Tarzan-like being who controls animals that do most of the fighting to protect their friends. Often very strong and able to use most weapons. Some magical ability but mainly nature-oriented.

The amount of studying needed to become an expert in a class also has much to do with the character's physical ability. Obviously, those trained with heavy weapons have to develop a large, powerful physique to wield them while those who focus on magic rely on its power instead of on muscle, and therefore spend most of their time improving their minds.

Science-fiction RPGs use many of the same class types as fantasy RPGs. There are brawny characters who are good with weapons but limited in technology, and there are geniuses of technology who are fairly weak. One advantage for science-fiction RPGs is that powerful futuristic weapons like blasters and laser guns don't always require a lot of strength to carry. Some of the classes in science-fiction RPGs include:

- *Military.* In games set in a *Star Trek*-like universe, the characters are often part of a military establishment, either aboard ships (which is usually modeled on the navy) or on the ground (modeled after the army or marines).

- *Explorers.* Sometimes they act like rogues if they are primarily after wealth and sometimes like rangers if they are charting unknown worlds.

- *Merchants.* Civilians who carry on trade between worlds, sometimes legitimately and sometimes underhandedly.

- *Scientists.* Can be either good or bad if they help create new inventions for friends or weapons of mass destruction for villains.

- *Medics.* A branch of science primarily aimed at keeping beings well, treating wounds and diseases, and performing life-saving operations.

MINMATAR GATE CAMP

Figure 6.2. *In the science-fiction game CCP Games' Eve Online, players can take on the persona of spaceships at times, and so the designers have to determine the attribute values for the ships in addition to the different alien races.*

As you might notice, there are similarities between the fantasy and science fiction archetypes. Military are similar to barbarians and knights, explorers to rangers, merchants to rogues, scientists to wizards, and medics to clerics. All classes can perform standard game actions—exploring areas, engaging in conversations, solving puzzles, fulfilling quests, and so on. Some characters need to be good in hand-to-hand combat while others support them with ranged weaponry and technology. Some characters are great casters of powerful magic or technology while others are concerned with healing those who have taken damage. And some are useful in special circumstances to avoid traps or gain entrance to forbidden places.

When creating classes, designers have to consider the purposes they will serve in the game. If a game requires a different character class for specific tasks, the designer can create such a special class, but most players will be reluctant at best to make take on the role of that character for a whole game. Creating a whole new character class can prove to be an exercise in futility unless that class' abilities are central to the game action—for example, an architect who can build up castles (and tear them down) if the game includes resource management, construction, and demolition as central play mechanisms (see Figure 6.2).

RPG Skills

Skills are specialties learned by characters while preparing for entry into a class or becoming more proficient in it. One way to distinguish one character class from another is to assign certain skills to a class that others can't perform. For example, the rogue class is often given the ability to pick pockets and crack locks that other characters can't. The skills can also be related to weaponry so that a certain class gains a positive modifier when using one weapon type—for example, a ranger getting a +2 modifier whenever she uses a bow of any kind. There can also be negative modifiers associated with weapons to deter players from trying to arm characters with inappropriate weapons. For example, a rogue might get a -1 modifier when using a battleaxe in combat because it is such a massive weapon.

Skills can also be related to some other specialty that is closely associated with classes—for example, the ability to regenerate mana for clerics and/or wizards or the ability to detect nearby enemies in forest locations for rangers. Some of these skills are automatic, meaning they take effect without the player needing to do anything, and others require that the player select an option either during combat or outside it.

Skills can also improve as the characters increase in level, so that as characters become more powerful over time, their skills improve as well. This is another useful way to differentiate character classes from one another. See Table 6.2 on page 138 for an example of such a Skill Chart. In addition to the skill's name and effect, the chart also indicates if it is automatic, meaning it is in effect at all times, or if it has to be selected to take effect. Of course, it takes a lot of testing to make sure that the skills are balanced and don't affect any attribute too critically, making the character class either too powerful or too weak.

Whatever skills are used in an RPG, they should all have direct effects on game play. In paper RPGs, there are minor skills that are used once in a great while (for example, animal husbandry, fishing, astronomy, and poetry, among others). While such skills are useful to help characters relate better to their characters, they can become nuisances in electronic RPGs since they have little effect on the major game actions. In MMORPGs, however, where players live for many hours in the game universe, additional skills can be useful in letting characters perform secondary actions (such as building and furnishing a house) that don't directly affect the central game play.

FRP Skills Chart		
Warrior		
Skill Name	*Type*	*Effect*
Melee Mastery	Auto	Positive Strength attribute modifier when wielding a club or axe
Resistance	Auto	Increases Defense attribute during a weapon combat
Berserker	Select	Increases all combat attributes for a limited time
Intimidate	Select	Lowers enemy's Defense attribute for a limited time
Knight		
Skill Name	*Type*	*Effect*
Sword Mastery	Auto	Positive Strength attribute modifier when wielding a sword
Leadership	Auto	Increases all party members' Defense attribute during any combat
Field Dressing	Select	Restores a limited amount of Hit Points after combat
Pursuit	Select	Reduces all enemies' Flee percentage
Ranger		
Skill Name	*Type*	*Effect*
Bow Mastery	Auto	Increases Dexterity attribute during combat
Camouflage	Auto	Increases Dexterity attribute during combat
Beast Control	Select	Turns one attacking animal into an ally for a limited time
Read Tracks	Select	Detects presence of nearby enemies
Rogue		
Skill Name	*Type*	*Effect*
Light Weapons Mastery	Auto	Positive Strength attribute modifier when wielding a knife or small bow
Stealth	Auto	Increases Dexterity and Agility attributes during combat
Pickpocket	Select	Increases chance of stealing item from another entity
Lock Pick	Select	Increases chance of picking locks and disarming traps
Healer		
Skill Name	*Type*	*Effect*
Club and Mace Mastery	Auto	Positive Strength attribute modifier when wielding a club or mace
Deflect Magic	Auto	Increases Agility attribute and reduces magic damage during combat
Reverie	Select	Restores some mana during or after combat
Herb Lore	Select	Transforms an herb item in inventory into a cure potion
Wizard		
Skill Name	*Type*	*Effect*
Staff Mastery	Auto	Positive Strength attribute modifier when wielding a staff
Resistance	Auto	Reduces magic damage and some weapon damage during combat
Channel	Select	Restores an increasing amount of mana during combat
Divination	Select	Detect nearby magic user or item or read mystic runes

Table 6.2. *This is what a Skill Chart for a role-playing game might look like. Note that the effects of some are automatic while others occur when the player selects the skill in combat or after.*

Additional Character Information

In paper RPGs, characters sometimes are given additional bits of information to help players better identify with their characters. Some games include *advantages* and *disadvantages*, which offer minor help or hindrance to characters over time. Advantages, for example, can include things as blessings, heritage, and reputation that occasionally give characters positive modifiers when performing certain game actions. Disadvantages are just the opposite and can include things like curses, psychosis, ignoble birth, and diseases, and they act as negative modifiers at times. Advantages and disadvantages are often applied to interactions with NPCs, and they are less useful in electronic RPGs where all NPC texts have to be worked out ahead of time.

Some paper RPGs also include *traits* as part of the character generation procedure. Traits are broader fields of expertise that the character is knowledgeable in. For example, a player with a wizard character may be more interested in the dark art of necromancy than elemental magic. Or a knight might be a connoisseur, not only able to detect the faintest traces of poison or spoilage in food but also to display an annoyance at inns that have limited menus. Again, this information is useful in paper RPGs where players want to bond to their characters, but it is less useful in electronic RPGs because it makes testing much more complex and does not necessarily affect game mechanics enough to be worth the effort to create.

Both paper and electronic RPGs often allow characters to select their dominant philosophy about life. In some games, this life philosophy is defined as good, evil, or neutral, and in other games, it is defined as lawful, chaotic, or neutral. Good or neutral means the character primarily does good deeds while adventuring while evil or chaotic means just the opposite. Neutral characters sometimes do good and sometimes do evil, depending on how they feel about NPCs or a situation at any given moment. One advantage to using this life philosophy in a game is that it can force players to make ethical judgments during play about what their characters will do, and different rewards can be offered depending on what action the character performs.

Initial Equipment

It is important to decide what weapons and clothing new characters start with plus any other equipment they will carry in their inventory. Beginning characters often have the lowest level weapons and armor (if any). They might start out in a shirt, trousers, and shoes, and then they earn better equipment through combat or solving quests. The initial attire needs to be appropriate to the race and class, for it would look odd to have an entry-level barbarian running around in a wizard's robe.

Other information that is important for beginning characters is how much money they have at the start of the game. If they have no money, they'll have to work to get some. However, if they have some money, they can buy a few inexpensive items to help them survive their first encounters (for example, some heal and cure medicine) or perhaps some light armor or a slightly better weapon. It is a good idea to limit how much money the character has at the start of play so that the player isn't forced into making too many decisions before comprehending how game play works. If given a sizeable amount of money at the start, the player may elect to buy arms or armor that isn't needed against low-level enemies. A beginning character might not be strong enough to wield a large weapon or have enough mana to cast advanced magic spells.

Likewise, it might be helpful to include some low-level items in a character's inventory at the start. Sometimes the characters are given nothing, but often they start out with a few low-level healing potions. Since the design team knows what kind of enemies the player will encounter early in the game, they can give a subtle hint to the player about what to expect by what they include in the character's starting inventory. If there are only healing objects in the inventory, the player won't expect enemies that are poisonous or otherwise infectious. If there are nasty enemies early on, the player should be prepared to meet them by being equipped with cure items as well as healing items.

Initial Skills and Magic Spells

In addition to items and weaponry, a beginning character can be assigned low-level skills and magic spells. As with items, assigning more than one skill at the start of play can confuse a player unfamiliar with the game system, especially if the player has to select the skill to enable it. It is often a good idea to hold back on skills until the player has explored the world a bit and has risen in level. Of course, beginning skills can be important for the survival of the character during the first combat encounters (for example, a skill that slowly replenishes mana for wizards).

Determining what magic spells a character has at the beginning of play is also an important design decision. Characters who are better in melee and ranged combat might not need any spells initially, but classes that depend on magic (clerics and wizards) need at least one attack spell and perhaps a healing or mana regeneration spell as well. Since magic is often powered by mana, the character needs access to some mana potions at the start as well. Otherwise, after casting a spell or two, the initial mana is used up and magic becomes useless. In science-fiction games that use psychic powers, the characters often need to replenish psychic energy as well, so they either need some replenishing item or the ability to naturally restore this power over time.

Physical Appearance

The player is usually given the chance to decide what his or her character will look like at the start of play. In paper RPGs, players make many selections for the character's starting age, weight, and height, as well as hair style, eye and skin color, facial hair, and any distinguishing marks (for example, tattoos or scars). They also might select whether the character is right- or left-handed. All this information refers to the physical appearance of the character. There is less concern for what the character is wearing, unless it relates to armor or is needed for a quest of some kind. Since the game takes place only in the players' imaginations, there is less need for precision when it comes to appearance.

Selecting a character's physical appearance for an electronic RPG, on the other hand, can be more challenging. Sometimes there is only one character available (for example, in Square Enix's *Final Fantasy X* or inXile Entertainment's *The Bard's Tale*) so the player doesn't have to worry about the appearance. At other times, the player gets to play around with the character's physical features (face, ears, nose, etc.) until satisfied with the final result, as in Bethesda Softworks' *The Elder Scrolls: Oblivion*. In MMORPGs, there can be many different variations of features to select from to give players as much freedom as possible in creating unique looking characters.

Once the designers decide how characters will be visualized in the game, they have to work with the art and programming teams to make sure the system they want will work. They may want to simply use a set number of pregenerated characters for players to select from, or they might want to let the player manipulate facial and body features at will. Obviously, being able to create as unique a character as possible requires extensive artwork, and the designers must confer with the art team to determine just how much work will be required to turn their ideas into reality. While it is useful to have as many distinctive-looking characters as possible, especially if players interact online in a multiplayer version of the game, the character artwork is not central to game play per se. The art team might point out that given the schedule for the game, they think it would be bet-ter to add more NPCs and enemy characters than spend too much time on a feature that appears only at the start of the game.

The other gating factor as far as artwork goes is what the char-acter will look like on the playfield. If the game uses a first-person point of view where the player looks at the world through the eyes of the main character (as in *The Elder Scrolls: Oblivion* and *Fallout 3*), then the player seldom sees the character, and therefore an exten-sive character visualization system might not be needed. If, on the other hand, the player sees the playfield in a third-person point of view, the main character will be visible at all times. In this case, the character appearing on the playfield is probably generic and doesn't have all the features the player selected during character genera-tion. The amount of art required to show a multitude of characters, each with different facial features, skin tone, facial hair and clothing, can swamp the art team. Additionally, the designers might want the character's appearance to change over time as new weapons, armor, and ornaments are acquired. The art team is much more likely to ask either for fewer options during character generation or to use generic figures on the playfield so as to complete the game on time and within budget constraints.

Experience Points and Leveling Up

One of the great rewards in an RPG is seeing one's character get stronger over time and acquiring new abilities as the character im-proves. During play, the character gets Experience Points (abbrevi-ated ExP or XP) for performing actions—winning a combat, solving a puzzle, or finishing a quest. When the XP reach a certain level, the character goes up an "experience level" and his or her attributes improve. Thus, a level 4 character is more powerful than a level 2 character. This mechanism is a way of rewarding the player for doing well in the game, and reaching a new level might require the player to make a number of choices.

Attribute Increases

As far as the player is concerned, the most important thing is that the character's attributes go up at a new experience level, either by auto-matic increases or by awarding the player a certain number of points to assign at will to the attributes. When using the latter approach, a point assigned to an attribute can actually raise it considerably and not just by a single point. The character's race and class often affect how much an attribute goes up when the player assigns a point to it. For example, the standard barbarian character gets stronger and healthier over time, so if the player assigns a point to the Strength attribute for a human barbarian, the Strength value might go up by 10 instead of 1. On the other hand, for a halfling barbarian, the assigned point might raise the value by 7 instead of 10 to account for the difference in physical size between the two races. Likewise, the same point assigned to a human wizard's Strength attribute might raise its value by only 4 while an elf wizard might have its value go up by 5.

While this approach works well for standard RPGs, it can be problematic for MMORPS where there might be dozens of level 4 barbarians running around the same area. Since players can usually look at other characters' attributes, it might seem odd that all level 4 barbarians, for example, have a Strength of 16. To help differentiate characters, the designers might decide to include modifiers based on a character's race, so that an elf barbarian would not be as strong as a human barbarian who in turn would be less strong than a dwarf barbarian.

Some computer and console RPFs automatically increment attributes as characters gain experience, such as in Bethesda Softworks' *The Elder Scrolls IV: Oblivion* (Figure 6.3). The player doesn't have to

Figure 6.3. *The player should be able to review a character's game statistics at any time, as shown here in Bethesda Softworks'* The Elder Scrolls IV: Oblivion.

worry about assigning any points. An advantage to such an approach is that the game is easier to balance, but some players might complain because they have less control over their characters' growth. It is important in such game to let players see the attributes to understand which ones have changed over time.

Another approach is to randomize the final values for increased attributes. For example, if a barbarian goes from level 3 to level 4, the minimum enhancement to the Strength attribute would be 6, but before this value is added, the game generates a random result between 0 and 4, and this result is added to the base value. Therefore, the barbarian's increased Strength value would be from 6 (minimum) to 10 (maximum). There would be much less likelihood of the same level characters having the same numeric values for their attributes with this approach. Of course, the designers have to be careful that a character class or race doesn't become too powerful too quickly through randomization.

Enhanced Magic and Skills

Depending on how the magic system is designed (see Chapter 8), the character might receive a new spell or have an existing spell also go up a level. So, the character might be given an Infernal Fire Ball spell at the new experience level while still retaining a less powerful Fire Ball spell received earlier. Another approach is to have the original Fire Ball spell increase in power at the new level and perhaps cost more mana to cast. The advantage of the second approach is that there are fewer spells for the player to remember and less clutter in the menus during combat.

The character can also gain new skills or improve current skills at the new experience level. For example, a wizard with the Restore Mana skill would not only have mana restored more quickly at a higher level but might also gain the ability to restore limited mana in other party members as well. Likewise, a ranger's ability with bows could be enhanced with a positive combat modifier, while she also gains another skill allowing her to detect nearby enemies. Sometimes the player might be allowed to assign points to improve existing skills directly or the improvements happen automatically as soon as the character reaches the next level.

As a rough rule of thumb, players should not be overwhelmed with too many choices after their characters go up a level. If there are too many points to assign to attributes, spells, and skills at a new level, players can become perplexed as to where best to assign the points. Having character information automatically go up at a new level relieves players of having to make too many choices but can also be alienating because there is less direct control over their characters' destinies.

Story Development

In addition to improving a character, a rise in experience level can have other effects in the game. If the rise in level is a result of the completion of an important quest, then one chapter of the game story might close and the next begin. For example, after deciding what changes to make to his character, the player learns that new areas of the game world have opened up and there are now new territories to explore, new NPCs to meet, and perhaps new armament and items to buy. There is often an animated sequence where more of the story is revealed and new goals are assigned to the character.

It terms of game play, the next set of dialogue options with NPCs can be triggered. It is important to decide whether unresolved sub-quests remain active, since they can be problematic if an NPC continues to repeat earlier dialogue while all other characters have something new to say. One approach is to change the original dialogue for remaining sub-quests slightly so that the NPC acknowledges a change in the game world while still requesting the character fulfill the sub-quest.

Experience Level Algorithm

The designers have to explain in the documentation how experience levels work and what happens at each level. Showing the information on a spreadsheet is very helpful because one can see at a glance what is supposed to happen with each character class as it goes up a level. The information in the spreadsheets can be stripped out, if necessary, and put in files that can more easily be accessed by the game engine. However, it is important for the designers to work out in detail with the programming team how experience levels work, and the data should be kept separate from the game engine itself because the designers are likely to tweak values frequently during the development stage.

In paper RPGs, the amount of points required to reach each new level increases at a fairly constant rate. For example, it might take 50

Human Warrior: Experience Level Chart										
			Attribute Raises			New Spells			New Skills	
Exp. Lvl.	Exp. Pts. to Level	Ext. Stat Pts.	Damage	Mana Pts.	Hit Pts.	First	Second	Spell Pts.	First Skill	Skill Pts.
1	8	1	3	0	9			0	Maces	0
2	24	1	4	1	11			1		0
3	96	1	4	1	14	Healing		1		1
4	175	2	6	1	18	Bolt	Home	1		1
5	400	2	6	2	23			1	Prowess	1
6	800	2	8	2	29			2		1
7	1,600	2	8	2	36			2		1
8	3,200	2	10	3	44			2		1
9	6,400	2	10	5	53	Fire Wall	Cure	2		2
10	12,800	2	12	7	64			3	Chase	2
11	25,000	3	12	9	75			3		2
12	40,000	3	15	10	87			3		2
13	60,000	3	15	10	100			3		2
14	75,000	3	21	12	114	Miasma		3		2
15	125,000	3	21	12	129			3	Battle Cry	2
16	200,000	3	30	15	145			4		3
17+	320,000	3	30	15	150			4		3

Table 6.3. *This is an example of how an Experience Level Chart for a human warrior might be structured. It shows the number of Experience Points needed to rise in level and the beneficial effects gained by the character at each new level.*

XP to go from level 1 to level 2, 100 XP to go to level 3, 200 XP to go to level 4, and so on, doubling the number of required experience points each time. The algorithm for such an approach is easy to describe, and the programmers can easily implement it in the game engine.

However, the designers might decide to make the curve less smooth and use unusual value increases as the game progresses. For example, they might have the number of XP required to level up double for the first three levels (e.g., ten XP for the first level, then 20 XP for the next and 40 XP for the third), but then for the next two levels require 2.5 times the number of XP (e.g., 100 XP at the fourth level and 250 XP at the fifth level) and then continually increase the XP total requirements thereafter. In this case, the programmers will have to rely directly on the point values supplied by the designers. In either case, whether the programmers can create a simple algorithm for the rise in Experience Level or have to rely on data supplied by the designers, the process needs to be worked out very early in the design process. It can cause massive headaches to switch from one approach to the other late in the development stage.

The number of Experience Points needed to go up a level can also be affected by race and class, making it harder for programming team to come up with a simple formula. The example of an Experience Level Chart (Table 6.3) shows what happens as a human barbarian goes up in level. In this example, the Experience Level is shown in the first column. The number of Experience Points the player needs to gather to go up a level appears in the second column; in this case, the warrior goes from level 1 to level 2 when the player collects a ninth Experience Point. The next column indicates how many extra points the player is given at each level reached to spend on the character's attributes. The next three columns show the automatic rises in value for the character's Damage attribute, mana, and hit point total. The next two sections show when the character gains new skills and magic spells and how many points the player can use to increase existing skills and spells.

Capping Experience Levels

In paper RPGs, there might be no set limit to how high a character can rise in rank, although the process of reaching the next level can get to be very long and tedious. Also, at very high levels, the only values that get increased are the character's attributes because he or she has maxed out on magic spells and skills. Therefore, many games put some cap on the maximum level a character can attain in the game. In electronic games particularly, the whole gamut of values have to be thoroughly tested to make sure that the game remains balanced and fun to play at all levels, and it can take a very long time to get characters at the highest levels for testing. Players of MMORPGs are known for "grinding"—killing multitudes of low-level creatures to earn enough XP to go up a level. At times, playing an RPG can seem more like work than play.

Some games have gotten rid of levels and instead reward players often during play by sporadically increasing attributes or improving skills or magic. Both Bethesda Softworks' *The Elder Scrolls: Oblivion* and *Fallout 3* use this approach, raising attributes constantly but without forcing the player to leave the game world to deal with the mechanics of character improvement. In *Oblivion*, the player earns experience points for using skills, and skills belonging to the character's class are easier to learn than those outside. In *Fallout 3*, on the other hand, most experience point rewards come from completing quests. Both approaches keep the player immersed in the game world instead of bringing up a special screen to deal with experience point allocations.

Creating Monsters, Villains, and Allies

An interesting game world has to be populated with many beings, both friendly who are willing to assist the character and hostile who only want to mix it up in battle. These entities—a term that includes both animals and humans—perform many functions to help or hinder the player and keep the plot moving along. Designers can wind up spending as much time creating these secondary characters as they do the characters that players will become. The non-player characters (NPCs) are also vital to game play because they serve so many functions—offering advice, advancing the storyline, providing sub-quests, and handling mundane matters like buying and selling materials or providing other services to the player. As with the main characters, considerable testing must occur to make sure that the enemies' attributes and powers are balanced while still providing the player with a challenge throughout the game.

Designers have only limited control over some aspects of these non-player entities (both friendly and hostile), since their actions are controlled by the game's artificial intelligence (AI) module. Designers have to work with the AI programmers to make sure the entities move and act as desired, but they don't actually create the AI routines. Some professional game engines (Epic's Unreal Engine and id Software's id Tech Engine) do allow direct control over the entities, but it can take some understanding of basic programming to get the entities to behave as desired.

Entity Types

The entities controlled by the game engine fall into seven broad categories:

- *Major Villain.* This is the antagonist of the game that usually doesn't appear as an interactive game object until the end of the game. Occasionally, the villain will pop up during play to engage the player character in combat, but these fights usually wind up with the player getting bested and the villain gloating (revealing more of his or her dastardly plan while doing so). This entity can require quite a bit of tweaking to make sure it offers a real challenge to the experienced player at the end of game while not being so powerful as to be unbeatable.

- *Henchmen.* These entities perform various services for the major villain and act as major obstacles for the player. They can actively interfere with the player's progress until defeated in battle. They often have a number of different attacks available, and they can help teach the player how to best use certain tactics before confronting the major villain. While they are tough opponents, they do not present the same challenge as the major villain. Defeating henchmen is one way for the player to get powerful armament and clues for finding the major villain. One approach to structuring the overall game story is to think of each henchmen as being a major chapter within the overall story. Once a henchman is defeated, a new chapter of the story begins. Note that henchmen do not always have to be humans, they can also be very tough monsters.

- *Minions.* These entities are the cannon fodder of most games. They have limited abilities and they often appear in random encounters. Special minions are used in set-piece encounters, for example, as opponents whose defeat ends sub-quests. They provide the player with items, gold, and experience points. Ideally, the minions grow in strength as the player's character does, so they always present a challenge, or they tend to flee when confronted by a much more powerful opponent. Sometimes minions are under the direct control of henchmen or even the major villain, and sometimes they are just creatures and scoundrels who occupy less desirable ecological nitches in the game world (e.g., dark forests, sewers, caves, and so on). For example, the ogre in Bethesda Softworks' *The Elder Scrolls IV: Oblivion* (Figure 6.4) is a minion that is found only in dark caves.

- *Active Allies.* These are the characters that help the player by joining the party or participating in combat against enemies. Sometimes the player has direct control over their actions, in which case they are handled like the main character in terms of selecting options during combat. Sometimes their actions are determined by the combat algorithm, and the same AI routines used to control attacks by the enemies can be used to control the attacks by allies. The allies often have their own stories going on during the game and their own set of quests that the player has to help resolve (or perhaps ignore, depending on what a given quest involves and how central it is to the main story quest). The player might have to deal with the minutiae of controlling active allies, assigning points when they go up levels, and dealing with

Figure 6.4. *An ogre from Bethesda Softworks' The Elder Scrolls IV: Oblivion presents an obvious threat. The musculature in the upper body and thick legs show him to be very strong. Compare this ogre to the "cute" Shrek in DreamWorks Animation's movies.*

the items and armament in their inventory just as for the main character.

- *Reactive Allies.* These entities are basically friendly to the player but they don't join the player in the major quest. In many cases, the major villain's plot involves harming one of the player's reactive allies through kidnapping, manipulation, or even murder. These entities sometimes have sub-quests for the player to perform and they often act as the agents for advancing the main plot. For example, a king might be hesitant to help the young hero find the villain until said hero removes a mighty dragon (henchman) threatening his kingdom. Once the dragon is slain, the hero is suitably rewarded and the king helps the player advance to the next chapter of the story.

- *Active NPCs.* These entities perform services for the player but they don't actively get involved in the story. They own the shops that buy items players collect in their travels, and they sell useful supplies like healing and cure potions, weaponry and other objects. They are hotel managers where the player's party can stay and rest, they are priests or clerics who can cure the party of illnesses, and they are porters that grant access to the world map for moving quickly between one location and another. They sometimes have minor sub-quests that reward the player with extra money or valuable items, but these quests usually don't involve anything too strenuous. These entities often have new dialogue available when one chapter ends and a new one begins.

- *Inactive NPCs.* These entities are window dressing to make the game world seem more populated. They interact with the player in dialogue that might have a few options, but generally they tend to repeat the same text over and over ad nauseam. As the game world conditions change, their dialogue can change as well, but they tend to reiterate the same information for long stretches of time. These entities usually have limited AI (perhaps for movement) and their text is useful for giving more flavor to the game by offering background information about the current location and what can be discovered nearby.

Entity Attributes

Those entities that engage in combat need the values for the same attributes as characters: Strength, Constitution, Health, Dexterity, and Luck. The algorithm for resolving an entity's attack is the same as for the player's character. Depending on what magic and items are given to an entity, it may be able to cast modifiers on itself to improve its attack value, on allied minions to improve their values, or on the player's character and allies to lower their values. It may also remove negative modifiers applied to it and its minions. The weaker the enemy entity, the less likely it is to have any serious magic. Aside from combat, the entities usually don't need other attributes aside from moving around the map level or the combat arena.

In simple dungeon-crawl RPGs, the enemies' values can be low compared to the character since the player will be spending a long time exploring the map and encountering many enemies. It gets boring to have to leave a dungeon frequently to load back up on healing medicines and other supplies. Likewise, in story-driven RPGs, most enemies the player encounters are relatively easy to defeat, again so the characters don't continually have to return to town for supplies. Enemies encountered while resolving quests are generally much tougher and have more magic and/or items at their command. The major villain and the henchmen are the most powerful enemies with many combat actions. Before facing these tough enemies, the player should be allowed to rest and save the current position because it gets frustrating to have to repeatedly spend a long time working one's way from a save point to the final confrontation with a henchman or the master villain.

In some games, the enemies' attribute values are based on the characters' current values. If there is a party involved, the game engine might use an average of the characters' values to determine the overall values for the whole group. When preparing for a battle, the algorithm first sets the enemies' attribute values as a percentage of the characters' values (individually or as a party), with low-level enemies having a low percentage and major enemies having a higher percentage. Thus, if a character's has a base Attack Value of 36, for example, a low-level enemy might get 25% of this value (9), while a high-level enemy might get 80% (29, rounding up from 28.8). Using this approach means that all enemies will present some challenge to the player throughout the game. The drawback is that the player might wonder why level 1 wolves found early in the game suddenly attack much more ferociously later on.

Entity Attribute (Monster) Chart

The attributes for entities can be defined in an Entity Attribute Chart (Table 6.4). Note that in addition to the basic attribute values, there are columns for magic spells an entity can use. Some of the information found on this example chart include:

- *Entity Number.* A unique number per entity that is used whenever the game engine needs to a pointer to the entity's data. This number is also used to point to the artwork used for the entity.

- *Entity Name.* This chart contains the singular name of the creature since the plural name is found on the appropriate Encounter Table. However, this chart could contains the singular and plural versions of an entity's name.

- *Attributes.* Basic values for attack value, defense value, dexterity, luck, fleeing, and Hit Points. It could also include a column for how much mana the entity begins with, assuming the mana is expended on casting spells the same way it is for the player.

FRP Entity Attribute (Monster) Chart

			Attributes						Magic Spells								
ID No.	Name	Type	Str	End	Dex	Agl	Flee %	HP	Magic %	1st Spell Name	Cast %	2nd Spell Name	Cast %	3rd Spell Name	Cast %	4th Spell Name	Cast %
1	Wolf	Animal	4	3	5	5	15	8	0	NA	0	NA	0	NA	0	NA	0
2	Boar	Animal	9	8	4	6	12	18	0	NA	0	NA	0	NA	0	NA	0
3	Eagle	Animal	10	9	9	15	10	16	0	NA	0	NA	0	NA	0	NA	0
4	Lion	Animal	12	11	9	12	5	30	0	NA	0	NA	0	NA	0	NA	0
5	Bear	Animal	15	10	6	9	3	50	0	NA	0	NA	0	NA	0	NA	0
6	Dire Wolf	Animal	25	15	8	16	0	120	0	NA	0	NA	0	NA	0	NA	0
7	Death Wolf	Magic Animal	30	21	12	15	3	190	10	Bolt	90	Curse	10	NA	0	NA	0
8	Were-Boar	Magic Animal	45	24	15	12	0	240	15	Poison	70	Curse	25	Petrify	5	NA	0
9	Hippo-bearamus	Magic Animal	60	30	14	10	0	600	25	Flash Fire	50	Hell Flame	30	Inferno	15	Heal Lvl 1	5
10	Dragon	Magic Animal	90	60	16	60	0	1200	30	Hell Flame	40	Bolt	30	Poison	20	Inferno	10
11	Ghost	Ghost	5	6	4	10	10	12	0	NA	0	NA	0	NA	0	NA	0
12	Ghoul	Magic Ghost	25	10	8	15	4	50	15	Curse	50	Poison	45	Petrify	5	NA	0
13	Shape-shifter	Magic Ghost	50	40	20	12	0	300	20	Bolt	50	Tsunami	35	Cure Lvl 1	10	Heal Lvl 1	5
14	Fire Fairy	Elemental	25	60	15	20	10	60	50	Flash Fire	40	Hell Flame	30	Inferno	20	Bang	10
15	Rogue Thief	Human	15	13	25	21	15	115	10	Bolt	90	Heal Lvl 1	10	NA	0	NA	0
16	Rogue Knight	Human	25	21	20	15	5	150	10	Poison	80	Cure Lvl 1	20	NA	0	NA	0
17	Rogue Wizard	Magician	12	10	30	30	10	90	90	Inferno	40	Tsunami	35	Lightning	20	Heal Lvl 3	5
18	Archer Prince	Henchman	100	80	25	20	0	800	15	Bolt	80	Heal Lvl 1	20	NA	0	NA	0
19	Woodland Queen	Boss	150	120	20	25	0	1200	30	Tsunami	50	Bolt	30	Poison	15	Heal Lvl 1	5
20	Forest King	Boss	300	180	10	10	0	3000	15	Inferno	80	Curse	20	NA	0	NA	0

Key
Strength = Attack and carry   Agility = Save from magic
Endurance = Defense and recovery
Flee % = Base chance to flee in a round
Dexterity = Initiative speed   Hit Points

Magic % = How often it attacks using magic
Spell Name (from Spell Chart)
Cast % = How often it uses that spell when attacking

Table 6.4. *This is an example of an Entity Attribute Chart. Each entry includes the type of enemy, its attributes and up to four magic spells it can use in combat (NA means that magic slot is empty).*

- *Magic Casting Percentage.* Determines the likelihood that an entity that can cast magic will use it as a combat action. Note that instead of using this value, the entity could be assigned an AI routine to handle casting magic so that it reacts to actions performed by the player (see Entity Combat Action Section below).

- *Magic Spells.* All the spells the entity can use during combat. (The level of each spell could be indicated as well if they have levels.) Note that each spell is given a percentage, which determines how likely it will cast that spell during combat. The percentages for all spells should add up to 100 percent.

The chart could include other information as well, for example, the entity's AI type, assuming the AI routines are broken into discrete types (e.g., aggressive, passive, reactive, and so on). If an entity can use items, skills, or other actions during combat, they can be included on the chart as well. Experience Points and money awarded for defeating the entity may be located on this chart or on the Encounter Table. Once the designers have worked out the details of the chart with the programming team, they can create the first version. It is a good idea to use spreadsheets to show the entity values since one entity can quickly be compared with others to find any discrepancies. The programmers can create a tool to copy the appropriate information from the spreadsheet to a file that can be read by the game engine.

If the designers want to include variable difficulty levels in the game, they can make individual Entity Attribute Charts for each level of difficulty, changing the values on the charts as necessary. Thus, if the player selects the "Easy" difficulty level, the game would use the chart with the lowest attribute values, making it easier to kill the enemies while the player takes less damage. This approach could also be handled programmatically, with the values on a single chart being diminished or increased by a certain percentage based on the selected difficulty level.

Entity Combat Action Selection

When an entity attacks during combat, the AI routines determine which form of attack it will use. There are several approaches to making this determination. Obviously, if the entity has only one form of attack—for example, a lion attacking with its claws—then it will perform this action every turn unless it flees or is killed. If the entity has several methods of attacking—for example, a human with several weapons and magic spells—then the AI routines determine the attack method.

One approach is to have the entity go through its list of possible attacks in order—for example, attack with knife, attack with sword, cast fire ball, and so on. The drawback with this system is that the player can soon predict what the enemy will do and counter the attack or minimize the damage. Another approach is to randomize the selection so that even though the player quickly learns the possible attacks by the enemy, he or she won't know which one will come next. This approach makes combat much more interesting because the next attack is unpredictable.

Entity Combat Action Table

Die Roll Range	Action Type
1–50	Sword attack
51–75	Knife attack
76–85	Fireball spell
86–90	Meteor Strike spell
91–95	Enhance Attack Skills spell
96–100	Heal spell

Table 6.5. *This is an example of an Entity Combat Action Table, which is created for each enemy type, in this case a rogue.*

A refinement to randomization is to weight the various options available to the entity. For example, there might be an Entity Combat Action Table that looks like Table 6.5. In this case, the entity will attack with the sword most of the time (50%), then sometimes go with the knife (25%), then occasionally cast a Fireball (10%), and rarely either enhance its own attributes (5%) or heal (5%). The advantage of this approach is that the entity shows certain preferences while still having a number of choices for actions during combat. Note that fleeing does not appear on this chart, although it could be added if the designers want it to be considered a combat action.

A final approach to selecting actions in combat is to use a scripting system that allows the entity to react to what the player does. When the time comes for the entity to make its choice of combat action, it first runs through a list of actions the player performed or other current conditions. If certain criteria are met, then the entity performs a certain action. If no criteria are met, the entity selects a combat action randomly. This approach is useful for henchmen and the major villain and allows them to seemingly react to what the player has done and to change their methods of attack each time the player fights them. If the player casts a Curse spell that weakens the entity, it might counter with a Remove Curse spell in a turn or two. Creating scripts for determining combat actions can become complex, so the designers should have a good sense of how the AI engine works before trying to create combat routines themselves.

Fleeing

It is sometimes useful to have enemies flee a combat if they are weak and facing very strong characters. Each enemy type might be given a flee chance on the Encounter Table, which is used to determine if it will escape from the combat, or perhaps this value could appear on the Entity Attribute Chart instead. The flee chance is usually very low because it gets frustrating to get into combat situations repeatedly with weak enemies only to have them flee at the first chance. Usually when enemies flee, the player is not rewarded with experience, gold, or items, although the design team can certainly decide that some reward is called for.

Depending on how the combat algorithm works, an attempt to flee can occur only once or every time the entity is about to engage in combat. The flee attempt is usually the first step in the entity's combat algorithm and might look something like this:

Determine Flee Attempt

Step 1. Check for a flee attempt before the entity's first combat resolution by generating a random result and checking the entity's Flee Value (either on the Encounter Table or Entity Attribute Chart).

- If the result is equal to or less than the Flee Value, the entity flees. Play its flee animation. Go to Step 2.

- If the result is greater than the Flee Value, the entity does not flee and continues the combat resolution procedure.

Step 2. Check if combat continues or ends.

- If no more entities remain on the playfield, end the combat.

- If more entities remain, go to the character or entity with the next highest Initiative value and resolve its combat.

Treasure Tables

Sometimes entities involved in a random encounter drop items after combat, even though it might seem weird that a level 1 wolf is running around with a short sword. To make the process more

Treasure Table
Map Used: Forest Prime Evil

Random %	Item 1	Item 2	Item 3*	Item 4**
1–20	Sword	NA	NA	NA
21–40	Club	NA	NA	Hatchet
41–50	Leather Hat	Heal Biscuit	NA	NA
51–60	Hatchet	NA	Heal Biscuit	Curative
61–65	Heal Biscuit	NA	NA	Heal Biscuit
66–70	Curative	NA	NA	NA
71–75	Leather Jacket	NA	Leather Hat	NA
76–80	Lockpick	Hatchet	NA	Heal Biscuit
81–84	Short Bow	NA	Heal Biscuit	NA
85–88	Spear	NA	Leather Jacket	NA
89–92	Chainmail	NA	Heal Biscuit	NA
93–95	Battle Axe	Curative	NA	NA
96–97	Jeweled Necklace	Heal Biscuit	NA	Curative
98–99	Silver Ingot	NA	NA	NA
00	Omni Visor	NA	NA	NA

* = Party of three only   ** = Party of four only

Table 6.6. *This example of a Treasure Table is set up to offer more treasure if the player is leading a party ("NA" means that items slot is empty).*

interesting, the results can be randomized by using a Treasure Table. See Table 6.6 for a simple Treasure Table. The algorithm for determining treasure dropped by entities after combat might go something like this:

Determine If Entities Have Treasure

Step 1. Check the entity's Loot percentage on the Encounter Table and generate a random result.

- If the result is greater than the percentage, then the entity does not drop treasure.

- If the result is equal to or less than the percentage, then it does drop treasure.

Determine Treasure Type Dropped

Step 2. Generate a random value and cross reference the result with the column of treasure items for the level.

- Bring up the treasure window when the combat is finished.
- Show the treasures in the window for the player to take.

Usually, items are fairly low-level and of limited use to the player. The treasures can be a useful way to replenish a character's stock of items during play without having to go to a town and shop for them. Also, the items collected after combat can be sold at shops for cash. As the character encounters tougher enemies, the resulting treasures can get better. If there are some special items the player needs to get in some map areas, they should not be assigned to a Treasure Table. Instead, such encounters should be scripted (see Chapter 11 for more details).

Sports Game Characters

There are "characters" in sports games, but these characters are either real-life athletes or fictional. They also have statistics (attributes) that are used in some games to resolve actions. Athletes don't have attributes like Strength, Hit Points, or Mana, but they have statistics relevant to the sport they play like Earned Run Average (ERA) in baseball, assists in basketball, and interceptions in football. Unlike RPG characters, however, the statistics for athletes tend to hover around the same value over their careers, as opposed to growing constantly as they play the sport. For example, a good batter in professional baseball has a batting average of about .250–.350 (meaning they get a hit 25–35% of the time they are at bat). If they fall below .250, they are considered on a losing streak. Batting above .350 means they are a superstar hitter, but even they can't break the .400 average for a whole season.

In some arcade sports games, the athletes' statistics are meaningless, and the player simply whacks away at a ball or tries to advance the ball or puck as far down field as possible. It is the player's ability that counts, not the athletes'. In games that are tied to professional sports, such as Electronic Arts' *Madden NFL* football games or 2K Games' *Major League Baseball*, the statistics are used in resolving some game actions. However, to use professional athletes' statistics in a game (as well as their likenesses and names), the developer needs one or more licenses, from the professional sports league, from the players' association, and sometimes from the individual athletes. It is possible to create artificial players with similar statistics, but most customers want real sports stars likenesses in the game, not some knockoffs.

Using Athletes' Statistics

Depending on the sport and how it is translated into an electronic game, the statistics can be very important to game actions or only tangentially so. There are many ways to use the statistics, from generating random numbers (say, from 1–1000 for baseball to generate a percentage result of .000–.999) and then checking a table to see if something happens. In a baseball game, a slugger has a wider range of possibilities than a poor batter and so is likely to wind up getting on base more often. In a baseball game, for example, one random result might determine if the player gets a hit and then a second random result determines how many bases the hit is worth. Some of the statistics can be modified to get even better results—for example, a homerun hitter might get a positive modifier to make him more likely to get a home run.

Another approach is to use a player's statistics in conjunction with the player's actions. For example, assume in a soccer game that the player is driving the ball down the field and kicks it to a teammate. The game generates a random result against the player's passing average, which in this case is very good. However, the player is not very competent with the controls, so even though the ball would normally get to the next player, in this case it gets intercepted. If the controller were in the hands of a very good player, the ball would get passed even though the random result indicated the player did not succeed.

The design team still has to work out with the programmers how some actions will be resolved. For example, in a baseball game, they have to determine exactly how a bat swing gets resolved. The algorithm might look something like this:

Determine Pitch Type

Step 1. Check the type of pitch being thrown and see if it is going to be a ball.

- If it is a ball and the player does not swing at it, have the umpire call "Ball" and go to Step 3.

- If it is a ball and the player swings at it but misses, have the umpire call "Strike" and go to Step 4.

- If it is a ball and the player swings and hits it, go to Step 5 to resolve the outcome.

Step 2. Check the type of pitch being thrown and see if it is going to be a strike.

- If it is a strike and the player does not swing at it, have the umpire call "Strike" and go to Step 4.

- If it is a strike and the player swings at it but misses, have the umpire call "Strike" and go to Step 4.

- If it is a strike and the player swings and hits it, go to Step 5 to resolve the outcome.

Resolve "Ball" Call

Step 3. Check how many times the umpire has called "Ball" so far.

- If this is the fourth "Ball," the pitching ends and the batter goes to first base.

- If this is the not the fourth "Ball," the pitching continues and the pitcher prepares to throw the next ball.

Resolve "Strike" Call

Step 4. Check how many times the umpire has called "Strike" so far.

- If this is the third "Strike," have the umpire say, "You're out!" and end the batter's turn.

- If this is the first or second "Strike," the pitching continues and the pitcher prepares to throw the next ball.

Resolve Hit Attempt

Step 5. Compare the thrown ball's path through the strike zone and compare it to the batter's "sweet spot" statistic to determine where the ball is hit and what will happen.

- If the result is "Foul Ball," have the umpire say "Foul!" and show the animation for where the ball lands. Then go to the next pitch.
- If the result is "Fair Ball," the ball is in play, so determine how far it goes.

The algorithm can get fairly complex because it has to determine things like dropped balls, what base the batter is to be awarded, whether or not a defending player can catch the hit ball or not, and any errors made by the runner or defending team. In any sport games, the designers work with the programmers to create algorithms that consider every possible action in the game.

One advantage to making an electronic version of a real-world sport is that the rules have all been standardized and the relevant statistics for the players are available. The designers select which rules will be used in the game and which statistics relate to those rules. They can ignore rules that don't apply to the game itself or statistics that don't affect game play directly. They do have to work out in detail with the programmer staff how the rules will be implemented and then check the game play versus the real game to keep actions within boundaries. If a football quarterback is passing for touchdown every time he touches the ball, then something is broken and needs to be fixed.

Conclusion

As is evident, it takes time to work out the attributes for the various entities in a game. In an RPG, there is also the task of assigning proper skills and magic/technology not only at the beginning of the game but also improving them over time as the character goes up in level. Many console RPGs limit the data for characters and give the player few if any choices about how improvements will be made. While these limitations can feel restrictive, they do make things easier on the design team since players often play through the game once or twice at most. A limited character generation system is better than a poorly designed one that can ruin the game by allowing multiple unbalanced characters.

In addition to determining the attributes for characters and enemies, the designers spend considerable time preparing the encounters and making sure the combat in an RPG feels balanced or that athletes work like their real-world counterparts in sports games.

Working through the basics in a paper prototype can help as a good first pass at the overall task, but it takes a huge amount of testing to ensure that the values are right and that the enemies seem to be acting intelligently in their combat choices.

Exercises

1. Determine all the attributes (statistics) your units will need in the game you're designing. Separate the major attributes needed to resolve major games actions like combat and movement from the minor attributes that have only a limited effect or are seldom used. Write up a brief description of each attribute and where it is used in during play.

2. Create a simple Character Generation Chart for a role-playing game.

   a. Include only three races and three classes in the system, and write a short description about the strengths and weaknesses of each race and class.

   b. Determine which attributes are needed, either using those you came up with in Exercise 1 or creating a different set for this exercise.

   c. Test all the possible character combinations using a simple combat system to ensure that no one class or race is too powerful at the start.

3. Once you have the attribute values, fill out the rest of the information needed in the Character Generation Chart.

   a. You should assign at least two skills to each class and add any other information you think is relevant (e.g., gender, philosophy, traits, etc.).

   b. Write up a short description of each skill and magic spell/technology assigned to each character class and race at the start of play.

   c. Decide what weapons, armor, and items each class and race will have at the start of the game.

4. Create an Experience Level Chart based on the Character Generation Chart created in Exercise 3.

    a.   Include 10 levels for each class.

    b.   Assign appropriate increases in attributes at each new level.

    c.   Indicate the levels when each character class or race receives new skills and/or spells/technology.

5.   Create a half dozen enemy types for your game (or a role-playing game) and assign them attribute values, weapons, magic spells, etc. as necessary.

    a.   Write up a short description of each enemy type, describing both its physical appearance and how it acts during combat (and other game actions if necessary).

    b.   The enemy types should include a mixture of low-level creatures, some tougher enemies and one boss.

    c.   Create an Entity Attribute Chart for the enemies including the magic spells/technology they know, their weaponry and armament.

6.   Once you have the Character Generation, Experience Level and Entity Attribute Charts done, test them using the combat system you created for chapter 5. Note that information about armor, weapons and other items is covered in the next chapter, so for this exercise use relative values for their attributes.

    a.   Perform a mathematical analysis to determine how many enemies of various types the player must defeat to rise in Experience Levels

    b.   Write up your results as an essay.

7.   Do some research on the Internet to determine which player statistics are considered most relevant in professional baseball, football, hockey and basketball.

    a.   Write up a short description of these statistics and explain which ones are best suited for an electronic version of each sport.

    b.   Then create an algorithm describing how various sport actions would be resolved using these statistics.

8. Create a chapter in your game design document in which you describe the major characters/units and enemies in your game.

   a. Define the attributes assigned to each entity type and how they are used to resolve various game actions.

   b. Include a brief physical description of each entity and a short list of actions in performs (in and out of combat).

   c. Check the Internet for images of entities that either look like or act like the ones appearing in your game and include them in the game design document.

CHAPTER 7

ON ITEMS

In many types of games, the playfield is strewn with objects for the player to find, and these items perform many different game functions, most of them positive. An item is different from an entity because it doesn't perform actions independently of the player's control. Sometimes the player has to act to acquire an item and at other times the item is acquired as soon as the player comes in contact with it. If players have to carry items with them in their travels, they are likely to have an inventory where extras are stored. These items are different from the weapons and other artifacts the character is wearing, and the player often has to take time to open the inventory to switch items or get something to use.

Items are different from tokens in board games. Tokens represent the player in an abstract way during movement around the board. Occasionally, there are extra items that can be collected or placed on the board to affect play. For example, the physical murder weapons appear on the board in Parker Brother's *Clue* and they are moved from room to room as players make guesses as to the identity of the murderer. No player owns a weapon, however. In *Monopoly*, on the other hand, there are houses and hotels that players buy and place on the board on their properties to raise the cost of rents for other players landing on those spaces. The players also get deeds when they purchase property and money as they go past the "Go" space or collect rents from other players. Most board games have a limited number of extra items because they are easy to misplace during and after play, and they can add considerably to the manufacturing cost of the game.

Item Categories

In electronic games, items can come in many varieties and do many things, as noted below. In action games, these items are sometimes called "power-ups" but they fall into the same categories as items in other game genres. Sometimes these objects are found on the play-field, sometimes they are given to the player as a reward, and at other times they are bought and sold in stores.

Health and Mana

Potions, scrolls, and other objects help restore a character's health (Hit Points) or cure negative status effects (poison, petrifaction, stun, and so on). Most games where combat is involved allow players to heal or cure themselves during the fight; otherwise, players would die quickly if they made the wrong decisions about what combat actions to use. These items are also used outside of combat to restore health to characters or remove persistent negative status effects. It is possible to have health items that can be used only during or after combat as well. Sometimes health and cure items have only one shot and are removed as soon as they are used, and at other times they provide multiple uses. These items are almost always removed from a character's inventory when used up.

Other items are used to replenish a magic user's mana and act the same as health items. A mana restorative might have only one use or multiple uses, depending on how the magic system is set up for the game.

Personal and Environmental Modifiers

Other potions, scrolls, and objects can be used to modify the character or an enemy during battle, either improving or weakening an attribute or putting a negative status effect on an enemy. These modifiers are usually temporary and last only for a certain amount of time or until the combat ends. Other modifiers apply to the game environment itself, for example, a thunderstorm or blizzard or a temporary slowdown of time. The effects can be quite spectacular—for example, earthquakes that shake the screen and snowstorms that cause a temporary whiteout of the playfield—and they sometimes damage entities so they can be used as weapons, too. Many of these modifiers can be employed via magic spells, the main difference being that an item can usually be used only once and is then removed from the character's inventory while a magic spell can be used repeatedly.

Weapons

In some types of games, the player acquires different weapons for characters and switches out weaker ones for more powerful ones

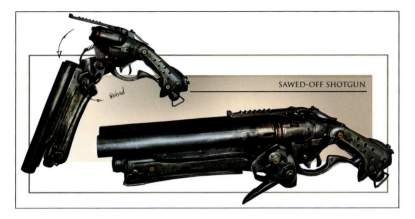

SAWED-OFF SHOTGUN

Figure 7.1. *This artist's sketch shows a sawed-off shotgun that appears in Epic Games'* Gears of War III.

(e.g., the sawed-off shotgun in Epic Games' *Gear of War III*; see Figure 7.1). Each weapon type has certain advantages and disadvantages. Occasionally, a weapon in an RPG is imbued with magic or an exotic technology as well, providing the character with several ways to attack during combat. Some modern weapons also have this advantage, being able to fire both projectiles and missiles.

In addition to weapons that are carried by a character, additional weapons can be put into the inventory for later use. Depending on how inventory is treated, a player might be able to put as many extra weapons and additional items into the inventory as there are open slots to hold them, or weapons might take up several spaces in an inventory, forcing the player to move other items around to make room for a spare weapon. Weapons are long-lasting and are not removed from the character's inventory unless destroyed, dropped, or sold.

Armor

These items provide protection during combat and they cover some or all parts of the body. Heavier armor provides better protection but can be cumbersome to wear and may not protect against magic/psionic attacks. Sometimes the armor protects against environmental hazards as well, for example, radioactivity or poisonous atmosphere. Armor can be worn on a character and carried in the inventory as well. As with weapons, the player might have to manipulate other items in the inventory to make room for spare armor. Armor is also long-lasting and is not removed unless dropped or sold. In some games, armor is removed if it is too badly damaged but it can sometimes be repaired at shops, by a special skill, or automatically over time (as in energy shields).

Ammunition

Weapons that shoot projectiles—solid or energy—will stop working if they run out. Ammunition is often scattered around the playfield for the player to find, and reloads for some projectile weapons can be bought in shops if the player has enough cash. Usually, very destructive ammunition types like missiles and rockets are rarer than standard bullets and arrows because they can do so much damage. In some games, the player has to select ammunition found on the playfield by clicking on it or moving it from a temporary holding box into the character's inventory, and in other games the ammunition is automatically added to the inventory as soon as the character comes in contact with it. In some role-playing games, ammunition appears as an object in the inventory that the player manipulates by moving it from space to space to make room for spare weapons and armor and other items. In other games, such as first-person shooters, ammunition is treated more abstractly and is simply added to the amount currently available for a weapon without taking up precious inventory space. However it is handled in the design, ammunition manipulation should not be a distraction to the player. If the action is fast and furious, ammunition should be easy to access, while in more realistic simulations, it can be a precious resource the player needs to address.

Resources

In real-time strategy and other strategy/simulation games, there are resources on the playfield the play can collect to build other materials. Some items—wood, metal, stone—are used to erect and improve buildings while others—food, water, herbs—are used to feed and heal workers and soldiers. Resources are often associated with terrain features, and the player sends gatherers to the map feature to collect the appropriate resource (for example, wood from trees, metal from mines, and stones from quarries). These resources can be gathered as long as the supply lasts, and the player might have to find new sources as old ones dry up. In some cases, resources are one-time objects the player finds while exploring the playfield, and they are removed when the player enters their spaces and cannot be continually mined. Resources generally have their own inventory system that differs from inventories carried by characters. The player usually does not manipulate objects in the resource inventory as he or she can with objects in a character's inventory.

Quest Items

The objective of a quest can involve the acquisition of an item or items the character must carry back to the entity that initiated the quest. Quests often involve a search for weapons and armor and special magic items. Sometimes the items are placed in the character's inventory and at other times they are held separately in a different inventory. These items can occasionally be used by a character until the quest is complete, at which time an item might go back to the original owner or be bestowed on the character as a reward. Quest items are usually removed from the player's possession once they have been returned to the NPC who initiated each quest.

Puzzle Objects

In most puzzle games, the player manipulates some game objects in various ways to achieve a specific goal. These items include playing cards, jewels, mahjong tiles, alphabet letters, jigsaw puzzle pieces, and many other everyday objects. In some RPGs, especially Japanese RPGs, there might be actual puzzles the player must solve to continue through the game. In Square Enix's *Final Fantasy X*, for example, the player has to figure out into which holes he or she is to place some large spheres found in the environment, and the correct combination opens up doors to temples, allowing the story to continue. Items used to resolve these puzzles are usually different from quest items, and they usually appear only near the location where the puzzle is found. They are not necessarily added to the player's inventory. In the adventure game genre, on the other hand, puzzle items are often carried in an inventory, and the player has to figure out where they are used to solve puzzles found in the game either individually or in combination. These puzzles are usually more complex than the simple puzzles found in role-playing and shooter games.

Sports Equipment

Many sports include items like balls, footballs, pucks, and other equipment that are passed around by players as they cross the playfield to score points. Opposing players try to intercept or otherwise appropriate the item to bring it back to their side of the playfield. Since most sports games try to simulate reality realistically, these items are governed by the natural laws of physics and don't do anything except move. They are also separate from the athletes' uniforms and any "inventory" on their persons like mitts, bats, and masks. The item remains until the end of the game when one side wins. There is usually no inventory system associated with sports games, although some equipment might have ammunition that is depleted (for example, arrows in an archery contest or rifle bullets in a biathlon).

Game Functions of Items

Most items in games serve a single function, although some armament in RPG and FPS games allow for multiple usages. The items sometimes have a few attributes associated with them (for example, Hit Points and Attack and Defense Values for weapons and armor), but more often they are used to modify one or more of a character's attributes, either by being worn or by being used by the player. Some items have functions that are special cases—meaning they modify, bend, or break the standard rules of the game. Other items are restricted to certain character classes. Because items serve so many purposes, the design team has to figure out during the design phase which purposes each item serves. They have to be able to explain to the programming team how the items work as well as describing what the items look like for the art team.

The programming team will want to group the items by type and to identify each function an item can serve. Grouping items together on an Item Chart (see the following section) is useful for both the designers and the programmers. It is better to overdesign the item list initially and cut back during production than to have to think up new items with different purposes later in development. If the developer has plans for extending the game with add-ons after the product ships, the programming team might include hooks in the code for functions that were considered initially but dropped due to time and budget constraints.

Item Chart

The Item Chart example is too large to appear on one page and has been broken into four tables (Tables 7.1 through 7.4) on the following three pages. The Item Chart shows how items can be organized by functionality for a fantasy RPG. It is broken down into categories that make it easier for the designers to change values and functions during testing. A simple tool by the programming team can be created to strip the appropriate values out of the spreadsheet as necessary so they can be read by the game engine.

- *Item Number.* Each item should have a unique number that can be used as a pointer to its artwork. Note that there are normally two kinds of artwork associated with an item. The first is the

FRP Item Chart

Item No.	Name	Type	Ammo	Remove if 0 ammo	Inven Art	Class						Race				Alignment		
						Warr	Pala	Arch	Rogu	Prie	Mage	Hum	Elf	Dwf	Hlf	Neg	Neu	Pos
1	Knife	Knife	0	0	1				+1						+1			
2	Bolo	Knife	0	0	1				+1									
3	Sword	Sword	0	0	2									+1				
4	Broadsword	Sword	0	0	2		+1			X	X		-1	+2	-1			
5	Sword of Zeus	Sword	1	0	21	X	+2	X	X	X			-1		-2	-2	+1	+2
6	Hatchet	Axe	0	0	3													
7	Battle Axe	Axe	0	0	3	+1		X		X				+1				
8	Berserker Axe	Axe	0	0	3	+2	X	X	X	X	-1			+2	-2	+2	-1	-2
9	Club	Club	0	0	4													
10	Morningstar	Club	0	0	4		+1							+1				
11	Royal Mace	Club	0	0	4		+2	X	X		X			+2	-1		-1	+2
12	Staff	Staff	0	0	5					+1			+1					
13	Mystic Staff	Staff	0	0	51	X	X	X	X	+2	+1	+1	+2			-2	+2	+1
14	Spear	Spear	0	0	6	+1							-1					
15	Cursed Spear	Spear	1	0	61	+2	X	X	X	X	X	+1	+1	-2	-1	+2		-1
16	Short Bow	Bow	0	0	7				+1									
17	Longbow	Bow	0	0	7			+1	X		X		+1	-1	-1			
18	Crossbow	Bow	0	0	7			+1		X	X	+1	+1	-1	-2			
19	Bow of Grace	Bow	0	0	71	X	X	+2	X	X	X	+1	+2	-2	-2	-1		+1
20	Claw of Terror	Claw	1	0	8	X	X	X	X	+1	+2	-1	-1	+1	+2	+3		-2
101	Leather Hat	Head	0	0	101													
102	Iron Helmet	Head	0	0	102						X		-1					
103	Great Helm	Head	0	0	103			X	X	X	X	+1	-2	+1	-1			+1
104	Athena's Cap	Head	0	0	401	X	X	X	X				+2			-1	+1	+2
105	Leather Jacket	Body	0	0	201									+1				
106	Chainmail	Body	0	0	202						X							
107	Knight Plate	Body	0	0	203			X	X		X	+1	-1	+2	-1	-1	+1	+1
108	Mystic Robe	Body	0	0	451	X	X	X	X	X			+2			-2		+1
109	Arm Shield	Shield	0	0	301						X		+1					
110	Great Shield	Shield	0	0	302			X	X	X	X	+1	-2	-1	-1			
111	Holy Buckler	Shield	0	0	501	X		X	X				+2	+2	+1	+1	-1	+2

Table 7.1. *An example of an Item Chart that could be used in a fantasy-role playing game showing the data for weapons and armor. This is the first half of data for weapons and armor; the other half appears as Table 7.2 on page 172.*

		Inflict				Protect				Special Attacks		Attribute Modifiers						Spell/Skill Effects		Gold		Text
Item No.	Name	Poi	Stn	Mut	Slp	Poi	Stn	Mut	Slp	Target	Effect	Atk Val	Dam Val	Hit Pts	Abs Dam	Dex Sav	Init	Spell	Skill	Buy	Sell	Desc
1	Knife											0								20	5	1
2	Bolo											1								50	25	2
3	Sword											1								50	25	3
4	Broadsword											2								150	75	3
5	Sword of Zeus		X							Magicians	×1.5 Damage	5				+1	+5	Bolt		0	1500	4
6	Hatchet											0								24	15	5
7	Battle Axe											1								0	80	5
8	Berserker Axe									Humans	×1.25 Damage	2				-2	+3		Prowess	0	500	6
9	Club											0								10	2	7
10	Morningstar											1								75	35	8
11	Royal Mace									Animals	×1.25 Damage	3				+1	+2			0	2000	8
12	Staff											0								21	9	9
13	Mystic Staff		X							Ghosts	×2.0 Damage	1				+3	-1		Mana Regen	0	900	10
14	Spear											0								30	15	11
15	Cursed Spear	X								Elementals	Auto-Kill	3				-3	-1	Curse		0	10	12
16	Short Bow																			30	20	13
17	Longbow											1								120	60	14
18	Crossbow											2					-1			0	140	15
19	Bow of Grace			X						Rogues	×2.5 Damage	3				+1	+2		Cure	0	2500	16
20	Claw of Terror	X								Humans	×1.5 Damage	2				-2	-1	Poison		0	120	17
101	Leather Hat												1		1					8	2	101
102	Iron Helmet												2		2					75	25	102
103	Great Helm						X		X				4		3	-1				0	900	103
104	Athena's Cap					X	X	X		Magicians	×1.25 Damage		2		1	+3	+2			0	1200	501
105	Leather Jacket												1	18	1					18	9	201
106	Chainmail												3	36	2					125	60	202
107	Knight Plate							X					5	160	5	-1	-1			0	300	203
108	Mystic Robe					X		X		Elementals	×1.5 Damage		2	40	2	+2	+2			0	1000	601
109	Arm Shield												1	50	2					100	45	301
110	Great Shield												3	120	4	-2	-1			0	325	302
111	Holy Buckler					X	X		X	Ghosts	×1.75 Damage		2	240	6	+1	+4			0	2100	303
112	Warding Shield					X	X	X	X	Elementals	×1.25 Damage		2	210	4	+10	+2			0	900	701

Table 7.2. This is the other half of Item Chart for weapons and armor (see Table 7.1 on page 171) and shows which items have status effects, special attacks, modifiers and spell/skill effects.

2D representation of the object as it appears in the inventory, and the second is the 3D model as it appears on the playfield or on the character. Note that the 2D representation of an object might use a different visual if the object has special properties (for example, a glow around an item that is needed to complete quest, a weapon that has multiple ways to be used in an attack, or a number to track ammo reloads).

FRP Item Chart II

Item No.	Name	Type	Ammo	Remove if 0 ammo	Inven Art	Warr	Pala	Arch	Rogu	Prie	Mage	Neg	Neu	Pos
						Guilds						Alignment		
401	Hercules' Insignia	Badge		0	601			X	X	X	X	–1		+1
402	Eros' Badge	Badge		0	602	X	X			X	X			
403	Ring of Ages	Ring		0	603								+2	
404	Fire Ring	Ring	3	1	604	X	X	X	X					
405	Heroic Amulet	Amulet		0	701				X	X	X	–1		+1
406	Mystic Amulet	Amulet		0	702									
407	Hateful Bracelet	Bracelet	2	1	801							+10		–6
408	Shielding Bracelet	Bracelet		0	802									
409	Jeweled Necklace	Necklace		0	901					X	X			
410	Hera's Boon	Necklace	3	0	902				X			–2		+2
411	Novice Wand	Wand	6	1	1001	X	X	X						
412	Poseidon's Wand	Wand	12	1	1002	X	X	X	X					
501	Lockpick	Lockpick		0	1101									
502	Hermes' Pick	Lockpick		0	1102	X	X	X		X	X			
503	Heal Biscuit	Health	3	1	1201									
504	Hercules' Potion	Health	3	1	1202									
505	Curative	Cure	5	1	1301									
506	Cure-All	Cure	5	1	1302									
507	Death Scroll	Scroll	3	1	1401		X				X			
508	Inferno Scroll	Scroll	3	1	1402									
509	Silver Ingot	Cash		0	1501									
510	Gold Ingot	Cash		0	1502									
511	Omni Visor	See Map		0	1601									
512	Home Again	Exit Map		0	1602									

Table 7.3. *This is the bottom section of Item Chart for a fantasy-role playing game showing the data for equipment and usable items. This is the first half of data for these items; the other half appears as Table 7.4 on page 174.*

- *Item Name.* The text string is used when the item's name appears in the game text as treasure or in the inventory. Note that if multiple copies of an item appear somewhere in the game, there might need to be a second column for plural names.

- *Item Type.* An identifier used to group similar objects together. In this case, Knife, Sword, Axe, Club, and Claw represent hand weapons used in melee combat, Staff and Spears represent pole weapons that can be used while standing behind other fighters, and Bow indicates a type of projectile weapon.

- *Ammo Number and Removal.* The first column indicates the amount of ammo the item carries. Note that some hand weapons have ammo because they can be used to cast magic spells, and the ammo refers to the number of spells that can be case. The value is also used for potions and other objects that can be used more than once before being removed from the inventory. The next column is used to indicate that the item is removed from

FRP Item Chart II

Item No.	Name	Status Effects Protect Poi	Stn	Mut	Slp	Absorb Damage	Dexer Save	Initiat	Spell/Skill Effects Spell Type	Skill Name	Gold Value Buy	Sell	Text Desc
401	Hercules' Insignia	Badge	X			5	-1	-1			0	750	801
402	Eros' Badge	X				0	+1			Seduce	0	750	802
403	Ring of Ages	Ring			X	1		+1			0	200	803
404	Fire Ring	Ring				0			Hell Flame		0	150	804
405	Heroic Amulet	Amulet	X			2		+1			0	300	805
406	Mystic Amulet	Amulet	X		X	0	+1	+2		Mana Regen	0	350	806
407	Hateful Bracelet	X		X		0		-2	Curse		0	20	807
408	Shielding Bracelet	Bracelet				4	+2				0	450	808
409	Jeweled Necklace	X		X	X	1		+1			0	5000	809
410	Hera's Boon	Necklace				2	+2	+1	Cure		0	1200	810
411	Novice Wand	Wand				0			Flash Fire		0	50	811
412	Poseidon's Wand	Wand				0			Tsunami		0	1800	812
501	Lockpick	Lockpick								Lockpick	0	12	901
502	Hermes' Pick	Lockpick								Lockpick	0	320	902
503	Heal Biscuit	Health							Heal Lvl 1		5	2	903
504	Hercules' Potion	Health							Heal Lvl 5		0	250	904
505	Curative	Cure							Cure Lvl 1		8	4	905
506	Cure-All	Cure							Cure Lvl 5		300	140	906
507	Death Scroll	Scroll							Auto-Kill		0	600	907
508	Inferno Scroll	Scroll							Inferno		0	1200	908
509	Silver Ingot	Cash									0	120	909
510	Gold Ingot	Cash									0	1000	910
511	Omni Visor	See Map							View Map		0	240	911
512	Home Again	Exit Map							Exit Map		0	280	912

Table 7.4. *This is the other half of Item Chart for equipment and usable items (see Table 7.3 on page 173) and shows which ones have status effects, special attacks, modifiers, and spell/skill effects associated with them.*

the inventory once the ammo is used up and applies primarily to potions, scrolls, and other limited use items.

- *Character Type Restrictions.* Some weapons cannot be used by certain classes, races, and/or philosophical leanings, and these are noted by the "X." If there are other distinguishing characteristics used in character creation, any limitation as to using the item can be noted in this section of the chart.

- *Status Effect Properties.* Some weapons and potions/scrolls can inflict status effects (poison, paralysis, petrifaction, etc.) on characters and entities while some armor and other items prevent the character from being affected. The status effect property items are noted by the "X."

- *Special Enemies.* Some weapons and potions/scrolls are particularly powerful against enemy types. The first column shows which entities are affected and the second column shows how the final damage against the enemy type is modified. In an extreme case, hitting an enemy of a certain type with a given weapon can kill it with one hit.

- *Attributes Modifiers.* If an item has attributes, each attribute should have its own column. In this case, weapons affect the attack value, dexterity, and initiative. Armor modifies the character's defense value, dexterity and initiative and also absorbs damage that would otherwise be applied to the character, which reduces its hit point total (in this case, if the total is zero, the item no longer offers any protection until it is repaired). Other items worn by characters can also modify the character's dexterity and initiative and can absorb some damage without being destroyed.

- *Spell and Skill Effects.* If the item can be used to cast a magic spell, the first column indicates which spell (note that healing and cure items can be at several levels as defined on the Magic Chart). An item that can be used to cast magic has a certain amount of ammo before it can no longer be used.

- *Buy and Sell Values.* The first column indicates how much it costs to buy the item in shops while the second column indicates how much shopkeepers will offer to buy the item. Note that many weapons and armor, especially high-end items, cannot be bought because they are gained through quests, but they can be sold. Quest items normally cannot be sold.

- *Help Text.* This number refers to the text string used to describe the item as it appears in the character's journal.

There might be other special functions that items do as well, which would appear in their own columns. However, as more special functions are available for items, they also make the chart itself larger and awkward to handle. In this case, the designers might have to break down the Item Chart by type into a number of smaller charts that handle the functions for each type separately.

Limiting Weapon Selection

In role-playing games, the designer's urge might be towards including a massive amount of weapons as well as armor, decorations, and other items to carry around. However, before plunging in and churning out ideas for weapons, the designers need to look at how player will get the weapons and how much damage they do to various enemies. Usually, the main character starts off fairly weak and can only use light weapons like a knife, short sword, club, or simple bow. Over time, as the character increases in strength, he or she can wield larger weapons. The restrictions applied because of a character's race, class, or alignment also has to be considered when designing weapons. It makes no sense, for example, to have item shops carry heavy, expensive weapons and armor at the beginning of a game if the players can't afford them or carry them. It would make more sense for these advanced items to appear in the shops later in the game when the player can afford them.

In other games genres, weapon selection is more limited. In a first-person shooter game, for example, the player might find about a dozen different weapons in the game. The different between the inventory in role-playing and first-person shooter games is that players can sell items they no longer need for money in role-playing games while in first-person shooter games the weapons, armor, and other items usually become a permanent part of the player's inventory when acquired. It can get very annoying to have to search through a large inventory of weapons to find the one needed to defeat a monster that is bearing down on the player.

Designing Weapons

The Weapons Chart (Table 7.5) is created for a first-person shooter game, and the information in it differs in many respects from the Item Chart for a role-playing game discussed earlier. There are more values for these weapons because combat is usually resolved differently than in role-playing games. Note that on the RPG Item Chart no values are given for damage done by the weapons; instead, the combat formula uses the character's Strength attribute to determine the basic damage from a weapon, and then various modifiers are applied to this value. In the FPS Weapons Chart (Table 7.5), the values are more absolute because combat is computed differently.

The weapons in this chart have the following values:

- *Name.* The weapon's name as it appears in the game.

- *Type.* Indicates what kind of weapon it is. Each weapon type differs slightly in how it is held by the player and what kind of damage it does.

- *Damage Range.* This value determines how many Hit Points are subtracted from the target for a successful hit. The value is

FPS Weapon Chart										
				Damage Multipliers						
Name	*Type*	*Damage Range*	*Range Close*	*Max*	*Head*	*Body*	*Limbs*	*Rate of Fire*	*Ammo Load*	*Reload Time (secs)*
Wrench	Melee	12-15	1-4		x1.5	x1.0	x1.2	NA	NA	NA
Knife	Melee	6-10	1-4	5-20	x1.2	x1.4	x0.8	NA	NA	NA
Chainsaw	Melee	25-40	1-4		x3.0	x1.0	x2.0	NA	NA	NA
M9	Pistol	15-30	0-50	51-150	x1.2	x1.0	x0.8	Fast	15	Fast
Glock 22	Pistol	20-40	0-75	76-200	x1.5	x1.0	x1.0	Fast	15	Fast
Walther PPK	Auto-Pistol	15-20	0-40	41-100	x1.2	x1.0	x0.8	Very Fast	9	Very Fast
Hunting Rifle	Rifle	18-30	0-75	76-300	x1.0	x0.9	x1.0	Slow	5	Slow
M16	Rifle	25-50	0-60	61-300	x1.5	x1.0	x1.2	Very Fast	20	Moderate
Barret M98B	*Sniper Rifle*	24-40	0-70	71-300	x2.0	x1.2	x1.0	Moderate	4	Slow
Browning Auto-5	Shotgun	10-15*	0-30	31-70	x0.8	x1.0	x0.8	Slow	4	Very Slow
Uzi	SMG	9-13	0-40	41-100	x0.8	x1.0	x0.8	Very Fast	30	Moderate
Heckler & Koch MP7	SMG	12-15	0-50	51-120	x1.0	x1.0	x1.0	Very Fast	40	Moderate
M1 Bazooka	Bazooka	60-120*	10-50	51-150	x1.0	x1.0	x1.5	NA	1	Very Slow
Ares M-92 Zapper	Electric Pistol	21-30	1-30	31-60	x1.0	x1.2	x1.0	Moderate	NA	NA
Ares B-6 Plasma Rifle	Pulse Rifle	70-100	1-60	61-150	x1.4	x1.0	x1.0	Slow	NA	NA
M67 Grenade	Grenade	10-120*	5-20	21-30	x1.2	x1.0	x1.6	NA	NA	NA
M74 Mine	Landmine	90-120*	1-5	6-15	x0.8	x1.0	x2.0	NA	NA	NA
* = May hit multiple targets										

Table 7.5. *This is a Weapons Chart that could be used for a first-person shooter game. Note how the values are more detailed than those appearing on the Item Chart for a role-playing game.*

randomized with minimum and maximum values so that the player can't always predict the effect of the attack on the target. Note that some weapons have an asterisk (*) to indicate that they do blast damage and can therefore affect multiple targets.

- *Range.* There are two possible ranges ("Close" and "Max") that determine how far from the player the target can be and still be hit. Weapons attacking at the Max distance suffer a negative modifier to the final attack value.

- *Damage Multiplier.* The damage applied to the target is modified by the indicated value depending on where on the body the target is hit.

- *Rate of Fire.* This column indicates how quickly some weapons can be fired. The values given are relative at this point and will be determined after testing.

- *Ammo Load.* If a weapon uses ammunition, this column determines how many projectiles can be carried by the player and fired before being depleted.

- *Reload Time.* This column is used to determine how quickly the player can fire a weapon. The values are relative and will be filled in after testing.

This Weapons Chart could be used in the game design document. Much of the information is a placeholder until the real values can be determined once enough assets are available to test the game at runtime. The chart contains more weapons than are normally found in a first-person shooter game, and a number will be removed after testing determines which ones are most fun for the player to use.

Item Types: Hand Weapons

A majority of weapons in role-playing games tend to be hand or melee weapons used when combatants are adjacent to one another and engaged in fighting. Since the invention of gunpowder, hand weapons have generally given way to projectile weapons. Fantasy games, however, are normally set in the pre-gunpowder era and so there are many more types of swords and knives. One reason hand weapons are so popular is that it allows players to come face-to-face with enemies as opposed to standing at a distance and shooting at them with a ranged weapon. In modern times since the advent of gunpowder, most weapons are ranged weapons, allowing one combatant to shoot at another from afar while often hiding behind some shelter. In science-fiction games, weapons can take on many bizarre forms and use different forms of energy and unusual projectiles as ammunition.

Knives

Knives are fairly small weapons having short sharp blades for stabbing or slashing. The do less damage than swords so usually it is not a character's primary weapon but it is often one of the first weapons a player receives early in the game. Some character classes like Ninjas are able to inflict more serious damage with knives. Most races can use knives of one sort or another, and some races like halflings might prefer the smaller weapon since they can wield it faster. To make knives more deadly, the designer can have a character attack more frequently with a knife because it isn't as massive as other hand weapons and therefore requiring less time to bring around for another attack. Many knives can also be used as a thrown weapon, but once it has been thrown, the player has to switch to another weapon until it can be retrieved.

One source for locating unusual knives is to check for societies around the world that use ceremonial or special knives, like the machete, which is used primarily to clear paths through tall grass. It is possible to create unusual knives made from icicles and wood, but they would likely break because they are brittle. Most knives are made of metal or stone. There are also everyday items that are not thought of as knives that can be used like them, for example, an X-Acto knife, a surgeon's scalpel, or a straight razor.

Swords

Swords have long blades used for stabbing or slashing an opponent. Blade lengths vary greatly with some swords being just slightly larger than knives and others being so long that two hands are needed to wield the weapon. Really large swords like the longsword of the late medieval period or the Scottish claymore may be too massive or too big for some races to use. An advantage of carrying a smaller sword is that a character can hold a shield for protection at the same time, warding off enemy blows while preparing to strike. A sword is often the primary weapon for some character classes in fantasy RPGs like knights and paladins although they can be used by most other classes, if not as handily. In science-fiction games, characters are sometimes equipped with futuristic swords like the lightsabers of the Jedis in the *Star Wars* movies. Because of their size, swords are generally too big to throw.

Swords come in many shapes and sizes, and they appear in almost every society around the world. Most swords are made from metal, with bronze and copper in the oldest societies, iron in more technologically advanced societies, and steel in modern societies. Some are highly decorated and encrusted with jewels, and in some fantasy games these jewels contain magic spells a player can use during combat instead of attacking with the weapon.

Clubs, Axes, and Other Hand Weapons

A number of other hand weapons have been developed over time in different cultures. Not everyone could afford to own a metal sword in medieval times, but they still needed to defend themselves and used various clubs and axes as weapons. Driving a nail through a club turned it into a simple war hammer that could pierce light armor with the sharp nail. The problem with these simple weapons is that they broke easily, but armorers created more solid weapons like maces and morning stars. Most of these weapons are one-handed, allowing the user to carry a shield for protection, and they get their destructive power from their weight and sometimes from their sharp edges or spikes. A few weapons like large battle-axes were so heavy the combatant needed two hands to swing them. These weapons could cause devastating damage to armor (and bodies), although they are generally less precise than swords.

In fantasy games, dwarves in particular seen to prefer axes and clubs as their primary weapons. Other classes and races might find most military axes and clubs too heavy to wield easily because of the metal used for cutting edges and spikes, but they can probably use lighter versions like hatchets, bats, and clubs. In many modern games, makeshift hand weapons are the first ones characters find as they explore the world, and tire irons, police batons, crowbars, and even chainsaws can be quite effective as eliminating the first enemies that pop up. Another weapon type that falls into this category is whips, which can get their attack power either from the power of a whip snap or from metal barbs attached to the end of the hand cord like the flail and cat o' nine tails. Smaller hand weapons like the hatchet, hand axe and tomahawk can also be used as thrown weapons, but then the character is defenseless unless armed with another weapon.

Extended Hand Weapons

There are some hand weapons that allow the user to stand at some distance from the enemy and still deliver a blow. These weapons are used to stab and to bash the enemy on the head. They typically have a long shaft of wood the combatant holds with both hands and a sharp blade or pike on the end. They can be rather simple like spears that have a single sharp point on the end or somewhat esoteric like the three-pronged tridents used by Roman gladiators. During medieval times some infantry carried poleaxes and halberds that were dangerous enough to stop mounted knights in mid-charge. In modern times, the bayonet can be attached to the front of a weapon to turn into jabbing weapons when ammunition has run out.

In some games, combat uses a grid system where some characters can be in the front line while others are in the back. A character in the back line can reach over a character fighting in the front line and use the long weapon without the danger of receiving a direct blow from an enemy combatant. Likewise, long hand weapons can be used against flying enemies that short-range melee weapons can't touch. Spears and lances are often associated with knights and paladins, but they are bulky and difficult to maneuver so they would probably not be used by weaker or shorter characters. Magic users are often armed with staffs of one kind or another. In many cases, the staffs are charged with magic spells but can still be used as long-distance hand weapons when the spells are exhausted. Some long hand weapons like the spear, javelin, and harpoon can be thrown, but again, the character needs some backup weapon until the thrown weapon can be retrieved.

Item Types: Ranged Weapons

Ranged weapons hurl an object at the enemy with the intent of causing damage through a powerful impact or explosion. Projectile weapons since the onset of the gunpowder era are much more damaging than hand weapons, and even light wounds can be devastating. The projectiles fired by such weapons can be as small as BB shot or as large as TOW missiles (Tube-launched, Optically guided, Wire command link). This category also includes thrown weapons since the weapon is the entity itself hurling the projectile.

Thrown Weapons (Non-Explosive)

These weapons are hurled at the enemy by hand and therefore inflict limited damage. One purpose to throwing a weapon is to slow the advance of the enemy before they can close in for melee combat. More massive weapons like javelins and spears can inflict more damage if they strike the target, and they are often thrown en masse at the same time by a whole group of combatants with the idea that some will hit a target and reduce the enemy's ranks. Once the weapon is thrown, however, the attacker either has to try to reclaim it or else switch to another weapon to continue the fight. Even a boomerang won't return to the thrower if it hits a target.

Some games do not use these kinds of weapons at all since almost anything that can be thrown can act like a weapon, and keeping track of the locations of all small objects in a 3D playfield is difficult. In other games, characters are given either a restricted number or an unlimited number of small projectiles like darts and shiruken (also known as fighting stars). If the number of projectiles is restricted, the player has to buy more or find more on the playfield. An unlimited supply of projectiles works well if the purpose is to delay the enemy rather than trying to inflict heavy damage.

Thrown Weapons (Explosive)

These are small bombs that can be tossed at the enemy and cause damage by explosion. They can be as small as firecrackers or as large as Molotov cocktails. Usually the weapon contains gunpowder or some other combination of chemicals, but some exotic weapons like an EMP (electromagnetic pulse) grenade can instead unleash a blast of energy. Because these weapons are thrown by hand, they do not travel very far, and so are used primarily as support for melee combat. Some grenades don't cause much damage but are meant to suppress the enemy by releasing smoke or tear gas or stunning them with a bright blast of light. There is usually some length of time between when the bomb is prepared to use, for example, pulling the pin on the grenade before throwing it and when it actually explodes. An alert enemy can react to the danger by ducking away or even picking it up and throwing it back at the attacker. When the bomb explodes, it causes damage over an area, with the greatest devastation being at the point of explosion and diminishing out along the blast radius (the maximum distance from the explosion where significant damage occurs).

While hand grenades are thought of as modern weapons, they were used as far back as during the reign of Byzantine Emperor Leo III (717–749) when jars filled with Greek fire were throw at enemies. They don't often appear in fantasy games, although Petrify Grenades appeared in Square's *Final Fantasy X*. While it is possible to create bombs that inflict modifiers and negative status effects for a fantasy game, they simply act like magic spells, scrolls, and potions with extra sound and visual effects. Grenades appear is many modern era and futuristic games since they are the normal component of a soldier's gear. They are best wielded by strong characters since the idea is to use them at a significant distance to keep from being damaged. In some games, if friendly units are within the blast radius, they too are damaged by the explosion.

Projectile Weapons (Non-Gunpowder)

These weapons are similar to thrown weapons in that projectiles are fired at enemies to inflict damage. Unlike thrown weapons, this class of weapon shoots projectiles with much greater force, reaching the target more quickly and usually inflicting greater damage when they strike. In addition to the standard forms of bows found in most fantasy games, this class also includes spear-throwers (atlatl), blowguns, slings, and even slingshots. As long as the attacker has ammunition, he or she can continue using the weapon. While the projectiles can be deadly, the weapons themselves have limited offensive capability, so hitting a berserk barbarian with a wood bow is much less effective than peppering one with the sharp-tipped arrows.

These weapons are usually meant to be used from farther back on the battlefield behind the infantry and not when the enemy is up close. During medieval times, the archers had little armor and carried only a dagger or short sword to protect themselves when the enemy got too close. It also takes time to draw an arrow from a quiver, notch it, and draw back the bowstring before shooting, and so the archers were often able to unleash only a few volleys before having to pull back behind the infantry. Bows appear most often in fantasy games and are the favorite weapons for rangers and for elves, although most classes and races in an FRP game can use them. Smaller or weaker character types might not have the strength or height to use a large weapon like the longbow, but they might be able to use crossbows if the mechanic for winding back the bowstring doesn't require great physical strength. Depending on the game, the projectiles fired by these weapons can have other uses too, for example, acting as smoke bombs or showering the enemy with burning arrows or inflicting negative status effects on them before they can close in for melee combat. After the introduction of gunpowder, bow weapons were used less frequently because the gunpowder made projectiles fly farther and impact with greater force.

Projectile Weapons (Gunpowder)

These weapons fire projectiles through the controlled detonation of gunpowder or similar exploding material. The ammunition generally affects only one target at a time, although shotgun pellets spread out as they move and therefore can hit several targets. The advantage of these weapons is that they can be used at both short and long range with equal effectiveness, as long as the attacker has ammunition. The amount of ammunition a character can carry both loaded in the weapon and carried in the inventory can be a limiting factor to reduce the deadliness of very powerful guns. Other limiting factors include the cost to purchase ammo or the weapon itself, reload time, and its fragility from repeated use. Occasionally, the weapon itself can be used in an attack either as a club hitting with the gun butt or as a spear if tipped with a bayonet.

Figure 7.2. *In Epic Games'* Gears of War III, *the soldier wields a Retro Lancer Assault Rifle that is used in short- and mid-range combat. Note the bayonet attached under the barrel comes in handy during hand-to-hand combat.*

Although gunpowder has been around since its discovery in China about AD 800, it was first used to propel Chinese rockets and fire cannons and eventually was used in handheld weapons in the 13th century in Italy. Guns are seen primarily as modern weapons and are usually not found in fantasy games (unless the projectile is a magic spell of some kind). During the 20th century, guns became much more powerful, firing more rapidly and carrying more ammunition. In first-person shooter games, there are usually a number of guns that get more powerful as players make their way through the levels—from pistols to rifles to shotguns to sniper rifles to powerful machineguns (e.g., the Retro Lancer Assault Rifle in Epic Games' *Gears of War III*; see Figure 7.2).

Projectile Weapons (Bomb)

Some of the most powerful modern weapons fire grenades, missiles, and bombs, which explode and cause massive damage over a large blast area. They can be used against multiple enemies that are grouped closely to one another at great distances, and the projectiles explode with enough force to disable or destroy tanks and other vehicles. The weapons have very limited ammunition because the projectiles are relatively large and have to be carried around. A soldier carrying a grenade launcher or bazooka might have to rely on a pistol after firing the explosive projectile. These weapons also have to be used at some distance from the enemy so the attacker isn't within the blast radius of the explosion. It is also dangerous for friendly units who are close to the target as well. The weapon itself is almost useless as a melee weapon because of its size and weight.

This class of weapon isn't very useful for a fantasy game set in any medieval period because gunpowder weapons would be anachronistic. The most powerful attacks in fantasy games are magic spells fired by expending mana, and their effects can be as devastating as grenade, missile, and bomb explosions. However, most modern era and futuristic games include at least one weapon that can fire explosive charges great distances.

Other Portable Weapons

There are other weapons used by the modern military that find their way into games, although they are not used as primary weapons to directly attack the enemy but more often as secondary weapons to slow down or damage the enemy. Some explosive devices like mines and satchel charges are placed in locations where enemy troops are expected to move through, and they explode on contact via some sensor, or when a lit fuse denotes it. Other weapons like dynamite and pipe bombs can either be thrown like grenades or planted on the ground and armed with fuses that give the combatant time to move away before the explosion occurs. Explosive devices generate large blasts, so the attacker has to make sure sufficient time is allowed to get out of the area before the device detonates. Other devices like caltrops and police strips are nonexplosive and are meant to hobble the enemy or stop vehicles with spikes that stick into the air and puncture skin and tires.

The flamethrower is an extremely destructive weapon that shoots out a stream of flammable liquid, igniting anything in its path. The amount of liquid that can be carried is limited, and there is a slight danger that a projectile could pierce the container, causing the liquid to explode and burn the person armed with the weapon. As with explosive devices, the flammable liquid will burn anything it comes in contact with, whether ally or enemy.

Occasionally, military units in games will be armed with mortars, a small portable cannon that shoots shells in a high projectile either directly at an enemy or in an area where the enemy is thought to occupy. It usually takes several soldiers to carry, set up, and fire the mortar, and they are limited by the number of shells they can carry in addition to their other equipment. In modern games, soldiers might be equipped with surface-to-air or surface-to-surface missiles. MANPADS (Man-portable air-defense systems) are shoulder-launched and often employ lasers to steer a missile towards enemy aircraft. Likewise, small surface-to-surface missiles are shoulder-launched and aimed at distant targets on the ground. Mortars and portable missile systems are relatively rare except in games that simulate modern combat, such as Infinity Ward's *Modern Warfare 2.*

Item Types: Exotic Weapons

Weapons in fantasy games can come in many different sizes and design, but their primary purpose is to damage an opponent by smashing, slashing, or piercing. The primary materials are metal, although wood is used for bows and staffs. Occasionally, a fantasy hand weapon will also be able to cast a magic spell, but otherwise the weapons and their effects are the same in fantasy games as they are in the real world.

Ray Guns

Weapons in science-fiction games often have a wider range of abilities and can draw on electricity, atomic energy, and undiscovered energy sources for power as well as explosives. Some of the most inventive weapons are found in games with a science-fiction setting (including some fantasy games that freely mix in science-fiction motifs). The first science-fiction ray gun was probably the weapon used by the Martians in H. G. Wells' *War of the Worlds* (1898), although the weapon itself was not named; the beam was described as a "heat-ray." In science-fiction stories and movies, directed-energy weapons have been called death rays, blasters, phasers, disruptors, and pulse rifles. These are basically lasers that focus electromagnetic radiation into coherent, high-energy beams. Similar weapons may shoot streams of hot plasma or beams of charged subatomic particles or even unknown particles. These weapons can be as small as pistols and rifles or large enough to mount on spaceships to use against enemy planets and spacecraft. Similar to the ray gun is the disintegrator gun that reduces its target to molecular particles. One advantage of such weapons is that they often don't use ammunition and can be fired endlessly. If such a weapon is included in a game, it should be given some offsetting factor, likely a low damage ability or a long time to recharge.

Unusual Projectiles and Power Sources

There are also weapons that use more exotic forms of projectile or sources of power. The railgun uses electromagnetism to accelerate a metal projectile down a set of rails and at a target. A close cousin is the coilgun (also called a Gauss gun), which has a set of metal bands running the length of the barrel to draw a metal projectile with electromagnetism. Both of these gun types are currently in development at various labs around the world. Another real-world weapon that appears frequently in science-fiction stories is the needlegun (also called a flechette gun), which fires a volley of small metal darts that fly at "hyper-velocity" towards a target.

There are also weapons that use bizarre forms of energy, for example, a gravity gun that can grab items flying at the shooter and toss them aside or throw items at enemies. One of the first appearances of this weapon was in Valve Software's *Half-Life 2* game. Another science-fiction weapon is the shrink ray that squashes an object, reducing it to a fraction of its original size. In 3D Realms' *Duke Nukem 3D*, the lead character Duke can reduce oncoming enemies with his shrink-ray weapon and then step on them (or freeze them with his freeze-ray weapon). A less lethal weapon is the stunner, which sends an energy beam that temporarily impairs the movement or consciousness of a living being without killing it. A psionic weapon uses a character's psychic energies to kill or immobilize an enemy.

Even though it doesn't necessarily make sense when compared to the firepower of other weapons, the lightsaber of the *Star Wars* universe is one of the best-loved film weapons in movies. It projects a colored beam of solid energy that cuts through just about any material and can be used to deflect incoming projectiles and other objects. While it cannot be used to fire a projectile, it can be used in hand-to-hand combat against another lightsaber.

Nuclear Weapons

Occasionally, a game will contain a nuclear weapon that a character can carry and possibly fire from a rifle. However, the blast from such a weapon devastates a vast area and leaves behind dangerous radioactive waste, effectively shutting off part of the playfield. Of course, in a game world, the devastation and radiation might be skipped over for the reward showing off the audio and visual effects of such a massive explosion. In games that have a patina of realism, nuclear weapons are almost never used at the tactical level but they can be employed at an operational or strategic level as effective methods of instantly killing huge numbers of people and destroying whole cities.

Other weapons of mass destruction—such as electromagnetic pulse or chemical and biological warfare bombs—might also be used sparingly. The problem with all these weapons is that they endanger the user's own units and cities as well as the enemy, and once a single bomb goes off, mutual retaliation can lead to Armageddon and the end of the play world as we know it.

Item Types: Armor

Before gunpowder became dominant on the battlefield, soldiers tried to protect themselves by wearing various kind of armor. Originally, armor was made from plant matter and animal hides, but as metallurgy developed, new forms of metallic armor appeared. The height of armor was during the Middle Ages in Europe when knights wore full suits of armor covering all parts of their bodies. The appearance of gunpowder on the battlefield negated the advantage of armor, for an individual projectile or explosion could pierce the heaviest armor. As a result, body armor disappeared because it was heavy and cumbersome and offered insufficient protection against projectiles. Helmets, however, remained popular because they offered protection to the head. In the 20th century, there have been advancements in body armor thanks to lightweight but protective synthetic compounds like Kevlar.

Head Armor

At one time, head armor might cover parts of the face in addition to the skull as in the Spartan helmet seen in the film *300* or the Roman galea worn by gladiators. During the Middle Ages, there were a number of different helmets, some of pure metal and some combined with chainmail. The Norman helmet of the 11th century consisted of

Figure 7.3. *Here are front and side views of sallet helmets with visors from mid-15th century Europe.*

a metal cap to protect the skull and a metal projection to guard the nose, while the Crusader helmet completely enclosed the head in metal. By the mid-15th century, once gunpowder made full helmets all but useless, smaller helmets became popular like the sallet that protected the head and neck (Figure 7.3). During the 17th through 18th century, metal helmets became more highly decorated with long tassels of colored hair sticking out of a spike on the top. By the mid-19th century most metal helmets had given way to cloth *kepi* caps, but they were revived in the 20th century during the First World War as a defense against machineguns and bombs. Modern armies still use lightweight helmets made of bulletproof materials like Kevlar. These modern helmets cover only the top of the head and the ears.

Of course, many other types of helmets have been popular throughout the ages, particularly by poorer foot soldiers who could not afford the expensive metal helmets. From cloth cowls and leather helmets of ancient and medieval times to the modern motorcycle helmets, police helmets, and hard hats, there are a number of head protectors that have appeared in games. In many role-playing games, characters start off with a simple cloth head coverings that offer minimal protection, and they acquire tougher headgear in combat or shops. Some fantasy races like the elves eschew head armor altogether while other races like dwarves and humans prefer heavy armor helmets. In science-fiction games, there are space helmets for space suits, aviator helmets for space fighters, and even Stormtrooper and Clonestrooper helmets from the *Star Wars* series that cover the head like medieval helmets. There are also helmets used in many sports events, such as hockey masks, football helmets, and batting helmets.

Head armor provides protection to a defender, and how it is handled depends on the combat system used in a game. Sometimes, a helmet simply provides a defensive modifier to the character that is cumulative with other armor. At other times, if damage is applied to different parts of the body, a helmet can reduce the amount of damage applied to the neck and head areas. Helmets may have their own Hit Points that are used up as they absorb damage during combat and eventually become useless. In fantasy games, helmets can be imbued with magic that offers other positive modifiers to a character as well, and frequently they are decorated with fantastic designs and geegaws like flaring wings off the sides. Normally, a character only needs one helmet at a time, which is worn and not carried in inventory. Of course, extra helmets can be carried as well, depending on how large a character's inventory is and how much extra weight can be carried.

Body Armor

This armor protects part or the entire torso. Its primary function is to protect the front of the body since opponents are attacking each other face to face, but sometimes it encases the body to offer protection on all sides. The first body armor was probably made from padded animal hides or vegetable material, but it offered only limited protection. The first empires to used metal armor consistently were in the Fertile Crescent and the Mediterranean. The Greeks and Romans favored metal breastplates that allowed them more freedom for maneuvering, but the height of body armor was reached during the Middle Ages when knights wore full metal uniforms during combat. Most of the knights rode horses, so their plate armor protected them from hits by other armored knights or from angry infantry if they got knocked to the ground. The advent of gunpowder diminished the protection offered by heavy metal, and so from the 16th century to the present most soldiers have worn simple cloth uniforms although some cavalry units continued to sport metal breastplates. Today, some armies do provide more protective uniforms for their ground troops such as the US Army's Interceptor Body Armor System.

There are also a number of forms of body armor that offer protection in one form or another, such as bullet-proof vests that absorb the impact of bullets, flak jackets that provide protection from shrapnel, bombsuits worn when defusing bombs, radiation suits that protect against radiation, and spacesuits that allow humans to survive in the vacuum of space. All these forms of body armor have made their way into games in one form or another. Body armor can be as light and simple as cloth and leather coverings, cloaks, and jackets or as heavy and cumbersome as chainmail and plate armor. In fantasy games, breastplates and other light armor is worn by most characters who engage in fighting. For weaker races like elves and halflings, the armor is sometimes made of enchanted materials such as the silvery mithril that was light yet incredibly strong.

As with head armor, body armor sometimes gives a simple positive modifier to a defender during combat and at other times it protects specific parts of the body from damage. The lighter the material, the less the protection—usually, although magical armor can be light and still very protective. Body armor can also be imbued with magic that enhances a fighter's other attributes as well. The problem with body armor is that it can be very heavy and bulky, which is not bad when it is worn but can cause problems if a player wants to keep several pieces in his or her inventory.

Extremity Armor

This armor protects the arms, legs, and other parts of the body. The Romans had some forms of protection for the arms and legs: the manica, which was an armguard and greaves, which protected the thighs. As medieval armor became more encompassing, more forms of armor were added. The gorget was a metal or leather collar that protect the neck, spaulders and later pauldrons were metal plates that protected the shoulder and upper arms, vambraces were made of leather or metal and protect the upper arms while the couter protected the elbows, and gauntlets offered protection for the hands. On the lower body, chausses protected the thighs while greaves protected the lower legs and sabatons covered the feet. When metal armor was abandoned, most of these specialized armor pieces also disappeared, although gloves of one kind or another were worn by cavalry as well as wrist guards.

In modern times, gloves are still worn but primarily to protect against the cold. Some gloves serve as other forms of protection, for example, armor gloves lined with Kevlar to handle sharp and splintered materials, lab gloves to deal with chemical and radioactive materials, and diving gloves used underwater. There are also special shoes that protect feet in dangerous environments, for example, steel-toed shoes and boots to protect against heavy falling objects, rubber-soled shoes worn where a person could be electrocuted, or combat boots worn by soldiers. In professional sports, there are many different kinds of gloves and other protectors for the shins, wrists, and arms.

In role-playing games, characters may wear protective gloves and footwear that offer some benefits during combat. Dwarves often wear metal sabatons as part of their armor set, while elves and wizards prefer lighter shoes that let them maneuver faster and halflings wear no shoes at all. Players can carry additional gloves and shoes in their inventory, but usually only one set is needed. Most shoes and gloves are made from cloth, leather, or chainmail, but exotic materials like mithril can be used as well. There are also specialized gloves that appear in games, for example, gauntlets that cast spells or heavy gloves studded with talon-like claws.

Shields

For millennia, humans also protected their bodies in battle with shields that were held in one hand while the other hand wielded a weapon. The defender put his arm through several straps to hold the shield to his body, and the shield intercepted or deflected enemy weapons. If necessary, the defender could quickly toss the shield aside if he or she needed his arm free for some other use. The earliest shields were made of wood and plant materials and eventually made from sturdier metals during the Copper, Bronze, and Iron Ages. Some shields like the buckler were relatively small and light while others like the kite shield were large enough to cover most of the body. During the Middle Ages, shields were carried by knights and foot soldiers in combat, but they also appeared on the coat of arms of the wealthy. While they offered only modest protection once gunpowder was invented, they were still used for a time by armies to protect against more primitive weapons, for example, during the conquest of the Americas by the conquistadors. They offered limited protection for anyone operating siege engines. Shields disappeared from the battlefield during the late 16th century, but they have made a comeback during the 20th century as protection for police when facing rioters. Modern riot shields are made of clear polycarbonate material that let police view the area while offering protection, and there are ballistic shields made of metal used by SWAT teams and others as protection against gunfire.

Shields appear frequently in fantasy games set in medieval times and they are best used by fighters in the front line who can not only protect themselves by deflecting or absorbing blows with the shield but also protect those behind them who are wielding two-handed weapons like halberds and poleaxes, shooting bows or casting magic spells. Tall, muscular races use larger metal shields while weaker races might use small metal or leather shields. Because of their shape, shields take up considerable space when stored in a character's inventory, but sometimes a character might need several types of shield to protect against both weapons and magic. They give a positive modifier to a combatant during a fight, and they can absorb damage that would otherwise be applied against the character, although they can be damaged or destroyed if they are given Hit Points like the characters.

In science-fiction games, a favorite form of the shield is the personal force-shield that covers some or all of the body. One advantage to this form of armor is that it can regenerate to full power if the person wearing it evades damage for a time, like the force field protecting Master Chief in Bungie Studios' *Halo* series. Some characters are able to generate psychic shields to protect themselves as well. These shields are often better at absorbing one form of damage over another, for example, being able to protect well against solid projectile but not so well against energy weapons.

Item Types: Potions and Scrolls

There are many kinds of items other than weapons and armor to be found in games. Some of the most common items are potions and scrolls. Usually these items are used for one specific function, and many are depleted after a single use. Some, however, can be reloaded and others can be used multiple times. Role-playing games have the greatest number of potions and scrolls, and they often take up considerable space in a character's inventory. In shooter games, characters often do not have inventories and the item's effect is applied as soon as the character comes in contact with it.

Health Potions

These potions restore Hit Points to a character either immediately as soon as swallowed or gradually over time. There might be several sizes available since characters in RPG need bigger boosts as they gain experience and their Hit Point total increases. Early in a game health potions normally restore a small amount of health and are cheap to buy, while better potions that restore greater amounts of health appear later and are more expensive. While most health potions are used on individuals, some can be used on all members of a party. The potions are used most often during combat to restore Hit Points lost to weapon and combat damage. They can also be used outside of combat, of course.

Sometimes a potion contains only one dose and is removed once it is used, and sometimes a given potion can be used several times before being exhausted. If health potions take up a lot of inventory space or are expensive, they might work better if they are not depleted in one use and removed from a character's inventory but instead remain as partial doses to be used later. For example, if a character has a slight wound and drinks a health potion that can restore 100 Hit Points, the wound is healed with 37 points being removed from the bottle and the remaining potion is still available to restore another 63points later. There is a danger, however, in using this approach if the character's inventory becomes littered with half-drunk potions, so a good solution is to combine partial doses whenever possible into full doses.

Cure Potions

These potions remove debilitating or negative status effects inflicted on characters during combat or for other reasons. Sometimes there is a one-to-one correspondence between a debilitating effect and the potion that cures it, and sometimes a potion can cure multiple effects. A few debilitating status effects like poison are sometimes allowed to linger after combat, and if so, the appropriate cure potions should be usable both in combat and out. If many different enemies in a game are wont to inflict debilitating effects, then cure potions should be readily available and be fairly inexpensive. But for debilitating effects that are inflicted rarely, the appropriate cure can be rare or more expensive.

Cure potions tend to be good for only one dose, although it is possible to have them contain multiple doses, especially if certain status effects are inflicted often. Players should know exactly how many doses they have left of each cure potion at a glance. During a turn-based game, the player has time to scroll through an inventory to find a specific cure potion to remove a status effect, but in a real-time game, having to find just the right cure can be distracting if the action is frantic, so having cure potions be generic and able to remove all status effects is helpful. There might even be cure potions that can remove status effects from a whole party.

Attribute Modifier Potions

These potions apply modifiers to friendly and enemy entities in combat. They usually boost a character's attributes or weaken an enemy, but they might allow the character to perform an unusual action like flying or moving through walls. They might affect a single individual or they might affect all friendly party members or all enemies in a group. Unlike worn objects, these modifiers apply only when the player uses the potion, and the usually modifiers last for a limited time before the character or entity returns to normal. These potions basically have the same effects as modifying magic spells (see Chapter 8). These potions normally have a single dose and are removed once the potion is used.

Scrolls

Scrolls usually contain magic spells, one spell per scroll type (see Chapter 8). They can contain healing and curing magic as well as spells that modify attributes or allow the player to temporarily employ a skill from another character class. Typically, a scroll is used only once and is then removed from the character's inventory. Most scrolls are used in combat, but healing and curing scrolls should be usable afterwards as well. An advantage of scrolls is that the allow characters to cast powerful magic spells they might not otherwise be able to use. Many of their effects are similar to those for potions and it is better to limit the number of scrolls (and potions) so that a character's inventory does not become cluttered with items whose purpose is not immediately clear.

Item Types: Auxiliary Equipment

Many games include items that are neither weapons, armor, nor potions. Some items are used only temporarily while the player is exploring a map or level and then they are removed at the exit or when they no longer serve a useful purpose. Other items stay with a character to be reused in different locations. Removing extraneous items from inventory lets the player know that they are not needed in the next area of the game.

Jewelry

This group includes items like rings, amulets, necklaces, and bracelets that can be worn on a character's body. They might simply be ornamental, but more often they serve a purpose. In RPGs, for example, a magic ring can improve one or more of a character's attributes when worn—for example, increasing the Strength and Defense attributes during combat. The modification occurs automatically so the player does not have to worry about activating the piece. Jewelry can also protect characters from being affected by debilitating status effects as long as it remains on the character. Most often the abilities of each piece of jewelry are predetermined, but occasionally the player can decide what the jewelry will do by enchanting it or having a jeweler alter it.

There are spaces on the player's figure on the inventory screen that shows where various items can be worn, and players can move jewelry from an inventory slot onto the figure only at appropriate spaces. While jewelry can increase the number of items to be found in a game, they also take up considerable room in the inventory if each object takes an inventory slot. To get around this problem, the inventory might include a pop-up window that is used for storing jewelry.

Jewelry can serve other functions in a game as well. A magic-user might be able to carry a wand on his or her person that is used to cast spells. The wands can be swapped in and out of the inventory as the player wishes, but this approach means the character can use only one magic spell at a time. Insignias, badges, and wreaths can be awarded to characters who have attained certain status in the game world, and in massively multiplayer online games, these marks of honor can be used to define membership in a player guild. These items can serve some game purpose or simply act as decorations, depending on the design. Selling excess jewelry is also a good way to earn money.

Eyewear

This group includes items that improve the player's ability to see things on the playfield. Usually, line-of-sight becomes severely limited at night or in smoky conditions, and items like night vision goggles and infrared detectors help the player detect entities and important items in the area. Although simple items like eyeglasses sometimes appear in games, they more often have a more important purpose by being enchanted or being high technology and modifying a character's attributes or providing protection when worn. Some eyewear like binoculars and sniper scopes can temporary make distant objects look closer when scouting the area for enemies or trying to snipe one of them stealthily.

In games with a first-person point of view, donning special eyewear can change the look of the game world. In Retro Studios' *Metroid Prime*, the player views the world through protagonist

Samus' head-up display through shows the view ahead and information displays, and she can change it into a thermal imager to detect enemy heat signatures and an x-ray imager to find things that can't be seen in normal light. Donning night vision goggles turns a dark setting into one where a minimal amount of light is enough to let the player to move around easily and locate enemies. Wearing a face-mask allows a character to see clearly when underwater. Unless such eyewear is needed throughout the game, it is a good idea to remove these items when no longer needed.

Detectors

This group of items helps players detect the presence of enemies or other important objects on the playfield. They are usually carried in the hand or sometimes mounted on helmet or on a vehicle the character can drive. Modern detectors are often electrical and require continual recharging to keep working. Some items like flashlights, torches, and lanterns illuminate dark areas, making it easier for the player to get through while spotting enemies. Other items like sonar, radar or a global positioning system (GPS) help characters determine their position in the game world. A few items like dowsing rods and spectral imagers can detect magical or psychic presences.

Detectors give visual and audio feedback about objects they detect, and the player should understand at a glance what the feedback is indicating. It might show multiple enemies as dots or use different colors to indicate different objects in the level, but trying to give too much information can confuse the player. There might be a special area on the main playfield screen where this information is displayed as in Valve's *Half-Life* where an image of a flashlight appears in the upper right corner that glows when it is in use and dims as the power is used up. Otherwise, a pop-up window can appear if the display includes a lot of information for the player to process.

Information Holders

These items store clues or other information the players need to solve puzzles and quests or to remind them where they are in the story. Some items like newspaper clippings, journals, and diaries contain materials for the player to read. They act as narrative devices to fill in the background story or expand the fiction of the game universe by giving insights about the races, lands, magical items, and other objects the player encounters. Likewise, audio-visual records like video tapes, computer disks, and memory chips give the same kind of information and sometimes they trigger extended cut-scenes, telling more of the game's story. Occasionally, information holders are sometimes included in quests, either directly as objectives of the quest or indirectly as part of the solution to a puzzle. For example, a character might find a computer disk that is useless until she tracks down a working computer to review the disk contents and learn the next location to visit to continue a quest.

These storytelling items usually do not go into the character's main inventory but have their own storage area so the player can re-play vital clues and information without having to sacrifice valuable inventory space. If players are sent on multiple quests concurrently, they should have some kind of permanent journal or notebook that is separate from information holders found during play where they can check which quests are open and which ones have been com-pleted. Role-playing games in particular tend to last for many hours, and it can be almost impossible for players to remember which NPCs originally triggered quests and where they can be found after they quit playing the game for a few days.

Lockpicks and Keys

In many games, there are three primary ways to open a door: first, walk up and turn the doorknob; second, complete a quest that auto-matically opens the door for you; and third, use a key or lockpick to open it. Occasionally, a character might be able to force a door open by brute strength, but the purpose of doors is to keep players from getting into areas where they don't belong. They also are useful for blocking players from hidden stashes of valuable items. Depending on how the game is designed, characters can be given a lockpick skill or even a magic spell for opening locks, but often they need the cor-rect key or a lockpick to open a locked door. If a characters is lacking the necessary skill or spell to open the door, whatever is hidden be-hind the locked door will remain unavailable, so items stored behind a locked door should prove useful to the player but not necessarily vital to resolving the game's main plot, unless there is some other method of getting into the locked area.

Even if characters have a skill or spell, they might not be able to get through a door until they find the correct key. Players can feel frustrated, however, if they can open most doors in the game

Lockpick Table

Random Result	Effect
1–70	Success
71–100	Failure

Note: Subtract 2 from random
result per Experience Level

Table 7.6. *Here is a simple Lockpick Table. Note that two is subtracted from the random results roll for each Experience Level, making it more likely to succeed as the player improves.*

world but are prevented from opening a few because special keys are required. It is possible to tie in the difficulty of locks to the level of the lockpick skill or spell the character knows, so that a low-level character is able to open only a few locks while a high-level character can open any lock in the world. Likewise, if lockpicks are items player collect, they can be given different levels, too, so that a Basic

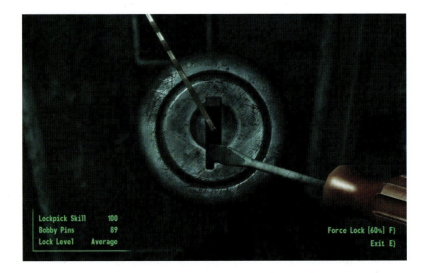

Lockpick Skill 100
Bobby Pins 89
Lock Level Average

Force Lock (60%) F)
Exit E)

Figure 7.4. *In Bethesda Softworks'* Fallout 3, *players can pick locks manually or attempt to force the lock automatically as long as they have lockpicks. The success at picking a lock relies on the character's Lockpick Skill.*

Lockpick is less useful than a Rogue Lockpick, which is less useful than a Master Thief Lockpick. Lockpicks and keys are usually not added to a character's main inventory but either have their own inventory screen or kept with other quest items.

Lockpicks are also useful for opening other features in a game, such as treasure chests, cabinets, and even safes. They might be used to disarm traps as well. The advantage of using lockpicks over keys is that in a large game world there can be hundreds of locked objects, and having specific keys for each lock can frustrate players, especially if they find a key and can't remember where it is supposed to be used. In science-fiction games, similar equipment such as an "electro-pick" can be used to hack into computers and security systems.

To make matters more interesting, lockpick attempts might be resolved using a Lockpick Table (Table 7.6) to determine the success of an attempt. As a player gains experience lockpicking, the random outcome can be modified to make the attempt more likely to succeed. Or the player might have to show some dexterity to be able to open a lock, as in Bethesda Softworks' *Fallout 3* (Figure 7.4), where players can attempt to pick tricky locks themselves or force an attempt automatically, assuming they have a pick available for the job.

Inventory

Many games include an inventory for storing items collected during play. Sometimes the player can manipulate the items in the inventory—for example, changing the weapon or armor the character carries or using a potion or scroll. At other times, the inventory is merely a listing of objects in the player's possession that can be used but are not directly manipulated—for example, different amounts of resources that have been gathered by beings controlled by the player. In some games, the inventory is available at all times, either for direct manipulation or for keeping track of items, and in other games the inventory is available only at certain times—for example, in a racing game, there might be an inventory of spare parts in a "garage" that can be accessed only between races. Many games have inventories that include active and passive sections where the player can manipulate some items but not others.

Some games, especially computer games, show the inventory at all times and it appears in a frame bordering the playfield view. In other games, the inventory is on a separate interface window that has to be opened by the player. It can be a challenge for the development team to come up with an inventory system that doesn't overwhelm the player with too much information while still providing quick access to items when they are needed. The designers have to figure out the functionality of each part of the inventory system, the programmers have to make sure everything works as designed, and the artists have to make sure that the items and controls are easily understood by the player. Having an inventory that is difficult to use can lead to the player getting confused and not wanting to continue playing the game.

Passive Inventory

A passive inventory is an interface screen or part of a screen where items are stored which the player does not directly manipulate. This type of inventory is found in many game genres including real-time strategy games, simulation and strategy games, first-person shooter games, and puzzle games. Items are often grouped together by functionality—for example, in an RTS game the current resources might appear in one area of the screen and be passive while the buildings and combat units available to build are in another area of the screen and are active.

A passive inventory is useful if it automatically takes care of dull and repetitive actions the player would otherwise have to handle. In many cases, the inventory acts like a spreadsheet, recalculating values as resources are collected by gatherers and doled out to builders. One drawback to such an approach is that the player might not notice if a resource has reached a maximum level or has been completely emptied. In either case, units in the game can become idle until they are given new orders.

Another use for a passive inventory is to show the player clearly what game items have so far been collected. Empty spaces can provide a clue for the player, indicating that some item are yet to be found. Filling all the empty spaces then completes a quest or puzzle or a level's objective. In this case, the player isn't necessarily interested in moving the items in and out of the inventory or trying to use them to perform a game action. The designer should consider early in the design phase whether items have a direct use in play and should therefore be active or if they simply serve as information displays so players understand how close they are to fulfilling the game's current goal. While it can be tempting to add functionality to an inventory system, the player can easily become distracted or angered by having to deal with too many trivial actions that detract from the more enjoyable actions in the game.

Active Inventory

An active inventory is one where the player has free rein to move things around and even discard items that are no longer wanted. RPGs have the most complex inventories, and their layouts and functionality can vary widely from one game to another. Because there are so many different enemies in RPGs that can perform many different actions against the player, it makes sense for the player to have a spacious inventory for storing many different kinds of items—extra weapons and armor, ammunition, food and potables, potions and scrolls, and so on. The inventory can be seen as a giant knapsack with enough storage to see the character or party through considerable periods of exploration and combat before having to find another source of supplies. Of course, it can seem a bit odd if there are too many slots available in the inventory, allowing the character to tote around multiple weapons and full complements of armor that weigh hundreds of pounds. Most inventories are based on storage space

Figure 7.5. *In Bethesda Softworks'* The Elder Scrolls IV: Oblivion, *a player can bring up the inventory interface to determine what weapons are armed, what armor is being worn, and what other items are being carried. Information about each group of items includes the cost of the item and its weight, and in this case how much protection armor provides and the armor's current condition.*

and not on the weight of the objects being carried (for example, as in Bethesda Softworks' *The Elder Scrolls IV: Oblivion;* see Figure 7.5).

The designers should decide initially how many item slots an inventory will have and then get feedback from testers to see if the number is too great or too small. It is better to have too many slots than not enough so players can carry whatever items they feel are required. Because players are marching off into the unknown throughout the game, they like to have a sufficient supply of potions, scrolls, and other supplies plus room for extra weapons and armor. Skimping on inventory space punishes players or makes them have to reload old saved games because they did not have enough of a certain supply to see them through the next level.

Inventory Interface Screen

Because it is so capacious, the inventory for an RPG usually has on its own interface screen. A typical RPG inventory interface often has the following information:

- *Character Representation.* This is an image of the character, and there are usually spaces around the image where various pieces of equipment are placed. There can be spaces for one or more weapons, various pieces of armor, and some accessories. The weapon is used to attack during combat, the armor protects the character, and the accessories provide positive modifiers to the character's attributes or ward off debilitating status effects. The player selects items for the character to wear and the removed articles go back into the inventory. Occasionally, an item cannot be worn because the character is of the wrong race, class, or alignment.

- *Open Item Slots.* Near the character's image is a grid of empty spaces or slots where items are stored. In cases where screen space is at a premium, the game might employ a menu system to show items in the character's possession. Sometimes any item in the inventory occupies a single slot while at other times items take up multiple slots as a way of showing the difference between large and small objects. While some games automatically sort objects so they take up the least number of slots, other games require the player to move items around to free up empty slots. Also, multiple copies of an item like a potion might each take up an individual slot or requite individual slots for each copy. One way to assist the player in finding items is to separate different item types into different areas, so that all potions go into one area while all armament goes into another area and all other items are assigned to a third.

- *Quest Item Slots.* Items that are needed to resolve quests are often given their own area in the inventory. The player doesn't always get to interact with these items, but they show what has been accomplished so far in completing the quest. The items are removed as quests are completed. These items can include both objects wanted by NPCs and also miscellaneous materials picked up during play such as keys, deeds, information holders, and the like.

There can be other information areas on the inventory interface as well. In some cases, the character's attributes are included on the screen so a player can see what happens when weapons and armor are transferred from the inventory to a character. One danger in designing the interface screen is overloading it with information. It can be very intimidating for the player upon first opening the inventory screen to see so many different areas on the screen. One aid for the player is to change the cursor to a hand or other icon as it moves over areas of the screen to show exactly which items can be manipulated. It also helps to have the name of an item pop up or become highlighted when the player moves the cursor over it.

Inventory interface screens in console RPGs often differed considerably from those in computer games. Generally, computers have traditionally had much higher screen resolution and the player sat much closer to the monitor, so more information could appear on each interface screen. Console games depended on televisions whose resolution, until recently, was much lower than computer monitors. Also, the player sat at a greater distance from the television, requiring the text in a video game be fairly large. The way television cabinets were designed also affected how much of the television tube could be seen. As a result, most console RPGs were forced to use multiple inventory interface screens because only a limited amount of information could appear per screen. As a result, text and other important information were pushed towards the center of the television screen so nothing important would be cut off. With the introduction of high-definition televisions, however, this restriction is now gone and a console version of an RPG game might use the same layout as the computer version. However, it can still be difficult to read all the text on smaller television screens, so developers should test their games on different size televisions and at different distances.

Store Inventories

In RPG and some other games, there are stores where players can sell items gathered during play and purchase new and additional items. The interface screen for the store needs two different methods for buying and selling goods. There is often a menu of choices when talking to the store owner, and when the player wishes to buy something, a list of the store's current stock appears with their prices. The player then selects the item to buy, often being able to select multiple copies on items like potions and other goodies, and then the transaction occurs. Sometimes a warning message pops up, asking players if they really want to buy the items, and this approach can help a player who accidentally picked the wrong item or too many copies of an item. The combined price of the bought objects is then subtracted from the character's current cash and the items are transferred into the inventory. If the player doesn't have enough cash, a different warning pops up so the player can adjust the number of items to buy.

Likewise, when the player wants to sell objects, the contents of the character's inventory appear and the player selects which ones

Figure 7.6. *This is a shop where players can buy weapons and sell items as found in Bethesda Softworks' The Elder Scrolls IV: Oblivion.*

to sell. The price for the items appears on the screen and the player may be asked to confirm the deal. Sold items are removed from the inventory and the character's cash is increased by the agreed upon amount. As with purchasing items, a pop-up screen might pop up to confirm the player's decision. Although warnings can be a bit annoying, they keep players from accidentally selling important items, which can force them to reload a saved game before the transaction occurred. The design team should determine whether sold items can be re-bought or are permanently removed from play when sold. If the player can sell quest items (perhaps to raise temporary cash), then they should be available at the same shop so the player can later reclaim them.

The interface screen for stores can vary widely from game to game, but the basic buying and selling of items remains the same (for example, as in Bethesda Softworks' *The Elder Scrolls IV: Oblivion;* see Figure 7.6). In addition, there might be other options the player can select, such as listening to gossip, repairing objects, removing debilitating status effects, and so on.

Resources

Resources are items gathered by players specifically to build, improve, or supply game objects. They differ from other items because players usually don't interact with resources directly but instead amass them to use for different game functions. Game play in real-time strategy and simulation games often involves gathering resources used to erect or improve buildings, supplying food to the population, and creating new objects (soldiers, vehicles, research, etc.) to be used towards the goal of winning the game. In many cases, there are units the player assigns to gathering the resources, and these units continue to bring in their assigned materials until either the resource runs out or the owner reassigns them to other duties. In a sense, money is also a resource because the player usually does not directly interact with it (except perhaps in games like *Monopoly* where directly manipulating money is important) but instead accrues it until needing to purchase something.

Resources are often objects found in the real physical world, such as wood, metal, plants, and animals, and the player doesn't worry about controlling their inventory because the resources are abstracted. Most of the time the player acts as an accountant rather than a foreman. Some resources such as gold and jewels are worth money and are not used in actual construction except letting a player purchase materials. Games can also include nonphysical resources such as research and libraries and even manpower allotments. One or more interface screens can be devoted to various resource management functions in a game, and the design team might include a technology tree to show how resources are used to improve game units over time. See Chapter 8 for more on technology trees.

When designing a game requiring resources, it is a good idea to keep the total number of resources limited unless the primary focus is on resource management and manipulation. In an RTS game, for example, the player gathers resources to create buildings and feed armies, and there might be a half-dozen resources to gather (for example, wood, metal, stone, plants, animals, water). Having to acquire six different kinds of wood and four kinds of metal makes the gathering process more complex and potentially much less fun. The design team can create a paper prototype of the resource system early in the development process to determine how many kinds of resources are needed and how they are used to create buildings, feed people, and supply other needs.

Money

Money, under one name or another, appears in many games as a method for paying for items the player wants to acquire. There might be several ways the player can earn money, from eliminating enemy creatures and fulfilling quests in RPGs to selling resources and manufactured objects in simulation games or even passing "Go" in *Monopoly*. Very few games focus on money management as the central game play mechanic, but players eventually learn that having some money on hand at all times allows them to buy items as they become available.

Some games are stingy when it comes to doling out money to the player, meaning that items found in shops are expensive. This approach is one way to force the player to go out into the world and explore new areas and confront new enemies. Being too stingy, however, can be frustrating, especially early in the game. If healing and cure potions are expensive compared to the financial payoffs received for removing low-level enemies, then players can feel trapped. They have to "grind" to get the experience points to rise in level until they can survive for long periods in the game world and gain enough money to buy decent armament and weapons. As a result, players are forced to stay in a limited area of the world that is relatively safe for more time than they want or enjoy.

Handing out money too generously, on the other hand, has its own problems. If players quickly accumulate enough money to buy whatever they need anywhere in the game world, they can quickly grow jaded of being so wealthy. The best items in most games should be found through adventuring in the game world, not just by visiting shops with a wad of cash. Occasionally, a game will force players to go bargain hunting for the best prices at different shop locations throughout the game world, but if the player is able to stockpile a hoard of gold, then eventually prices mean nothing. However, most players prefer receiving too much money instead of having to scrape by with empty pockets.

It's interesting to note that MMORPGs have had some problems with how money is managed. On the one hand, players have been known to pay real-world money to other players so they spend a long time grinding away in minor combats to build up a character's level, and they will also pay to acquire rare items in a game, which most MMORPG publishers outlaw. The companies, on the other hand, want players to stay online as long as possible, especially if players are on a pay-to-play plan, and so they are stingier with monetary rewards, which leads to players grinding away to get the cash they need. There are companies involved in illegal "gold mining" that offer large amounts of game-world money they have spent the time gathering for real-world cash. Gamers say they don't want to spend time doing boring things (grinding) to get the gear and money they need to do more exciting things (fighting dragons). But as long as the publishers need players to stay online to make money on the MMORPG, they will try to prevent players from trading game money for real-world money. The problems associated how players earn money in a game world is likely to persist.

Conclusion

Items take many different forms in games from the weapons acquired in RPG and FPS games to the resources in RTS and simulation games. The task of the design team is to define how these items are to be used to perform game actions. Grouping diverse items together by functionality helps the designers explain how they work so that the programmers can write the code that makes the items work as planned. The programmers would no doubt moan in agony if they had to write individual code for the thousands of items that can appear in an MMORPG, for example, but if those thousands of items are reduced to a hundred groups of related items that behave similarly, their task of writing the code becomes much easier. It is up to the designers to explain to programmers understand how the items are grouped by functionality. Likewise, they have to be able to describe the physical appearance of items as they appear in the inventory and on the playfield for the art team and provide visual references whenever possible to inspire them.

Role-playing games usually have the most items to deal with because as characters grow in ability and power, they need ever better armor and weapons and more powerful potions, scrolls and other supplies. Players also need sufficient money to purchase the items they expect to use next, so the game has to include a well-balanced monetary system that gives players adequate financial rewards for their efforts while keeping prices reasonable for items players use repeatedly and more costly for items players have to strive to earn. While items are not as exciting to design as combat, they are central components of the game and need to be as carefully tested and balanced as other game actions.

Exercises

1. Make a list of the item types the player will find in the game world you're designing.

    a. Break the list into item types that are worn, items that are carried in an inventory, items that are resources for building, and items that are acquired through completing quests, both major and minor.

    b. Define each item type's functionality in the game.

    c. Then try a first pass at defining the attributes you plan to assign to each type and their relative values.

2. Do research on the Internet to find five examples of five different weapon types, as described in the text. The weapons should all be from the same era.

a. Determine a ranking for the weapons in each group based on the amount of damage each does, how many targets it affects per attack, their maximum range, how long it takes to reload, and so on.

b. Write up your reasons for creating the rankings you did.

3. Create an Item Chart for a role-playing game containing at least 75 items. The chart should include weapons, armor, accessories, scrolls, potions and whatever other items players can find on the playfield or in shops. Do not include quest items in the chart. Also, ignore the buying and selling of objects at this point. Determine which items need attributes and assign placeholder values to them in the chart.

4. Come up with Weapons Chart for a first-person shooter game set in a genre other than fantasy, science fiction or modern warfare.

a. You might consider horror, supernatural, American West, the ancient world and even cartoons as possible genres and settings for the game.

b. The weapons should cover a spectrum of types, from hand weapons to very powerful weapons.

c. Determine the attributes you will need for each type of weapon.

d. Create a Weapon Chart for the game in the genre you selected containing at least 12 weapons.

e. Check various websites on the Internet to locate at least three Weapons Charts for other FPS games and compare your chart with them. Make whatever changes you think are appropriate to your list based on the data from the other games.

5. Create an inventory system for a role-playing game.

a. Using simple schematic drawings of the Inventory interface, show what items are worn by a characters and what ones are carried.

i. What other data should be displayed on the Inventory screen(s)?

ii. Can you fit all the information you think is important on one screen, or do you need multiple screens to show everything?

iii. How do you differentiate quest items from items the player can use?

       b.   Define the controls for manipulating objects on the Inventory Screen for both a computer version (using keyboard and mouse) and a console version (using a controller).

6. Design the interface for a shop where items can bought and sold in a role-playing game.

       a.   Create simple schematic(s) for the shop interface screen. Include any other important information that the player needs in addition to the prices.

       b.   Define the controls used in buying and selling objects. Include the controls for both a console and computer version of the game.

       c.   Add the buy and sell values to the Item Chart you created in Exercise 3.

7. Imagine you are designing a role-playing game and you want to add a game mechanic about gathering and using resources found on the playfield. The resources could be used to build new and more powerful items, improve buildings and cities, modify a character's appearance, and so on.

       a.   How would you incorporate resources into various game mechanics in the role-playing game?

       b.   What kind of interface would you need to design to manipulate the resources and what kind of information would you display for the player?

       c.   What additional charts and tables would you need to handle the resources and their applications?

       d.   Discuss the advantages and drawbacks of adding resource management to a role-playing game.

8. Write up the first draft of the chapter discussing items and/or resources for your game design document.

       a.   Group items together by type and write up a short description for each type.

       b.   Incorporate all charts and tables that relate to items and resources.

       c.   Create brief physical descriptions for the items, and, if possible, try to find visualizations that approximate what you think each item (or item type) should look like.

CHAPTER 8

ON MAGICKS AND TECHNOLOGIES

"Any sufficiently advanced technology is indistinguishable from magic."

—Arthur C. Clarke

"...any sufficiently advanced magic is indistinguishable from technology."

—Larry Niven

The concept of magic has been associated with fantasy since ancient times, and it has become a primary factor is separating fantasy from other literary genres. Technology, on the other hand, has long belonged to the realm of science fiction, which speculates on the effects that futuristic technology will have on people. Occasionally, the two concepts overlap in the same genre as in some Japanese RPGs where dragons coexist with spaceships and in the literary genre of "steampunk" where magic co-exists with technology after the Industrial Revolution.

Magic and technology add a whole new dimension to games because they expand the basic physical rules of the game universe. In addition to using arms during combat, wizards and clerics among others can cast spells of great power, and combatants on distant worlds brandish weapons of mass destruction like the BFG 9000 from id Software's *Doom*. Magic and technology offer players new approaches to game play and some exciting visual effects as well.

It takes time to design a really good magic or technology system for a game. The system has to be self-consistent and feel "right" to players. Each has its own sense of evolution and progression as players advance through the game and gain ever more powerful spells or weapons to use against ever more threatening enemies. Of course, magic and technology have more uses than simple weaponry and they can be employed in many different game activities. It is up to the designers to decide early in the design phase what magic or technology will do in the game universe and how it will work.

Magic in Games

In traditional paper RPGs, magic is used in combat, of course, but it also has many other uses that are not necessarily reflected in electronic RPGs. For example in a paper RPG, casting a love spell on an NPC can help a player unearth some secret information because the Dungeonmaster handles the NPC's dialogue and therefore can improvise as the situation progresses. Casting a love spell on an NPC in an electronic RPG is more burdensome for the designers. If the spell changes an NPC's opinion of a character and therefore the responses the NPC gives during a conversation, the designers have to create a whole new set of branching dialogue responses for this altered mood (see Chapter 10 for more on branching dialogue). There can be hundreds of NPCs in an electronic RPG, so writing up the branching dialogue for all their responses to a love potion spell takes extra time and requires more playtesting. Also, there is usually a limit as to how many spells a character can know. If the character is able to learn dozens or hundreds of spells, it becomes a daunting challenge to make them all different as well as easily accessible through the interface. As a result, many of the subtler magic spells used in paper RPGs don't make their way into electronic RPGs.

Limiting Magic in Games

Magic sometimes needs to be limited if it is too powerful. If a wizard can run around and zap everything into dust by unleashing a barrage of fireballs, the game quickly becomes unbalanced, and players will opt for wizard characters over all others. Conversely, if magic is too weak, then players will select fighters instead. Balancing the power of magic is a primary responsibility for designers of RPGs.

There are several ways to limit the power of magic. One way is to make the casting time last longer for more powerful spells. A small fireball that does only limited damage might take only a second to appear, with a visual effect showing the spell being cast. On the other hand, a spell that spews all-consuming flames can take several seconds to cast. The player then has to make sure that the caster is protected while the spell is being prepared and cast.

Another method to limit the effectiveness of magic is to use directionality. Less powerful spells can be made to act intelligently and hunt down a target while very powerful spells can be limited by the direction in which the character is standing when the spell takes effect. Thus, a low-level fireball can track its intended target while the large flame wave has a limited spread and affects only targets that it comes in contact with as it moves across the playfield.

Many RPGs use mana as a way of limiting magic. The term mana is derived from peoples of the South Pacific and refers to a power that resides in people and other objects. It is similar to "the Force" from the *Star Wars* universe. Mana is the source for powering magic in many RPG systems, and it is drained as the caster employs magic. The more powerful the spell, the more mana it drains. It is equivalent to the Health attribute. Characters who are adept at magic gain a large pool of mana over time so they can cast ever more powerful spells. In some games, the mana is replenished naturally, as the magic user draws mana power from nature. In other games, the ability to replenish mana is an attribute assigned to a few classes. But in most games there are potions or other items that replenish mana. It does no good for a wizard to set out on a long trek through a countryside that is populated with monsters and enemies and not have a way to replenish mana as well as health.

Categories of Magic

Magic in electronic games fall into three broad categories:

- *Attack Magic.* This form of magic is used to attack enemies during combat and is an alternative to weapon attacks. The caster sometimes uses a learned magic spell and sometimes unleashes the spell from a scroll or other magically imbued item. The spell can create a physical object (e.g., fireball, lightning bolt, enchanted creature) or it can use some unseen force (e.g., mental energy or ethereal object) that targets a nearby enemy (Figure 8.1).

- *Defense Magic.* This form of magic creates barriers and other forms of protection such as shields and armor that interfere or intercept enemy attacks. The spell can create a physical object (stone wall) or an unseen force (force field) that prevents an

Figure 8.1. *In many fantasy games, magic spells are used for powerful attacks as here in Gas Powered Games* Demigod.

enemy moving close enough to attack or otherwise absorbs damage the character would suffer. The spell object disappears either after having its own health reduced to zero or after a certain amount of time has passed.

- *Modification Magic.* This form of magic has many different effects, but all spells somehow modify the target they are applied to. The effects can be beneficial (e.g., healing, curing status effects, improving attributes) or detrimental (e.g., poisoning, instilling status effects, weakening attributes) to a character, or they can change the terrain on the battlefield or transform one thing into another. These spells can sometimes be used outside of battle to repair characters or restore things as well.

- *Conjuration Magic.* This form of magic creates creatures out of thin air that take part in the battle, usually on the caster's side. Necromancy is the term often used for magic that creates demonic creatures or resurrects the dead. The conjured creatures act as allies and try to attack the opponents or any creatures they have conjured. These creatures are subject to positive modifiers by the casting player and negative modifiers by the opponent.

Magic Chart (Levels)

ID No.	Name	Level	Type	Target Type	Attack Value	Restor Ht Pts	Mana Cost	Status Effects Remove			
								Poi	Stn	Mut	Slp
1	Flash Fire	1	Combat	One Enemy	12		5				
		2			18		8				
		3			25		12				
		4			36		17				
		5			50		23				
2	Hell Flame	1	Combat	One Group	30		18				
		2			50		32				
		3			75		46				
		4			130		60				
3	Inferno	1	Combat	All Enemy	120		50				
		2			200		90				
4	Bolt	1	Combat	One Enemy	15		6				
		2			21		14				
		3			32		22				
		4			48		30				
5	Lightning	1	Combat	One Group	26		15				
		2			52		27				
		3			90		40				
6	Bang	1	Combat	All Enemy	160		60				
7	Tsunami	1	Combat	All Enemy	200		90				
17	Heal	1	Any	Party Member		40	5				
		2		Party Member		60	10				
		3		Party Member		90	15				
		4		All in Party		130	20				
		5		All in Party		180	25				
19	Cure	1	Any	Party Member			6	X			
		2					12	X		X	
		3					18	X			X
20	Curative	1	Any	All in Party			25	X	X	X	X

Table 8.1. *This Magic Chart allows spells to improve over time, changing attributes as the spell gets stronger.*

The creatures usually have standard combat and movement attributes, which are defined in the Entity Attribute Chart (see Chapter 6). They can also have a time limit applied to them so that they disappear after a certain amount of time if they have not been killed by combat.

If magic spells grow more powerful over time, either automatically as a character's experience level goes up or manually by assigning points to improve spells, the attributes can change as well. The Magic Chart (Table 8.1) is designed so that spells improve over time as the player goes up in level. Note that the chart includes only attack and heal/cure spells and does not associate spells with colleges of magic. The chart includes the following information:

- *Identity Number.* Each spell has a unique number, which is used as a pointer to its artwork. As with artwork for items, there are two kinds of artwork associated with each spell. The first is the

2D representation of the object as it appears in a selection menu, and the second is the art used on the playfield, which includes its appearance, appearance while on the map, and its special visual effect when interacting with the target.

- *Spell Name.* The text string is used when the spell's name appears in the game text on a selection menu.

- *Spell Type.* This identifier indicates whether the spell can be used only during combat or at any time, in or out of battle.

- *Target Type.* This identifier indicates the selectable target for the spell. For combat spells, the target is either one individual enemy, a group of enemies in the same space, or all enemies on the playfield. For health and cure spells the target can be one friendly unit, including the player, or the whole party.

- *Attack Value.* This number is used to resolve each attack against a target, assuming the spell reaches the target.

- *Restore Hit Points.* This number indicates how many Hit Points are restored to each target of the spell.

- *Mana Cost.* This number is the cost in mana to cast the spell. If the character does not have enough mana available, the spell cannot be cast.

- *Status Effects.* The four columns are used to indicate with an "X" which status effects are removed when the spell takes effect. The four effects are poison (Poi), petrifaction (Stn), silence (Mut), and sleep (Slp).

It is also possible to have a magic system where spells continue to stay at the level at which they are first learned for the whole game. In this case, each new spell has its own entry on the Magic Chart, which is itself simplified. However, there are definite tradeoffs in making each spell unique, for the player has to remember what effect each spell has during the heat of battle. Also, the interface needed for listing many spells can be clumsy to use, slowing the player's reaction time. In a real-time battle, the player can get frustrated having to sort through a large menu system to find the appropriate spell to cast. In computer games, spells can be attached to hot keys on the keyboard, allowing faster casting of commonly used spells. In console games, a more extensive menu system is required because there are fewer buttons on the controller, although some games such as Ascaron's *Sacred 2: Fallen Angel* and CDV Software Entertainment's *Divinity*

Magic Chart (Simple)

ID No.	Name	Type	Target Type	Atk Val	Atk Mod	Def Val	Hit Pts	Def Mod	Ini Mod	Agi Mod	Restor Ht Pts	No. of Turns	Mana Cost
1	Flash Fire	Combat	One Enemy	12									5
2	Hell Flame	Combat	One Group	30									18
3	Inferno	Combat	All Enemy	120									50
4	Bolt	Combat	One Enemy	15									6
5	Lightning	Combat	One Group	26									15
6	Bang	Combat	All Enemy	160									60
7	Tsunami	Combat	All Enemy	200									90
8	Poison	Combat	All Enemy										30
9	Petrify	Combat	One Enemy										36
10	Curse	Combat	One Enemy										25
11	Drowsy	Combat	One Enemy										70
12	Magic Shield	Combat	Party Member			10	30					10	30
13	Zeus' Sinew	Combat	Party Member		+3			+1				5	50
14	Athena's Wisdom	Combat	Party Member		+1			+2	+1	+2		6	60
15	Apollo's Lyre	Combat	Party Member					+3	+2	+3		5	70
16	Hermes' Wings	Combat	Party Member		+1			+2	+1	+5		6	60
17	Heal	Any	Party Member								40		5
18	Heal-All	Any	All in Party								1000		30
19	Cure	Any	Party Member										6
20	Curative	Any	All in Party										25

Table 8.2. *This Magic Chart has spells staying at the same level throughout the game. Note that the second half of this chart (Table 8.3) appears on page 220.*

II: Ego Draconis allow players to assign a limited number of spells and other actions to buttons.

The Magic Chart (Tables 8.2 and 8.3) shows a simpler system where each spell has only one effect. The data fields are basically the same, with the addition of more attributes:

- *Attack Modifier.* This value is added to the character's Attack Value when attacking with a weapon.

- *Defense Value.* This value is used to resolve weapon combat as long as the spell object (in this case a magic shield) exists on the playfield. The shield intercepts attacks that would otherwise hit the character it protects.

- *Hit Points.* This number indicates how many Hit Points the spell object can absorb before being destroyed. This defense spell object remains on the field for a certain amount of time or until it is destroyed.

- *Defense Modifier.* This value is added to the character's Defense Value when involved in a weapon combat.

Magic Chart (Simple)

ID No.	Name	Inflict				Remove				Protect			
		Poi	Stn	Mut	Slp	Poi	Stn	Mut	Slp	Poi	Stn	Mut	Slp
1	Flash Fire												
2	Hell Flame												
3	Inferno												
4	Bolt												
5	Lightning												
6	Bang												
7	Tsunami												
8	Poison	X											
9	Petrify		X										
10	Curse			X									
11	Drowsy				X								
12	Magic Shield												
13	Zeus' Sinew									X			
14	Athena's Wisdom											X	X
15	Apollo's Lyre												
16	Hermes' Wings										X		
17	Heal												
18	Heal-All												
19	Cure					X							
20	Curative					X	X	X	X				

Table 8.3. *This is the other half of the Magic Chart (Table 8.2) that appears on page 219. It shows the status effects of spells, either inflicting them on the enemy, removing them from an ally, or protecting a character against the status.*

- *Initiative Modifier.* This value is added to the character's Initiative Value at the start of each turn and increases the character's chance to attack first in the turn.

- *Agility Modifier.* This value is added to the character's Agility Value when determining if a magic attack affects the defending character.

- *Number of Turns.* This value indicates how many turns a spell is in effect (unless it is destroyed before the time limit is reached).

"Schools" of Magic

Another way to group magic spells is by assigning them to certain "schools" of magic. The most common schools are based on the four elements of the ancient Greek theories about matter: air, fire, earth, and water. Sometimes a fifth school, ether, is added to the mix as well. These schools serve several design purposes: they make the names of the spells more obvious and they offer a way to balance each school's power so that no one becomes dominant.

As described below, coming up with names for magic spells can be challenging. Using schools of magic simplifies the naming process. A Fireball spell obviously comes from the School of Fire Magic while a Boulder Attack spell belongs to the College of Earth Magic. Sometimes characters have to align themselves to a school of magic, and their ability to cast spells from this school is greatly enhanced while spells from other schools are not as powerful. Ideally, there are an equal number of spell types for each school, so that they are equally attractive to players.

The schools of magic can also conflict with one another in a sort of yin-yang way. In many games, earth and air magic are opposites as are water and fire magic. Thus, water magic might be particularly effective against a fire dragon while fireballs can steam-fry krakens. Likewise, playfields can be associated with certain schools of magic, enhancing or reducing the magic from other schools. Thus, in a world of fire with lots of lava and hot rocks, water magic might be very ineffective while fire magic has extra power.

If a spell doesn't fit easily into an elemental school, it can be assigned to a neutral school like ether. Spells that heal and cure magic in particular should be neutral unless each elemental college has its own forms. However, duplicating spells for all elemental colleges can lead to a huge list of different spells, which can cause confusion during play.

Magic Spell Attributes

When creating a magic system, the designers have to define how each spell works by explaining how it works, what it looks like when cast, and what attributes is has. The programming team needs to know what is involved in casting the magic spell and how it behaves once it appears and moves across the battlefield, and the art team also needs to know what visual representation are needed both during casting and when the magic appears on the battlefield. Here are some of the attributes and abilities that might be needed to create magic attack spells:

- *Time of Appearance.* How long does it take for the spell to appear in the game once the player casts it? Is the caster immobilized while the spell is being cast, or can the character move and still cast the spell? Is there a graphic (for example, sparkles around the character's hands) that shows the spell being conjured? Is there a special effect (e.g., a puff of smoke) when the appearance time is ended and the spell takes effect?

- *Spell Characteristics.* What does the spell look like once it appears? Does it move across the battlefield, and if so, how fast? What happens when it strikes the target? What is the spell's attack value? Does the spell have Hit Points (meaning it can take damage before going away)? What special visuals are involved in the movement and resolution of the spell's effect on the target? How powerful is the spell and how many Hit Points does it remove from the target? How much mana does it cost to cast the spell?

- *Targets.* Does the spell affect one target, a group, or all enemies? Does it also cause collateral damage on nearby friendly units? Does the spell target one specific enemy type only (for example, a spell used against zombies and other reanimated dead monsters)? Are there some enemies that are resistant to the spell?

- *Artificial Intelligence.* If the spell moves across the playfield, how intelligent is it? Will it track a moving enemy? Or does it move in a straight line and affect only those objects in its path? If the object of the spell is an entity, how does it behave as it moves and attacks the enemy? Is it smart enough to get around terrain features or does it stop as soon as it comes in contact with blocking terrain?

Defense spells have similar attributes, with some changes to the attributes for defense value, the number of Hit Points it has, and perhaps an attack value if it interacts with an attack spell that stays on the battlefield for any length of time (for example, a creature that the attacking caster unleashed through a spell).

Modification Spell Effects

Modification spells have many effects and can be broken up into subcategories, each with its own set of attributes in addition to standard attributes for casting time and duration. Some subcategories include:

- *Health.* These spells restore some Hit Points to the target. Some spells are used on individuals while others can restore health to the whole party. The amount of Hit Points restored can depend on the type of spell if each spell belongs to a separate college of magic or if the level of the spell and amount it repairs increase over time. The amount of mana needed to cast a health spell needs to be carefully adjusted to give the player a reason has to consider whether it is better to use a magic spell or a health potion. If a magic spell restores only a small amount of health while eating up a lot of mana, it won't be used much by players who need the mana for attack spells. If the inventory space for health potions is restricted, however, players will depend more heavily on magic to restore Hit Points. The player should always feel that magic is a cost-effective way to restore health.

- *Status Effects.* These spells inflict debilitating status effects on the opponent that weaken the entity, slow it down or otherwise prevent it from attacking at full strength. The designers have to determine if the effects are temporary or if they last until they are counteracted by another spell or item. Some status effects include poison, petrifaction (turned to stone and unable to move but taking no damage in this condition), paralysis (unable to move but able to take damage), sleep, silence, fear, charm, curse, slow, berserk, confuse, and blind. An interesting effect is "doom" which starts a counter and unless the effect is counteracted, the entity dies when the counter reaches zero. Most status effects are in effect only while the character is engaged in combat but some, like poison, might continue to have an effect after combat ends.

- *Cures.* These spells counteract status effects and return the entity to normal. Occasionally, they may restore health as well as remove a status effect. The spells might target only one status effect (for example, a cure for poison) or it might target any kind of infliction. Spells that restore characters to life also fall under this rubric, because they remove a status effect (death) from an entity.

- *Attribute Modification.* The spell enhances one or more of a character's attributes for combat or decreases an opponent's attributes. These spells often have a duration of the effect that needs to be specified (which might be different from modifiers for armor and jewelry that are permanent while the item is being worn). The designers also have to work with the art team to make sure that there is visual feedback to help the player know that modifier effects are currently active. In addition to placing modifiers on a character, there are some that remove or dispel them from the enemy, setting the attributes back to their base values (although modifiers for worn equipment are usually not negated).

- *Transformation.* A few spells are used to change the identity of one object to another either temporarily or permanently. Such a transformation could neutralize an oncoming danger such as an attacking creature or attack spell, or it could have beneficial effects of changing something relatively useless into something useful, for example, turning lead into gold. More than likely, the final transformed object is predetermined and the player does not have to select what the object turns into, since doing so takes time and could be dangerous in real-time combat.

- *Rare Outcomes.* Some spells cause temporary changes that are beneficial for a character or allow the character to do things for a short time that would otherwise be impossible. The effect might give the character an unusual advantage in combat or allow access to places that are otherwise unreachable. Some of these effects include being invisible, hovering (rising in the air without being able to move), flying (rising in the air and being able to move), being immaterial (allowing the character to pass through solid objects), illuminating a dark area, locating an object, reading runes, breathing underwater, exiting dungeons, and so on. All these modifiers require special code to enable the effects, so it is important for the designers to discuss their ideas with the program team early in the process to make sure that they can be implemented in the current game engine. If a rare outcome spell is used only once, it might not be worth all the effort to create when a workaround could be possible.

Magic spells can be attached to items as well, so a player can wield a Flaming Sword or Mace of Lightning that attack with magic as well as physical damage or the player can wear a Jewel of Avoidance that improves the Agility attribute. Once the basic magic system has been laid out, the designers can assign spells at the appropriate level to different items in the game. Some spells can also act as skills for character classes, for example, a Gentle Healing skill for a cleric that has almost the same effect as a Heal magic spell.

Naming Conventions for Spells

As discussed earlier, many games use the ancient Greek concept of four elements making up the universe—air, fire, water, and earth—for naming magic spells. Air magic can include blowing winds and lightning strikes, while fire magic includes fireballs and sheets of fire; water magic includes hail and windstorms; and earth magic include boulders and pelting stones. One drawback to using this naming system is that it is difficult to come up with new names for spells that differ from those appearing in other games. It's easy to understand that a Fireball spell is likely to produce a fiery ball streaking across the map to strike an enemy. A name could be attached to the spell—for example, "Mordor's Fireball" to make it seem unique, but a fireball is a fireball no matter what it's called.

It is less easy to understand esoteric spell names that are based on other societies or technologies. Gamers in the Western Hemisphere are likely to understand that a spell called "Thor's Hammer" refers to the Norse god of thunder and would therefore assume it is an attack spell based on lightning. Gamers in the Eastern Hemisphere (China, Japan, Korean, and India are all very large game markets) might not recognize Thor and might instead assume the "hammer" means the spell sends out a warhammer to attack an enemy. A Western audience, on the other hand, might have no idea what a magic system based on the Chinese myth of Feng-Du (the ten courts of hell) means or that "Wu-Guan-Wang's Torture" refers to an attack spell where bees swarm out to attack an enemy.

It is possible to set up a completely original naming system for a game, but the problem remains that it is difficult to come up with such a system where the names are obvious enough for the player to know immediately which ones to use during the heat of battle. However, there is a certain cachet to coming up with a clever system and it can become a useful tool by marketing to promote the game as being original.

Assigning Magic Spells to Characters and Enemies

While it is possible to limit some magic spells to certain races or classes, most of the time it's a good idea to let the player experiment with all the different spells in the game. There can be limitations to the spells based on race or class—for example, dim-witted barbarian warriors only being able to learn some low-level attack and healing spells—but too many limitations can irritate players. They want to experiment with all the different magic spells in the game even if they wind up using only a few repeatedly.

There are some general rules about magic spells that apply to most games:

- *Weak magic early in the game.* Beginning characters might get one or two simple spells (or none at all) to use early in the game. There is so much information for players to grasp at the beginning of a game that forcing them to master a sophisticated magic system early on can lead to confusion. Over time, the spells can become more powerful as enemies become more powerful.

- *Teaching by doing.* A complicated magic system can be confusing to players, so it is a good idea to include a tutorial on the system as part of the game itself. If players can create their own magic spells and/or modify them, then they need to be shown the process. The tutorial can extend over time so that everything doesn't have to be explained up front. It is better to give the player a few simple concepts to experiment with and then introduce subtleties and advanced techniques once the player understands the basic of how the magic system works.

- *Balance the spells.* One of the more challenging tasks facing the design team is to make sure the magic system is balanced so that no single spell is too powerful. Powerful spells should have some compensating factor to offset their power—for example, a long casting time or a huge drain on the character's mana. Another way to balance the spells' power is to assign weaknesses to spells—for example, fire spells have no effect against water creatures and vice versa.

- *Enemies with special magic.* It can be annoying to run into a major villain or a minion that employs a form of magic that the player hasn't seen before. If the player gains that magic after defeating the enemy, then the player is rewarded. If the magic can't be learned, then the player feels robbed and may complain that the game cheats.

Technology in Games

In science-fiction games, highly advanced technology can act like magic in that it does amazing things that are seemingly beyond the normal laws of physics—because those laws haven't been discovered yet. Intergalactic travel, laser weapons, anti-gravity platforms, and other wonders have no basis in real physics—at this time. They might sometime become reality as we learn more about how the universe works and how to harness the vast forces working in it. Thus, while Einstein's Theory of Relativity shows that mass cannot travel *at* the speed of light, there are some ideas by respected scientists that suggest mass can travel faster than the speed of light by using wormholes. As long as the explanation for an effect can be explained using scientific reasoning, it falls under the rubric of science fiction instead of fantasy.

Straddling Science Fiction and Fantasy

There are some concepts that straddle both science fiction and fantasy. For example, some researchers are investigating psychic powers where the mind is supposed to cause effects in the physical world through sheer willpower, which does not appear to be much different than a wizard casting a spell to make something strange happen in the physical world. Also, creatures from horror fiction such as werewolves and vampires seem not much different from angels and demons that people believe exist in a spiritual world, and yet these monsters can be dispatched by real-world objects like silver bullets and stakes through the heart. The difference between science fiction and fantasy/horror is that science fiction gives everything a patina of reality where futuristic inventions and powers are based on extensions of current knowledge. Fantasy and horror, on the other hand, cannot explain in a scientific method how extraordinary objects and powers come into being. However, there are "laws" that apply to the supernatural—for example, garlic and crucifixes affecting vampires, wolfbane and silver bullets affecting vampires, and holy water and exorcism rites affecting evil spirits.

Science fiction runs a gamut of realism from space operas, where scientific rationales for space travel and zap guns are barely considered, to "hard" science fiction, which extrapolates current science theory into the future and examines realistically how new discoveries will affect people. Even in the wildest science fiction there is usually at least lip service paid to scientific theory as a way of explaining the wonders of the imagined universe for example as in Bethesda Softworks' *Fallout New Vegas* (Figure 8.2).

As a result, designing a game in a science-fiction universe is difficult, especially if the intent is to create a game set in a hard science-fiction universe rather than a space opera one. The game designers

Figure 8.2. *The setting for Bethesda Softworks'* Fallout New Vegas *is a wide-open post-apocalyptic world. The player can travel through the vast world without being channeled along in a certain direction by the main plot.*

need a solid understanding of current scientific theories and an appreciation of where the leading edge is for various scientific disciplines. One way to look at the matter is that games that emulate the television and movie series based on Gene Roddenberry's *Star Trek* with its starships, phasers and tricorders are in the tradition of hard science fiction, while games that try to feel like George Lucas' *Star Wars* with light-swords, Jedi Knights, and the Force are more in the tradition of space opera. With less hard scientific explanation needed, space opera games are slightly less difficult to design than hard science-fiction games.

Combat in Science Fiction vs. Fantasy

There are several important differences between combat in fantasy and combat in science fiction. First, if a game includes space travel, there is an option for recreating combat between spaceships. There are a number of flight simulation games set in outer space where players engage in spaceship-to-spaceship combat. Some of the better-known games include ORIGIN System's *Wing Commander* series, MicroProse's *Lightspeed* and *Hyperspeed*, and LucasArts' *Star Wars: X-Wing* series. While these games are set in space, the spacecraft usually handle like terrestrial aircraft engaging in dogfights,

Figure 8.3. *The gravity gun in Valve Corporation's* Half-Life 2 *can be used to pick up objects on the playfield and toss them around at will. It is definitely a concept out of science fiction.*

and there is limited attention to the real physics involved in combat outside an atmosphere. Sound effects give drama to the action even though space does not support the transmission of sound waves. Momentum is ignored as ships turn on a dime and bank and yaw like airplanes through an atmosphere. The spacecraft are armed with futuristic weapons that shoot energy and explosive projectiles, and designers have to specify the attributes for these weapons as they would in any military simulation.

A second advantage of combat in outer space is that it is possible to portray combat between fleets. Space combat is sometimes the main focus of a game and sometimes it is only part of a larger strategic campaign involving stellar empires. Some example of games that include fleet combat are Petroglyph Games' *Star Wars: Empire at War*, Taldren's *Star Trek: Starfleet Command*, and Mad Doc Software's *Star Trek: Armada* series. One problem with designing this kind of game is determining whether combat will be shown on a flat 2D map or in true 3D. The overall scale for such games can span galaxies but most combat occurs at an operational level.

Third, it makes more sense for futuristic science fiction that combatants use ranged weapons instead of melee weapons in combat since most fighting in modern combat is done at a distance with rifles and other long-range weapons (Figure 8.3). Some space operas games still have close-range combat with lightsabers and other exotic melee weapons. But realistically, soldiers greatly prefer killing enemies at a distance rather than engaging in fierce hand-to-hand combat. Ranged weapons therefore demand a more spacious combat arena. Many real-time strategy games have science fiction settings, from Westwood Studios' granddaddy of all RTS games *Dune II: The Building of a Dynasty* and their *Command & Conquer* series to Blizzard Entertainment's *StarCraft* series to Gas Powered Studios' *Supreme Commander* series. These games are operational in scale, allowing the player to keep an eye on the whole battlefield. Because combats units are small, they can engage an enemy at a distance. The advantage of science fiction weapons is that the player can see the energy projectiles flying across the battlefield and know exactly which units are engaging in fighting.

A final difference science fiction has over fantasy is that combat can take place on exotic worlds or even in the vacuum of space. Planets can have poisonous atmospheres or crushing gravity that affect the ability to see the enemy and to move. In space, trying to shoot a gun can result in the attacker flying backward from the repercussion from the weapon, assuming the game observes Newton's third law of motion.

There can also be dangerous and bizarre creatures inhabiting the alien worlds as well. In this sense, science fiction and fantasy both share a similarity, although fantasy often draws on mythologies of all cultures for its creatures while in science fiction the creatures are completely unlike anything found on Earth. It can be quite enjoyable to describe an alien three-eyed shaggy beastoid that hops around on five legs and shoots lightning out of a horn in the middle of its forehead, rather than trying to put another spin on the familiar centaur or griffin. Of course, if the game has a hard science fiction tone to it, all the creatures should be explained well enough so they seem naturally adapted to their alien environments.

Technology Trees

Many science-fiction games include a technology tree (or tech tree) of some kind to deal with the improvement of game objects over time. Since science fiction is about the future, it gives a solid foundation for considering the evolution of weaponry and other items over the course of the game. Tech trees start off with game objects at a certain primitive state and over time evolving in complexity and having a greater effect on game play. A game might take a passive approach and simply have researchers develop new technology which then appears after a certain time has passed, or it might be more active by giving the player the option of selecting which new technologies to research and then going out and gathering the resources to develop them.

In science-fiction games, the research usually delves into subjects far beyond the current level of scientific knowledge with the intent of developing powerful new weapons or other game objects. In a space opera setting where the laws of science are stretched almost to the breaking point, the result can be massive weapons that split the fabric of space and other objects that allow instantaneous travel across vast interstellar distances. In a hard science-fiction setting where the intent is to extrapolate reasonably beyond the current level of technology, the new discoveries need to be given a reasonable explanation for how they work. It helps a designer to keep up to date with modern science and understand the leading edge of different scientific disciplines. Players can be impressed with terminology that incorporate the most forward-thinking scientific concepts—dark matter and dark energy, string theory, quanta, brane theory, and so on. Of course, it is best if these cutting-edge terms are used correctly.

The designer must determine the starting point of the tech tree. In MicroProse's *Sid Meier's Civilization*, which starts at the beginning of human civilization, the tech tree starts with prehistoric developments of pottery, writing and bronze making among others and goes up to space age technology. In a later game, Firaxis' *Sid Meier's Alpha Centauri*, the setting is in the future where four intelligent species are trying to conquer space, and each species has its own tech tree that focuses primarily on weapon and vehicle development but includes a few other objects like housing facilities and reactors. The tech tree in *Alpha Centauri* does not try to cover as large a time scale as in *Civilization* and therefore has a more limited range of possibilities.

Creating a Technology Tree

The first step in designing a technology tree is to decide whether such a complex game mechanic is called for. In a first-person shooter game, players continue to find new and more powerful weapons as they explore the levels. The weapons are not tied together in a progression where a new weapon is developed from an earlier weapon. Instead, each weapon is already fully developed and ready to use. While it would be possible to add a tech tree to such a game and force the player to research new weapons, the game mechanic could prove irritating to players who just want to run through a level and blast away the enemies blocking their path. Likewise, a tech tree could be added to a role-playing game, but there are already many quests and story elements for the player to keep in mind and having to worry about developing new weapons and armor might not be worth the effort. In addition to the work required to design a good technology tree, the development team also faces the extra effort of testing, balancing, and debugging the data.

The next step is to determine the starting point for the technology tree. Is there one discovery that acts as the starting "seed" for the tech tree or are there several possible seed points available to explore even at the start of the game? Having too many possibilities early in the game can confuse players and lead to frustration. One way to prevent the tech tree from getting out of hand is to have different "branches" all lead to the same major technological breakthrough. If there are several ways to get to this breakthrough, then players can continue from mission to mission no matter what earlier branches have already been explored or ignored.

Next is to determine the major nodes on the tree where important discoveries become available to the player. In an RTS game, the designer might want a major discovery to appear every third mission and several minor discoveries to be available every mission. Some discoveries can be predecessors that must be completed before a major discovery becomes available. The designer has to test the game every step of the way to see if the discovery is so important that players won't be able to continue without it. If so, then many clues should point players toward those discoveries that must be made early on. Using this approach, however, can give players they feeling they are being led by the nose and that they don't have much free choice in deciding which new discovery to go after.

The important job for the designer is to balance the game so that important technologies are always available by the time the player needs them, no matter which way the player progresses through the tree. It makes more sense to redesign any missions that absolutely require previous technologies to be completed. Players get angry if they reach a point in the game where they can't continue because they didn't do something the way the designer wanted them to earlier in the game. There should always be some kind of workaround to keep any mission from turning into a blockage that prevents players from completing the game.

Functionality and Resources for New Discoveries

During the process of thinking through the node structure of a technology tree, designers should define the functionality for every object on the tree. While some objects can be predecessors for later discoveries, most objects should have some definite purpose for being designed. They should somehow improve play by allowing the player to do some game actions faster or make items more powerful or easier to collect. Occasionally, a "red herring" can be included, which is a discovery that has no real purpose (it offers a great opportunity for comic relief), but these useless discoveries should appear seldom or players will stop trusting the tech tree mechanism.

Most of the time, players have to invest resources of some kind into developing the new technology. The resources can be collected assets like wood, metal, and stone or they can be abstractions like cash, manpower, and education. It is a good idea to limit how many assets are needed to create new technologies and to be consistent as to how they are used. Obviously, there should be enough resources available in the game world to support research and development of new inventions, especially in the case of multiplayer games. Sometimes resources can be seeded across the playfield randomly for the player to find, but during testing the designers should make sure that each player has access to enough resources to keep up technologically with the other players.

The final step in the process is to come up with appropriate names for the discoveries and some text that gives reasonable explanations for how each one works. If players don't know that a newly discovered "photon assembler" is a powerful weapon that shoots energy beams, they might not test it out to see what it can do. "Photon assembler" could be anything from a camera to a magnifying glass, so it is not a very useful name to alert the player as to the object's usage. "Photon blaster" would be a better name because it describes the object's purpose, although "blaster" is a rather clichéd science-fiction term.

Example of Creating a Technology Tree

Assume a designer is tasked with designing a simulation game about the evolution of humans, starting from the Stone Age. One of her first steps is to determine how technology advances over time, and so she starts to list out all the weapons used by early man. After some research, she selects the stick and the rock as the earliest known

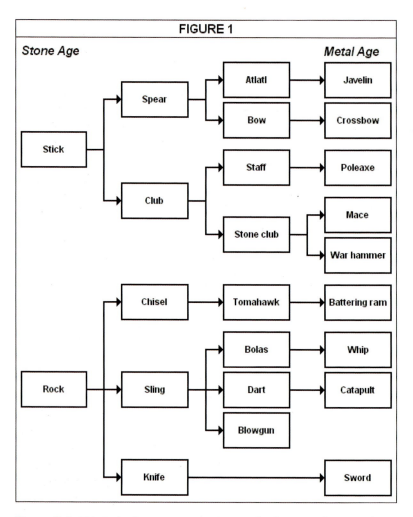

Figure 8.4. *This is the first pass at creating a technology tree for a simulation about human development from caveman to civilization. The boxes at the far left are the at-start technologies available to the player, and the other boxes are innovations to be researched and developed during play.*

weapons employed by Homo habilis some 2.3 to 1.4 million years ago. She then considers how more advanced weapons were developed from simpler ones and ends up grouping them into the technology tree shown in Figure 8.4. She develops some simple charts listing the combat values of these weapons—the Attack Value, whether they are one-handed or two-handed, if they are used direct in hand-to-hand fighting or as projectiles, and so on.

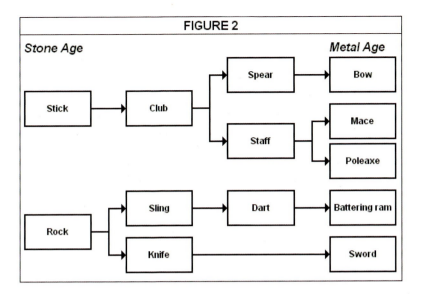

FIGURE 2

Stone Age

Metal Age

Stick → Club

Spear → Bow

Staff → Mace

Poleaxe

Rock → Sling → Dart → Battering ram

Knife → Sword

Figure 8.5. *The designer reduces the number of weapons by removing redundant weapons that have the same basic effect during combat.*

Testing the weapons values in a simple paper prototype, she realizes that there is considerable redundancy, so she decides to simplify the number of weapons and creates a revised technology tree as shown in Figure 8.5. Satisfied with this section of the tree, she turns her attention to other early human inventions. She decides to base all these innovations off the other earliest discoveries of man: controlled fire. She creates a first pass at the different innovations, tests her assumptions and revises her list to come up with the technology tree seen in Figure 8.6 She continues building out the tree to the point where the simulation is to end, with the rise of the first civilizations such as Sumer and Pharaonic Egypt.

Once the tree is complete, she turns to refining the values for items in the game and how they interact. Since one primary game play mechanic is gathering the resources needed to build various objects in the game, she decides to limit the number of resources to five items: humans (to gather the resources), food (to feed the humans), and the raw resources of wood, stone, and metal used in building the various structures. The values are incorporated into a Resource Chart, such as the one appearing in Table 8.4. During this whole process, the designer continues testing assumptions via her paper prototype to ensure that the values she is assigning are reasonable

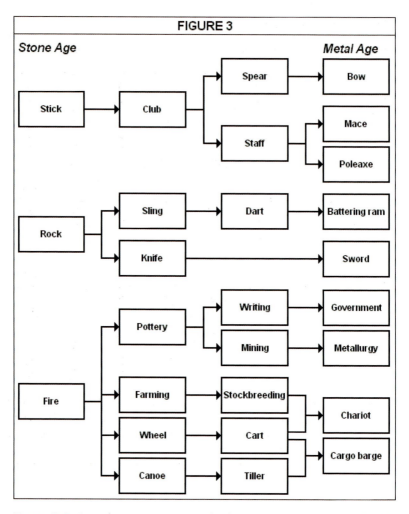

Figure 8.6. *Once the weapons are set, the designer moves on to expanding the technology tree, adding innovations stemming off another at-start technology: fire. Note that the tree does not strive to be correct chronologically since the point of the game is to show the possible order in which new innovations are generated, not when they were created.*

(Figures 8.4 through 8.6). Once the first pass at a database for the game is ready, she turns to a simple interactive prototype created by a programmer and artist to see how the game action feels in real time. She can then tweak database values as necessary before the real art and code assets are created.

Resource Chart: Cost to Build						
Structure Type	**Resources**					
						Time
Habitat	*Humans*	*Food*	*Wood*	*Stone*	*Metal*	*(in mos)*
Cave	0	0	0	0	0	0
Hut	1	1	2	0	0	1
Shack	3	7	4	1	0	1
Cabin	8	18	10	2	0	2
House	12	21	18	4	1	4
Manor	20	36	30	8	6	24
Castle	100	240	60	80	36	60
						Time
Military Structures	*Humans*	*Food*	*Wood*	*Stone*	*Metal*	*(in mos)*
Barracks 1	15	24	27	10	6	8
Barracks 2	24	60	60	36	15	18
Archery range	6	9	15	4	2	4
Stable	15	24	30	12	6	12
						Time
Commercial Structures	*Humans*	*Food*	*Wood*	*Stone*	*Metal*	*(in mos)*
Granery	6	9	21	6	0	4
Farm	15	24	25	9	3	12
Masonry	9	14	20	18	6	15
Forge	30	45	24	32	21	24
Market	27	36	35	27	15	18
Temple	40	75	35	30	21	42
School	12	16	25	15	12	27

Table 8.4. *The designer creates a Resource Chart to determine how many resources (humans, food, wood, stone and metal) are needed to build various game objects. Notice that as society develops from the Stone Age to the Metal Age, metal becomes increasingly important in object creation.*

Conclusion

Designing a whole magic or technology system is no trivial matter. It takes time to work out all requirements for the system and requires considerable testing and balancing. While working on the system, the development team should decide if the current project is likely to be the first in a series of games. If so, then additional time and effort can be devoted to thinking up magic or technologies that goes beyond the current scope of the game. It is better to have a consistent magic or technology system that runs through the whole series than to change the system from game to game. As a matter of fact, if there is talk of creating add-on modules to enhance the shelf life of the first product, the programming team can create hooks in the code to enable the implementation of the new magic or technologies in the add-ons.

A good designer should be familiar with the classics of fantasy and science-fiction literature, which can act as wellsprings for ideas about magic and technology. Additionally, a designer working on a science-fiction game should have a good understanding of current ideas regarding the cutting edge of science and technology. The education of the designer never stops, not only to keep up with the current state of game technology but also to keep finding new sources of inspiration for materials that can be incorporated into games.

Exercises

1. Work up a document in which you describe the fundamentals for a magic system that can be used in a fantasy game.

    a. The fundamentals should arise from a single world mythology (e.g., Chinese, Mayan, Inuit, etc.), an ancient philosophy for defining how the universe works (e.g., Heraclitus, Confucius, Zoroastrianism, etc.), or a pseudo-science of your own creation (e.g., Tarot, Table of Magical Elements, channeling, etc.).

    b. Define what makes the magic work in the system you described.

        i.   Is something exterior required to power the magic like mana, or is each spell self-contained?

        ii. What are the steps involved in performing the magic?

        iii. What are the limits as to what the magic can do or affect?

2. Do some research on the Internet for science fiction writers and come up with five different examples of futuristic technology. Some topics you could research include weaponry, medicine, the arts, education, food production, and so on.

a. Discuss how these technologies might be used in games set in three of these science fiction sub-genres:

    i. Post-holocaust

    ii. Space opera

    iii. Steampunk

    iv. Hard science fiction

    v. Alternate history

b. Write an analysis of your findings as they would apply towards designing a game.

    i. How close does the futuristic technology come to magic in effect?

    ii. How does the power needed for magic compare to the power needed for the technology?

3. Come up with a list of 20 original magic spells or technological innovations that could be used in a game, based on what you learned from the firsttwo exercises. Include spells/technology that can be used in *and* out of combat.

a. Write up a short description of each spell/technology.

b. Determine whether the magics/technologies have more than one level (meaning they can be improved over time). If they have more than one level, describe the different effects at each higher level.

4. Define which game mechanics (e.g., combat, exploration, puzzle solving, etc.) the spells/technologies you came up with in Exercise 3 can be used for.

a. Determine the attributes needed for these magics/technologies and compare them to the attributes you've defined so far for other game mechanics. Do you need to create new attributes to make the magic/technology work or can you use existing attributes?

b. Determine the order in which magic/technology become available during play. What must players do to acquire new or improved magics/technologies?

5. Create either a Magic Chart for a fantasy game or a Technology Chart for a science fiction game. You can use the magics/technologies you created in Exercise 3 and the attributes from Exercise 4 when designing the chart. If the magic/technology improves over time, include the changing attribute values at all levels.

6. Incorporate the magics/technologies you have so far created into the Character Generation System and Entity Attribute Charts from Chapter 6 and the Item or Weapons Chart from Chapter 7. At this point all items in the game should have values assigned to them. Test the game in paper prototype to ensure that everything is well balanced.

7. Create a Technology Tree for a fantasy, horror, supernatural or other "non-realistic" genre game.

    a. You can use either technology or magic as the basis for the tree.

    b. The tree should go through at least eight stages of evolution.

    c. Write up brief descriptions for each new innovation and define what game mechanics it affects.

8. If you game include magic or technology, write a first draft of the chapter for your game design document. (If you don't have a magic or technology system in your game, then analyze either type as it is used in an existing science fiction or fantasy game. Some ideal candidate for such an analysis are the *Magic: The Gathering* and *Pokémon* trading card games published by Wizards of the Coast. Note that there are many other similar card games by other publishers, and any one will do as long as its genre is science fiction or fantasy.)

    a. Group the magic/technology by type and write up a short description for each type and its effects on game play.

    b. Give a brief description of what the magic/technology looks like when used.

CHAPTER 9

ON PUZZLES
IN GAMES

Puzzle games are a staple of the industry and more people play these kinds of games than play RTP, FPS, RPG or any other genre. Most puzzle games are very simple and straightforward and therefore easy to learn. These simple puzzle games include crossword, Sudoku, find-the-word, word jumble, solitaire, and similar games. Ideally, after a few minutes, the player gets the idea of how the game works and then continues playing until exhausted or the end is reached. It is possible to add bells and whistles to these games—extra artwork, more audio, tons of additional levels, and so on—but the basic game play is simple and doesn't change even with the addition of all the extras.

Coming up with an initial concept for a puzzle game is not terribly difficult, but designing one that appeals to large numbers of players is challenging. There are lots of puzzle games available by download over the Internet and many are free. It is difficult to make a living just doing puzzle games.

Puzzles appear in other games as well, and these are the primary focus of this chapter. These puzzles take the forms of quests and sub-quests in action-adventure and role-playing games. While not as overt as a puzzle game using playing cards or domino tiles, these quest puzzles follow the same construction rules as simpler puzzle games. Additionally, in many RPGs and some RTS games, there are actual puzzles the player must solve to continue playing, and they force the player to stop and think through the steps needed to complete the puzzle.

Elements of Puzzles

Puzzles are primarily abstractions that focus on one particular activity. They include props like playing cards, mahjong and domino tiles, colored beads, numbers and letters, and other objects that a player manipulates in some way to achieve the puzzle's goal. In some cases, the props are tied to the real world—particularly games using letters to spell words and numbers that are manipulated mathematically. In many cases, however, the props are not tied to the real world and the identities of props could be switched without affecting the game play. For example, the illustration appearing on a jigsaw puzzle could be switched with any other illustration without changing how the puzzle is put together. Likewise, in the popular game of Sudoku, the nine numbers that fill the grid could be replaced by any other symbols. There is no manipulation of numbers mathematically in the game, since it is a puzzle about pattern recognition.

Puzzlemaster Kim Scott defines a puzzle as "a problem that is fun to solve." He also defines them as "Puzzles are a toy with the goal of finding a solution." Of course, some puzzles are a pleasure while others are a pain. A homework assignment in mathematics might be seen as a pain by many students, but the homework problems are all puzzles to be solved and some students enjoy the mental challenge of coming up with the correct solutions.

Most puzzles are solitaire experiences, and players are not trying to compete against other persons but against themselves. Therefore, the designer doesn't have to build in any penalties for cheating because players are only cheating themselves. The fun in playing a puzzle is the Eureka factor, the "Aha!" when the player comes up with the correct solution to solving the puzzle, where all the pieces fall into place. Usually, players ponder over the puzzle, trying out various approaches until they find one that works. The solution might seem imponderable at first, but eventually a sudden insight appears that cuts through the confusion and leads to the solution. That sudden moment of realization can almost feel physical. In a way, detective novels are fictional puzzles where the reader tries to stay ahead of the sleuth who is gathering clues and come up with the name of the guilty party who committed the crime.

The basic elements of a puzzle are:

- The initial problem that is presented to the player.

- The rules that guide how the puzzle is to be solved.

- The solution where everything is made clear and puzzle is complete.

In electronic games there are other elements needed for a puzzle game:

- The props that are used to solve the puzzle.
- The background on which the props appear and are moved around.
- The interface through which the player manipulates the props.

Additional elements for an electronic game can include audio and special visual effects, but these aren't central to the game itself. Note that "props" includes the various objects the player controls either directly or indirectly. In Psygnosis' *Lemmings*, for example, some of the props are the lemmings that move around on the background, and the player selects actions for some of the lemmings such as bashing and climbing to clear a safe path for the rest of the creatures to escape the end of the level.

Categories of Puzzles

Puzzles fall into several broad categories, with each category appealing to a different type of player. Some games are cerebral while others are visual. Some categories like image games are universal, appealing to a worldwide audience without requiring modification, while others like word games have to be heavily modified from culture to culture.

Word Games

These games involve players spelling out or manipulating words in some way. Sample games include crossword puzzles such as TikGames' *Word Cross* (Figure 9.1), acrostics, code-breaking games, Hasbro's *Scrabble* and *Boggle* board games, and the television show *Wheel of Fortune*. These games test the players' understanding of their native language and particularly their ability to spell out words. The reward comes from either filling in a grid with correctly spelled words or getting the highest score for spelling words correctly based on a point system.

While these games are popular all across the world, they suffer from the fact that they don't usually translate easily from one language into another. The number of letters in words and idioms vary greatly from one language to another. Even a simple crossword game

Figure 9.1. *TikGames' Word Cross is a word game based on the concept of filling in a crossword grid and similar to Hasbro's Scrabble.*

can be difficult to complete for people speaking the same language, thanks to local differences in spellings and idioms. For example, the English use "colour" and "honour" while Americans use "color" and "honor," and they call a car "trunk" a "bonnet" and their "television" the "tube." There are also diacritical marks that indicate different usages of the same letter in a language—for example, in French, the letter "e" can appear as is or else have a separate glyph attached to it to indicate an accent *grave* (è) or *acute* (é).

Image Games

These games use images instead of words, and players try to rearrange an image, find differences between two altered versions of the same image, or search an image for clues that lead to the puzzle's solution. Sample games include rebuses, mazes, jigsaw puzzles, the popular book series "Where's Waldo," and electronic games like *Tetris* and PopCap Games' *Bejeweled* (Figure 9.2). These games rely heavily on the player's pattern recognition abilities and ability to draw inferences from shapes and colors. The reward is finding hidden objects or restoring a shattered image to its original appearance. Because

Figure 9.2. *PopCap Games'* Bejeweled II *is an image game where players try to match the same color jewels to remove them from the grid.*

these games don't rely on language, they can easily translate from one culture to another and therefore appeal to a worldwide audience.

Logic Games

These games rely on the player's ability to reason out a solution to a problem. Sample games include riddles, brainteasers, logic mazes, Sudoku, Rubik's Cube, Hasbro's *Clue,* and the computer games *Battleship* and *Minesweeper.* They often have a mathematical basis and require the player to use inductive or deductive reasoning to find a solution. Detective novels fall into this category as well, since the reader is like a player trying to deduce from the clues who committed the crime. The reward of logic puzzles is getting all the pieces in the game to fall into place and relate reasonably to one another by the end. They, too, are easily translated from one culture to another and therefore are played worldwide.

Memory Games

These games rely on the player's ability to remember specific items such as facts or locations in a real world (or game world). Sample games include card games like Concentration, trivia games like Hasbro's board game *Trivial Pursuit* and the television show *Jeopardy*, and the parlor game *20 Questions*. These games rely on the player's short-term memory to remember patterns and long-term memory to remember facts. The reward is coming up with the correct answer or finding the right match. Visually oriented games like Concentration can often translate easily from one culture to another while word-oriented games like *Trivial Pursuit* need extensive translation to work globally, even though the knowledge might be familiar to many cultures.

Dexterity Games

An advantage to electronic games over paper and board games is that the game props can move across the screen. The player can interact with the game either by directly manipulating these props or by manipulating other props to indirectly influence the behavior of the moving props. Early arcade games are example of these games that depend on the player's dexterity to succeed. The player might maneuver a character around the screen as in Namco's *Pac-Man*, Nintendo's *Donkey Kong*, or Gottlieb's *Q*bert*, or shoot at moving props as in Atari's *Centipede* and *Missile Command*. Generally, to keep the player from memorizing some simple pattern for moving the controls and automatically winning the game, the pace of the game speeds up or slows down, or objects appear on the screen randomly that force the player to react to them. Eventually, no matter how good a player is, it is almost impossible to win these games. Of course, since the idea is to have players pump quarters into the arcade consoles, the publishers don't want a game to last too long. Occasionally, a really good player can stretch out a play session for tens of minutes, but the average player is normally defeated after a couple of minutes.

Games that require hand-eye coordination are very popular with young players because they can respond quickly to changes on the screen. As players age, however, they come to prefer games that exercise the mind more than the fingers. Since many action and role-playing games include puzzles of some kind, it is a good idea to consider the audience when designing the puzzles for these games. If the rest of the game is action-oriented, than adding puzzles that require good dexterity is appropriate. If the main game requires the player to consider various strategies as they progress, then the puzzles should require more thinking than quick reactions as well.

If a puzzle-within-a-game has to be solved for the player to continue, it is a good idea to have the puzzle match the rest of the game in look and theme. If a puzzle is a secondary activity that is not central to finishing the game, then it can act as relief and a change of pace for the player. In this case, there can be rewards for winning the puzzle game but the payoffs should not be mandatory for resolving a major quest. For example, in Square Enix's *Final Fantasy X*, the player has to solve a logic puzzle by putting spheres in the right sockets to gain access to temples, but the game also includes a sport similar to soccer called Blitzball that the player can engage in at will later in the game.

Games Combining Categories

Many games use elements from several categories. For example, the game of Hangman combines an image with spelling out a word. A player tries to guess a word of a certain length by selecting letters. If the word contains a selected letter, the opponent player writes that letter in a space under the image of a gallows. If the selected letter is not part of the word, then the opponent player gets to add one part of a body to the noose, starting with the head and working down to the feet. If the player spells out the word before the body is drawn completely, he or she wins. Otherwise, if all parts of the body are added to the image before the word is spelled out, the opponent wins. The main play element is selecting the letters, and the image of the hanged body is simply a way of keeping track of wrong guesses. The image adds a sense of urgency and grim humor to the actual game play.

It is relatively easy to come up with game concepts that combine puzzle categories. For example, in word games requiring players to spell out a word using letters on cubes, the cube could spin around slowly, requiring quick reflexes by the player to stop the cube with the right letter showing. Or a logic game could include images—for example, a Sudoku-like puzzle where the player has to fill in spaces on the grid with images from nine paintings by Renoir that have been broken apart and have to be reassembled correctly in groups of nine pieces.

Randomization in Puzzle Games

Many puzzle games have only a single solution, and once the player has come up with the solution, there is little reason to go back and redo the puzzle. The player already knows what has to be done to solve the puzzle and the Eureka factor is missing. Jigsaw puzzles, trivia games, and crossword puzzles are some games that have single solutions.

Other puzzle games employ randomization to vary the starting conditions or to otherwise change some mechanics of play. These games can be played repeatedly because each time through is a new and different experience. Solitaire cards games, dice games, and arcade games use randomization to keep players coming back for more. Randomization can include shuffling the cards so that the order of cards in a solitaire layout changes with every deal, or it can include the result of the dice roll to determine how far a token will move on a board or what number combination takes on major important (as in Craps). Randomization also is used to vary combat resolution in many games and affects many other game mechanics in electronic games.

Depending on the type of game being developed, the designers might decide to include puzzle solution as a game mechanic. If the expectation is for players to repeatedly replay the game, then it is best that the puzzles have some randomization factor. For example, players might be allowed to visit a casino to raise money by playing some games of chance. The odds, of course, should be weighted in favor of the player instead of the "house" since players can get discouraged if they can't raise the money they need. Each gambling game requires randomization so it can be replayed. Otherwise, there will only be one payoff the first time the player wins the game and understands the solution for winning. If players can repeat the game and get the same result every time, there is no challenge or fun, even though they might make a ton of money playing it.

If the expectation is for customers to play through a game once or maybe twice, then puzzles probably don't need randomization. Not only does randomization require more extensive testing, it can lead to frustration if the player gets stuck trying to solve it. For example, consider a situation where players need to open a safe by inputting the correct combination, which is randomized at the beginning of the game; they can be stopped in their tracks if they can't figure out the combination. They might input the combination a handful of times before finally giving up and moving on to another game. They can't go online to check a walkthrough of the game either because the safe combination is created randomly.

Some RPGs allow a player to continue playing the game even after the central story has been completed. If the state of the world remains the same as it was before the defeat of the main villain, then having to come up with new solutions to puzzles the player has already solved is simply extra work for the design team. However, if the world changes after the first story ends—for example, unleashing new and more powerful monsters—then creating new solutions to puzzles might be called for since the game world feels fresh and different to players.

Designing Puzzles that Appear in Games

The approach to designing puzzles that appear inside games differs from designing a puzzle game that is *sui generis*—that is, one unique in character that stands on its own. First, a puzzle-in-a-game serves either as a temporary hindrance that must be overcome to continue the game or as an enhancement that adds more play value to the game world. It should not be so interesting in itself that the player ignores the rest of the game. If a puzzle is that interesting, it should probably be released on its own. Examples of such puzzles-in-games that enhance play value include the levels in Valve's *Half-Life* games where there are no enemies to shoot and the player must instead figure out how to get from the start of the level to the end by getting around obstacles or manipulating objects in the environment. Likewise, in Valve's *Portal* (Figure 9.3), the whole game revolves around the

Figure 9.3. *Valve Corporation's* Portal *is a puzzle game with a compelling story. It employs a simple game mechanic where the player creates portals on flat surfaces of the playfields to warp between one area and another.*

player learning how to use twin portals to teleport through the levels and solve puzzles along the way. Square Enix's *Final Fantasy* games include a number of different card games and Chocobo races.

Second, a puzzle-in-a-game should be a natural extension of the overall environment and not feel shoehorned into the game world. The Tetra Master card game in *Final Fantasy IX*, for example, has pictures of monsters from the game on the cards and feels like a natural part of the universe. On the other hand, the sphere puzzles needed to open the temples in *FFX* feel forced and don't really fit in as a natural game mechanism. In standalone puzzle games, the environments can include whatever is needed to make the puzzles work. They generally aren't part of a larger story, although they may use licensed characters to widen their audience appeal, such as Nintendo's *Wario Land* and *WarioWare* games that feature lots of mini-games and puzzles and feature characters from the popular *Super Mario Bros.* series.

Third, a puzzle-in-a-game should be relatively short. It might take the player a few attempts to work out the solution of the puzzle, but if solving it takes too much time or effort, the player might resent being taken away from the main game play for so long. These puzzles should also be used sparingly. Too many mini-games or puzzles can get to be distracting, and each one has to be thoroughly tested and balanced.

Fourth, a puzzle-in-a-game should be easy to learn. The interface should seem obvious and there should be a limited number of controls to learn. The player already has to remember the different interface screens and controls for the rest of the game, and having to learn even more for something that offers a limited payoff can become irritating. There should be lots of audio and visual feedback for players so they can understand what they have to do. Some games where the puzzle elements are mean to challenge the player for only a short time will highlight the interactive parts of the puzzle as the player nears them—for example, highlighting a switch that is thrown to raise a platform.

Fifth, the props needed to complete the puzzle-in-a-game should be relatively close together and near the puzzle's environment. It is annoying to have to crisscross the world map repeatedly to find objects scattered among locations to solve minor puzzles. The main quest, of course, can force the player to explore all areas of the game world, but sub-quests should be localized to a central location or several adjacent locations. Having to travel to multiple locations while completing a sub-quest can also cause the player to forget who initiated the quest. It can be annoying to have to chat with all the NPCs in a town to find the one that initiated a minor sub-quest. A journal in which minor quests are recorded, as well as who initiated them and where, is incredibly helpful.

Finally, the development team needs to keep in mind that a triple-A product is likely to be released internationally, and therefore any puzzle-in-a-game needs to be able to work in multiple languages and cultures. Hence, including a word or memory puzzle game can be problematic unless the team is willing to rework the puzzle for every major market. Logic and image puzzle games require the least amount of effort to prepare for an international market.

Quests as Puzzles

In some action games (first- and third-person shooters) and in role-playing games, there is a story that drives the action of the game and gives the player motivation to explore the world and engage the entities found therein. There is usually some central conflict with a major villain that has to be resolved, but the final confrontation does not take place until the player has explored the world and prepared for the climactic battle. The central story is a quest by the character to acquire the objects needed to defeat the villain, and the quest can be broken up into multiple sub-quests that in turn must be resolved before the final quest can be completed. For example, the protagonist might need a magical suit of armor to be able to confront the major villain in his lair, and the whereabouts of the armor is currently unknown. The hero has to travel from place to place and help various NPCs resolve their problems to learn where the scattered pieces of armor have been hidden. After much trial and tribulation, with minions of the villain constantly doing their best to stop the hero, the last piece of armor is found, and now the player can head off to the villain's lair for the final showdown.

In working out the details of a game's story, the designer can approach the main quest and sub-quests as puzzles, using the elements of a puzzle described earlier.

- *Initial Problem.* This is the goal of the quest, the objectives the player must fulfill to be able to complete a sub-quest or confront the major villain.

- *Rules.* These are the restrictions the player faces towards meeting the goal and how they can be overcome to acquire the quest objects. For example, the gateway to a new area of the game world is closed until the player brings its guardian some secondary quest object.

- *Solution.* Once the quest is complete, the player receives whatever object—weapon or item—that is required to gain access to the main villain for their final confrontation. Defeating the major villain is, of course, the solution to the game.

Since the puzzle is in an electronic game, there are other elements to keep in mind:

- *Props.* Items required to fulfill various objectives during the quest. Props can be items picked up along the way or entities that have to be eliminated (for example, removing a monster that guards a treasure or bringing some item to an NPC). These quest-related items are sometimes kept in a character's general inventory and sometimes in a special area of the inventory for items that the player acquires but does not use.

- *Background.* The various locations throughout the game world the player must visit to complete the main quest. The props placed in the locations should be appropriate to them. For example, it doesn't really make sense for a minion of the main villain who rules a subterranean, molten area to wield a Sword of Ice that is a prop necessary to complete the main quest.

- *User Interface.* The manner in which the player manipulates the props to make things happen. The props can be active (for example, weapons or items) the player uses while questing or passive (for example, keys or passwords) the player simply needs to have in the character's inventory to fulfill an objective.

The puzzle-quests-within-a-game are often nested as well, meaning that players might have to complete a series of sub-quests to get to the final solution of the main quest. The quest structure is a like an onion, where there are layers within layers and players have to peel off each layer by solving a sub-quest to get to the heart where the last prop is found that is needed to complete the main quest. When using this structure, it helps to have some method to inform the player, whether through a journal, an NPC, or some other method, of the immediate goal to complete a sub-quest and the long-term goal that completes the game.

Military Missions as Quests

In working on an RTS or other wargame, a designer can use the principles for puzzle creation when designing the combat missions. Each mission should have a central problem to resolve, whether it be holding an area against enemy forces for a certain amount of time, trying to capture as much territory as possible or killing all the enemies on the battlefield. The main objective of the mission is the goal and the designer has to come up with the rules for fulfilling the mission. There can be several smaller objectives (like sub-quests) the player must first satisfy before the main mission can be accomplished—for example, capturing several high hills around an objective where artillery can be placed to bombard enemy forces occupying an area. The props, of course, are the military units assigned to the mission, and the background is the battlefield and surrounding terrain.

The designer must make sure that the player understands the main objective during a mission briefing, but he or she doesn't have to spell out exactly what the player must do to complete the objective. Indeed, a good mission design lets the player experiment with a number of different solutions, and designers are often surprised by the cleverness of players during testing.

Creating maps for the mission is itself a puzzle for the designers. Recreating a real battlefield in a game is fairly straightforward since there are maps of real-world battles available as references. Creating maps for fictional battles is more challenging, since the designers have to take into account how terrain features affect movement and combat. Before rushing in to create a map, the designer should figure out on paper the paths the players can use to get to the mission's objective and then think out how terrain will offer protection, allow ambushes, or block fire. To prevent players from simply rushing all units towards the central objective, the designer might want to add secondary objectives, such as uncovering weapons caches or rescuing captured allies, to entice players into scouting the area carefully and being ready to change their strategy as conditions on the battlefield change.

Adventure Games

A game genre that has not been covered much so far is adventure games, which shares similarities with role-playing and first-person shooter games. An adventure game tells a story, includes NPCs with whom the player interacts and often has shops where items can be bought and sold. The main difference is in game play. Where RPG and FPS games often include combat as a primary game mechanic, in adventure games there is often little or no violence at all. Instead, an adventure game tells its story by having the character solve puzzles to open up new areas of the game world and ultimately to resolve the plot. In effect, an adventure game is a series of puzzles for the player to solve.

Puzzles in Adventure Games

The solutions to the puzzles in adventure games are often combinatorial, meaning that the player combines items to create the solutions. The player travels through the game world collecting game items and getting clues from NPCs, and then combining items at specific locations in specific ways that solve the puzzles. TikGames' *Interpol: The Trail of Dr. Chaos* (Figure 9.4) is an example of a simple adventure game where the player gathers and manipulates many items to work through the puzzles and the story. For example, the player tries to

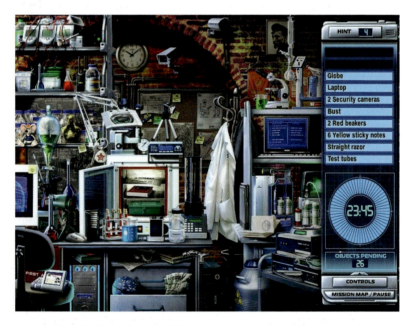

Figure 9.4. *TikGames'* Interpol: The Trail of Dr. Chaos *is a simple adventure game where the player has to solve a number of simple puzzles to progress through the story.*

enter a building but is kept out by a guard because he doesn't have the correct ID swipe-card. Getting past the guard is the puzzle, and the player scours the game world until he finds a swipe-card left on a table in a restaurant. Returning to the building, the player learns he still can't get in the building because he doesn't have a mustache like the employee on the ID card. So, the player continues looking around until he finds a bottle of glue in one location and a paintbrush in another. He can then take some bristles from the paintbrush and glue them to his lip. Now that he looks like the employee, the guard lets him into the building.

Part of the enjoyment of adventure games is exploring the game world and finding NPCs to interact with and items to collect in one's inventory. Many adventure games are humorous, eerie, or fantabulous with well-written text and interesting characters. Players continually have to visit locations and talk to NPCs until they figure out what to do to complete a puzzle and move on to the next area in the game. Trying different combinations of items and mulling over possible solutions to the puzzles is the other enjoyable aspect of these games. There are problems, though, with these games because it is difficult to gauge how challenging any given puzzle will be and players can get very frustrated if they can't figure out the solutions to the puzzles. One person's extreme challenge in a puzzle can be a snap for another person. Even testing the game on multiple new players isn't always helpful because some might find a puzzle impossible to solve while others find it too easy. Add to the fact that walkthroughs of most games are available through the Internet, and players can simply hunt down the solutions rather than unraveling them through trial and error.

Changing the Challenges

One way to prevent players from cheating when playing adventure games is to include randomization in some of the puzzles. For example, the combination on a safe or the coordinates that have to be input into a GPS system could be created randomly at the start of the play, and the player would then have to experiment and try different combinations until finding the right one. Another approach is to include dexterity puzzles with the thought puzzles, for example, having to find one's way through a room filled with heavy stamping presses where players have to time their movements to travel down a conveyor belt without being squashed. Of course, using dexterity or randomization can prove frustrating to brilliant players who can solve puzzles but not coordinate their hand-eye movements or who resent being forced to try random inputs until hitting on the one that works.

Some of the first adventure games like Infocom's *Zork* series were text-based where players had to type in directions for movement and performing actions. Later, games like Sierra On-Line's *King's Quest* and *Leisure Suit Larry* series and LucasArts' *Monkey Island* series include graphics and have the player interact with the game by clicking on actions and items. The genre reached its zenith of popularity with Cyan Studios' *Myst*, which sold some six million copies worldwide, but fewer adventure games are being published because the audience for such games has shrunk. Other game genres are telling interesting stories with more kinds of action for the player than simply experimenting with combinations of items and actions to find a solution. A game like Ubisoft's *Assassin's Creed* or Square Enix's *Lara Croft and the Guardian of Light* that combines intellectual puzzle-solving with fast action is the heir to the slow moving, puzzle-centric adventure game of yore. However, the older audience that favored traditional adventure games is not the same as the younger audience that enjoys action over puzzle-solving, but there is certainly room for both if designers do their jobs correctly and make compelling games with good stories, fascinating locations, and interesting characters. They have to allow players to get through the game world successfully using their brains or their brawn, meaning that plot bottlenecks are created where either problem-solving or dexterity is used to get through to the next area of the game.

Conclusion

Adding puzzles to a game can make the product more interesting to players as long as the puzzles feel part of the game world and are used simply to make the game only slightly more complicated with the addition of a new game mechanic to learn. Simple puzzles can work in action games like first- and third-person shooters, where players want to focus on exploring the environment, finding treasures, and eliminating enemies. While more challenging puzzles can be added to complex games like role-playing and simulation games, which are slower paced and force players to plan their actions, they also slow down the pace of the game and can wind up being so challenging that players either give up trying to solve them or resort to walkthroughs to get past them. Continuous and extensive testing by new players can help a development team determine the effectiveness of the puzzles and whether they add to or detract from the players' overall enjoyment.

The elements of puzzles can still be used by designers to help define the structure of the overarching story in a game and to determine where important items should be located. Both large and small quests can be considered puzzles that players must solve, and their resolutions can be richly rewarding for players who want to exercise their minds as well as their hand-eye coordination.

Exercises

1. Search the Internet for free sites that offer puzzle games.

   a. Try out several games in the different categories described in this chapter.

   b. Write up an analysis of your findings regarding how the puzzles are structured.

      i. What are the basic elements of each puzzle type?

      ii. Can some puzzles only be played over the Internet or would it be possible to make physical versions of them?

2. Come up with the concept for a simple combinatorial puzzle that includes two or more categories (word, image, logic, memory and dexterity).

   a. If possible, try making a physical version of your game.

   b. Write up the idea as a two-page pitch paper making sure that the first sentence can stand alone as the high concept.

3. Design a card game that uses a *modified* card deck.

   a. Start out with a standard 52-card deck and then replace or change some or all of the cards. For example, you could add another suit or two, change the card values (number of pips or identities on the face cards), alter the shape of the cards, add additional cards to each suit, and so on.

    b. Test the game and revise the rules until it is enjoyable to play.

    c. Write up a short analysis of how you came up with the idea and what changes you made through testing.

4. Do research on the Internet to find three examples of puzzles in role-playing and other games that have no direct connection to the plot (that is, the puzzles are not integral to quests or sub-quests). Some examples include the Chocobo races and card games in various Square Enix *Final Fantasy* games. Create a short presentation on the sub-games you found and explain if they enhance the player's enjoyment of the game or simply become a distraction.

5. Create a puzzle-within-a-game for a first-person shooter game that somehow must be solved to complete the game.

    a. Define the goal of the puzzle, any items that must be collected, and what the player must do to complete the puzzle.

    b. Determine the environment in which the puzzle appears and then where the items used to solve the puzzle are located in the playfield.

    c. Test the puzzle in paper prototype and make any changes as needed to help keep players on the right track towards solving it.

6. Create three linked missions for a wargame or real-time strategy game that have at their center a puzzle the player must solve to complete the missions.

    a. Define each mission's objective clearly so the player knows what to do to complete it.

    b. The puzzle can become apparent to the player from items or information uncovered during play.

    c. The puzzle's resolution should become apparent by the conclusion of the third mission.

    d. Prepare a presentation so you can demonstrate your concept to others.

7. Research adventure games on the Internet and find at least five examples of where a puzzle is explained in detail. Analyze the elements of each puzzle to determine what props they involved and what steps the player must follow to complete each one.

8. Design at least one puzzle for the game you are designing. The puzzle could be a quest or mission. If you are making a game with quests and missions, design the puzzle so that it can be incorporated into your game. (Note: If you don't plan to include quests/missions/puzzles in your game, create one that *could* appear in it.)

   a. Make sure to include the set up for the puzzle, the props the player must collect to solve it, and the locations where the props are placed.

   b. Write up your ideas for the puzzle so that you can test it once you make the maps for the game (this is an exercise in Chapter 11).

Part III: IMPLEMENTING THE DESIGN

CHAPTER 10

STORYTELLING IN GAMES

Until recently, the difference between movies and games was pretty dramatic. Games were about players performing a few limited actions to achieve a goal or series of goals while movies told stories of characters involved in some conflict that was resolved by the end. Early arcade and video games had little room for the elements of stories—interesting characters, well-developed conflict between them, dramatic tension leading up to a big climax, and then the denouement as the story wound down and the characters went about their lives. Movies also featured lots of dialogue, lots of action, and lots of music, all of which early electronic games lacked.

As the technology for games developed in the 1980s and the storage capacity for game platforms increased, real stories began to appear in games where the player took on the role of the protagonist whose actions and dialogue were controlled by the central processing unit (CPU). When 3D graphics became the norm in the 1990s, game worlds became much larger and more visually interesting, and using CDs for game data storage allowed even more dialogue, music, and sound effects. Nowadays, the border between movies and games is blurring, and in the future the two could possibly merge in interactive movies where viewers make their own decisions about what paths to follow through the story.

Stories in Games

While many games aren't interested in telling stories, others are anxious to narrate grand epics of massive scope in huge worlds populated with a large cast of characters. Puzzle games usually have no stories, although a few such as Interplay's *The Lost Vikings* and GT

Figure 10.1. *This is part of the introductory text that kicks off the main story in* Bethesda Softworks' The Elder Scrolls IV: Oblivion.

Interactive's *Oddworld: Abe's Oddysee* do have background stories that give the player reasons for solving the puzzles. Likewise, arcade games generally do not include stories, save a few notable exceptions such as Cinematronics' *Dragon Lair* and Atari Games' *Gauntlet*. The early text-based adventure games like Infocom's *Zork* series had minimal storylines, although as the genre grew, newer adventure games developed more complex stories with more interesting characters. Early action games like Nintendo's *Super Mario Bros.* and *The Legend of Zelda* have minimal stories, but as they too grew larger in scope, their stories also expanded and became more complicated.

Role-playing games usually have the largest stories where the hero undertakes a series of quests to defeat the evil machinations of the master villain (Figure 10.1). These stories usually involve the player visiting many different locations and interacting with many different characters both good and evil along the way. The stories are often structured like a huge novel divided into books and chapters, with each book involving the resolution of a central sub-quest and smaller quests at multiple locations acting as chapters of the book.

Simulation games and wargames will sometimes include stories as well, although if a wargame is based on a real battle, the story is replaced by historical facts. Real-time strategy games are often set in fantasy or science fiction worlds and tell of nations competing against one another for dominance. In such games, there is less emphasis on individual characters since they focus on armies in conflict. Where the scale of the game is tactical (as in an FPS game) and focuses on the exploits of a few soldiers, as in Electronic Arts' *Medal of Honor* and id Software's *Return to Castle Wolfenstein*, the exploits of the soldiers are framed within a larger overarching story.

Advantages of Stories in Games

There are definite advantages of having a story in a game. First, it gives an overall structure and meaning to the game action, and provides an Aristotelian beginning, middle, and end to the action. Games without stories can end unexpectedly at any time, and the player never senses the action building towards a climax. Second, a story provides motivation for players, a reason to be running around the game world and destroying everything in their path. As long as the climax is still ahead of them, players know there is more to come, and if they've liked what they've experienced so far, they'll want to continue experiencing even more. Third, taking on the identity of a character in the game world helps the player identify more closely with the conflict that drives the action. Players feel they have a personal stake in the outcome of the game if their characters get killed while performing heroic actions. They can become so immersed in the game world they lose track of time in the real world.

Fourth, if the designers have created interesting characters, a substantial game world and a compelling story—in other words, a strong intellectual property—the game can breed multiple add-ons and sequels and make the developers a lot more money. Finally, this intellectual property can draw the interest of other industries, to make both accessories like toys and action figures and also movie and television series tie-ins. The financial reasons for including a story in a game can be as strong as the players' motivation reasons.

Disadvantages of Stories in Games

There are, of course, disadvantages of using stories in game. It takes time to figure out the plot for a story that can last through 20 hours of play and often much more. The plot can get so convoluted that players lose track of why they are undertaking the quests they have been given. Second, there is a danger that game play will take second place to storytelling, and some cut-scenes, the animated sequences where much of the plot of a game is explained, can go on and on with the player growing more and more impatient to get back to the fun of stabbing and killing. Occasionally, some of the most exciting action in a game occurs in these cut-scenes, and players can be disappointed if they can only watch events occur without being to interact with the changes in the game world. Third, creating the assets to represent the large cast of characters, multiple locations, and multitude of items is expensive and takes time since artists have to create everything from scratch. In addition, most games include voiceovers where actors record the dialogue of the many characters, and preparing for the recording sessions is expensive and can require several callback sessions for last minute changes.

Fourth, it takes considerable time and testing to check for any dangling plot elements, and the more quests and sub-quests there are in the plot, the longer the debugging process takes. Finally, there is the danger that if development takes too long, the team will be forced to make last minute changes to the plot, perhaps having to cut out whole subplots and truncate the storyline. These changes require that expensive art and audio assets be dropped, new dialogue be written to explain holes in the plotline, more voiceover sessions be made, and additional testing be done to ensure that the changes work.

Problems with Game Stories

While games have stories, they have been criticized for the weakness of the stories. There is a certain sameness to many role-playing games, especially those set in fantasy worlds. These games rely heavily on the same literary tropes (i.e., clichés) as their paper RPG ancestors, which in turn drew heavily from the fiction of J.R.R. Tolkien's epic *The Lord of the Rings*. In Tolkien's novels, the world of Middle-Earth is replete with humans, elves, dwarves (well, at least one last remnant of the proud race), and orcs, which also have been incorporated as characters and monsters in most role-playing games. It sometimes seems that designers are more interested in coming up with variations for the magic and combat systems in electronic RPGs than developing new and interesting fantasy worlds.

Weak Characters

Another criticism about game stories is the weakness of the characters. This weakness comes both from poor writing and poor acting.

Until relatively recently, the stories in games were written by the designers who created the game world and the beings in it, but nowadays professional writers are often brought in to help punch up the story and create more interesting dialogue. Some of the dialogue found in old video games is absolutely appalling, an attempt to mix middle English with modern idioms and an occasional out-of-place joke or two. The stories in these older games were also poorly structured, and the plots felt either overly melodramatic or completely non-dramatic. The hero's objective might be painfully obvious, as in rescuing a kidnapped princess from the master villain or in taking simple vengeance against the blackguards who killed his family. Recent games have started to take on more interesting plots where things change over time and the hero's motivation also changes, possibly from mere revenge to having to sacrifice himself to save the world. Still, many games want to be epic in scope where the hero has to save the land, the world, and even the universe from destruction at the hand of the master villain who plans to unleash some nameless horror upon the world…and yadda yadda yadda.

Game characters also face weak characterization because of the limitations imposed on them by the game mechanics. There are only so many actions a character can perform in a game because there are only so many controls the player can master and remember during play. The most common action of characters in games is combat, which can take up a huge portion of the active game play (as opposed to passively exploring the game world). Defining a character by his or her abilities in combat is very limiting, even if those abilities are awesome to players. As a result, the characters in games seem more caricatures than real people.

Too Much Information

To understand what the player is expected to do, there can be a goodly amount of exposition that has to be given before the real play begins. In games the situation is even worse because the player not only needs to understand the backstory of the game—what has happened up to the point where the game begins—but also has to learn the controls. As a result, the early part of a game can have a lot of explanation both about the game world and characters and about how the game mechanics work. In RPGs, in particular, the evil plans of the master villain have to be revealed in enough detail to give the player a sense of the ultimate goal of the story and what to do next. Then, as the player explores the world, she gathers allies who have to explain why they want to join in the quest. Usually, there are henchmen working for the main villain that the player faces before the final confrontation with the main villain, and their machinations and purposes for acting also need justification. As a result, RPGs are filled with extensive story information as well as details on how to play the game.

Even though a game can have a complex storyline, the game play is fairly simple and straightforward: Explore, fight, dicker, and fight some more, using controls that should be easy to learn lest the players give up in frustration. To keep things interesting for the player, the game offers new areas of explore and new monsters to fight, but eventually the game can drag down. Unlike a movie that lasts a couple of hours or a book that might take several days to finish, a game usually lasts ten hours or longer, and in the case of RPGs (especially MMORPGs), they can last for 40–100 hours or more. There are more places to visit and more NPCs and more monsters and more fights in games than in any other media.

Despite being larger than other forms of entertainment, RPGs and other games face the problem of endless repetitiveness, forcing players to do the same actions over and over again hour after hour. Where a movie can build constantly to an emotional climax, games stretch out the action for so long that players feel less emotional involvement in progressing the story and more excitement in finding new items and entities and exploring new places. When the final confrontation with the main villain comes at the end, players are often relieved—not so much with concluding the dramatic confrontation with the antagonist but in knowing that the game is close to being finished, barring the long, long fight with the villain that caps the action. RPGs often feel like long-distance marathons where only the strongest-willed survive to the end.

Structuring Stories in Games

Many people trying to get into the game industry have the mistaken belief that the designer's primary task is to come up with an interesting story on which to hang the game. While story is an important element of design, it is not the overriding one. Coming up with interesting game mechanics is far more important, and a game with a mediocre story can sell well as long as players become totally immersed in game play. A good story can make the game characters more interesting, but the real story being told during a game is the player's. A player's emotions are more invested in how cleverly he or she handles the problems presented by the game mechanics than in the character's dramatic problems. Players don't much care for other NPCs telling them what emotions they should be feeling or nagging them to hurry up and do something to stop the villain. In games, players have much less emotional attachment to the character they control than in how well they perform.

Designers do need to understand the basics of storytelling, of course, and they should take classes in creative writing at college if at all possible. There is a craft to story construction that can be learned by anyone, even though only a few learn to tell stories compelling enough to sell...or create games around. There are many sources available online and in bookstores for learning the craft of storytelling, so this chapter will look at structuring stories for games instead of teaching the basics of plotting.

Quest Structure

As described in the previous chapter, one approach to structuring the story in a game is to use quests and sub-quests. The primary quest involves stopping the major villain from completing a master plan of world conquest or whatever. To complete this quest might require that the main character fulfill a number of conditions before being able to undertake the final confrontation—for example, getting the special weapon that alone can slay the villain or acquiring a set of keys or runes or other objects that open the final path to the villain's lair. The series of actions are sub-quests with specific goals the character must achieve to continue. The sub-quests can involve stopping the minions of the main villain or doing favors for certain personages who then give the character some object needed to complete the main quest.

The advantage of such a quest structure is that the goals are all fairly clear-cut and the story itself is scalable. The designer can create a simple flow chart outlining the actions needed to complete a given goal to determine if a quest is too complex or too linear (see Figure 10.2 on page 270). If it turns out the scope the game is too ambitious and needs to be cut back, some of the goals can be removed or shortened. Likewise, if the game is too short, additional sub-quests can be added to give the player more to do. If the player controls a party instead of a single character, each member of the party can have his

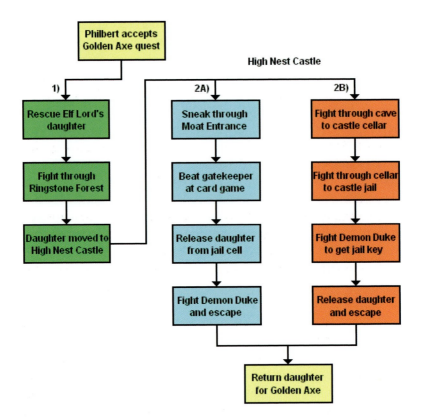

Figure 10.2. *A flowchart is a useful tool for helping the design team map out the plot elements of a game.*

or her own story arch with sub-quests leading to a climax that affects the main story's quest.

Note that the story structure described above works well for a game that has a definite ending. If the project is an MMORPG, the main difference would be that there is no one overarching quests. Instead, the online game contains a series of sub-quests that can be extensive but don't substantially change the conditions in the game world. MMORPGs are persistent worlds, where things don't change much over time. The reason for this stasis is that beginning players can join the game at any time, and if some of the more challenging and rewarding quests are not available because that part of the story has been finished, the newcomers feel cheated. If some NPC has a quest to find a magic sword, that quest should be available to all players at all times, even if the NPC initiating the quest winds up with tens of thousands of copies of the magic sword.

One example of a quest structure in a game can be seen in BioWare's *Dragon Age: Origins*. The game story starts with an introductory sequence in which the player selects from six available characters and lives that character's early history (also learning the main game mechanics) until being inducted into a group called the Grey Wardens, a group dedicated to destroying the evil beings that are overrunning the world. The main story then kicks in with the player surviving the treachery of a noble who betrays his king at an important battle and the ensuing slaughter that follows. The player takes on the leadership of the Grey Wardens and is tasked with four major sub-quests: getting humans, elves, dwarves, and a council of mages to join in the final battle against their common enemy. Before the final battle can begin, however, the player has to deal with the treacherous noble. The climax is the battle with the great dragon that leads the enemy forces.

There is a problem, of course, with using quests as the backbone of a game story. Eventually, a sensation of sameness develops as the player goes from one sub-quest to the next, and there isn't always a sense of increasing tension over time nor an urgency that builds to the climax. There is, however, a sense of reward as the player completes various quests and acquires new armament and objects of power to use against the next set of enemies. As long as rewards are doled out on a regular basis, the players are content and willing to continue questing towards the final show down with the villain.

Zigzag Structure

A quest-based story structure allows players to know things their characters don't, primarily the master villain's master plan. Occasionally, a cut-scene animation pops up and shows what the villain is currently up to, thus providing a sense of urgency that the villain's plan is coming to fruition. A different approach to telling the story is to keep the player as much in the dark about what is happening in the world as the character is. In a quest-based story structure, the players understand throughout the game what they have to accomplish before they can confront the major villain—for example, collecting all the keys or runes or arms that enable them to meet and beat the villain. If players are given only limited information and set on one quest at a time, the designer-storyteller can then change directions abruptly at any time during the story and even change the goal of the quests as the need arises. This approach is like a zigzag, where the player starts out in one direction to achieve a goal and then, as circumstances change dramatically, us forced to change directions because the goal has changed. This reversal of purpose can happen several times during the game, with each major change in the plot providing new quests and new objectives.

As an example, say that the hero, Sir Clyde, learns his fiancée, Lady Genteel, has been kidnapped by the evil wizard Gort. Clyde's first goal is to track down Gort's whereabouts to rescue the fair lady. Just as Clyde breaks into Gort's dungeon to confront the villain, a giant Ruby Dragon arrives and kidnaps Lady Genteel. Much to Clyde's surprise, he learns from Gort that Lady Genteel is actually a "daughter of the sun" and is doomed to be sacrificed to bring back the red dragon race. Putting their mutual animosity aside, Clyde and Gort team up to track down the Ruby Dragon. No sooner do they fight their way into the dragon's mountain lair then they see the sun god Heliyos abscond Lady Genteel and flee with her to the highest heavens to become his wife. The Ruby Dragon is now willing to join up with Clyde and Gort to rescue the lady so as to save dragon-kind, and so the humans leap on the dragon's back to fight their way to the gates of the Third Heaven where they find that all the gods at war and Lady Genteel is again missing, having been abducted by the Dark Lord of the Underworld… And so it goes.

One advantage of a zigzag story structure is that the player is never quite sure of what will happen next and whether or not the next destination will be the final one. This kind of story structure has been used in many Japanese RPGs, and it provides players a different kind of emotional involvement in the game action. Because one never quite knows what will happen next, the designer-storyteller can spring major surprises on the player with sudden reversals of fortune and other "I didn't expect *that*" variations.

A major drawback to the zigzag story approach in that the player usually has to be kept on a tight leash at all time and given little freedom to explore the game world. Each new area of the game world the player visits has a limited number of discoveries to be made, and the player is restricted from wandering out of the current location to explore other new areas. Going back to explore areas of the world that have already been visited generally does not provide much reward except the chance to buff up the characters. There are usually fewer sub-quests available because of the travel restrictions or the sub-quests are all localized.

One way to restrict movement is to allow travel between major locations only by using a strategic world map and forbidding entry to new locations until the current chapter of the story is finished. It is possible by the end of the game to open up the game world and allow the player access to all locations, but by then most of the new discoveries have already been revealed so there is little novelty in visiting these same areas again.

Mission Structure

Games with simpler stories, such as real-time strategy games and even shooter games, can tell their narratives in a more linear fashion by using missions. Each mission acts like a self-contained chapter in a story and advances the story a bit. In many cases, the mission has nothing to do with telling the story, but cut-scenes appear between missions to advance the plot and set up the next mission. Each mission normally takes place on a single map or level, which can have its own narrative structure, as described in the next chapter. Once a mission is completed, the player moves on to the next mission and another part of the story may unfold through a cut-scene. To add variety, the player is sometimes allowed to select the next map to visit or the mission to undertake from several available, but the storyline usually does not advance until all maps or missions are completed in a strict linear fashion.

One advantage to this structure is that the player has a pretty good idea of when the story will end. The pace of the story is continuous and there are seldom any dramatic turns of fortune to worry about. The characters can be flat and two-dimensional, and there is little time given to character development (although there can be leveling to improve characters). A drawback to this structure is that if players get stuck trying to complete a map or mission, they may decide to give up playing the game if they can't figure out how to get to the end.

One way to make a mission-based story more interesting is to force the player to switch sides once in a while, as in Bungie's first-person shooter *Halo 2* where the player switches between playing the human Master Chief and the alien Arbiter. A similar approach was used in Sony's role-playing game *Arc the Lad: Twilight of the Spirits*, which switches between the fraternal brothers Kharg of the humans and Darc of the Deimos as they seek to destroy each other's race. Seeing the same situation from multiple viewpoints adds depth to the story and allows the designer to make good use of dramatic irony.

Hero's Journey Structure

One approach to building a story for a game is to use the mono-myth of the Hero's Journey, as described in Joseph Campbell's 1949 book *The Hero with a Thousand Faces*. After studying myths of many

The 17 Steps of Joseph Campbell's "A Hero's Journey"
Departure
The Call to Adventure
The hero is warned that his or her life is going to change.
Refusal of the Call
The hero initially refuses the call.
Supernatural Aid
A magical guide appears to prepare the hero for the journey.
Crossing the Threshold
The hero leaves the known world for the unknown.
The Belly of the Whale
The hero's lowpoint, but also the transition from the old life to the new.
Initiation
The Road of Trials
Series of tests the hero undergoes early in the transition.
The Meeting with the Goddess
The hero experiences power of love (internally or externally).
Woman as the Temptress
The hero is tempted to stray from spiritual journey by earthly desires.
Atonement with the Father
Central point of journey where hero meets powerful being that muse be defeated to continue.
Apotheosis
A period of repose for the hero before the return trip.
The Ultimate Boon
The hero's achievement of the quest goal, often transcendent in nature for the hero.
Return
Refusal of the Return
The hero is reluctant to leave and return to normal.
The Magic Flight
The hero begins the journey back with the quest goal.
Rescue from Without
Guides and rescuers assist the hero to start of continue along the return journey to everyday life.
The Crossing of the Return Threshold
The difficult return to everyday life while retaining wisdom learned during the journey.
Master of the Two Worlds
The hero learns to balance the material and spiritual in the everyday world.
Freedom to Live
The hero can now live in peace, free from the fear of death.

Figure 10.3. *The 17 stages of the hero's journey, based on Joseph Campbell's* The Hero with a Thousand Faces, *can provide a solid structure for a game story.*

cultures in various times and areas of the world, Campbell found a pattern in many of them, which he describes in the book's introduction as "A hero ventures forth from the world of common day into a region of supernatural wonder: fabulous forces are there encountered and a decisive victory is won: the hero comes back from this mysterious adventure with the power to bestow boons on his fellow man."

Campbell talks about the seventeen stages of the monomyth, starting off with the call of duty that leads the hero to head out from the known world into the unknown world. The hero is often guided initially by some supernatural helper that helps him (or her) overcome his initial insecurity and cross the first threshold into the unknown. The hero then undergoes a series of trials and sometimes encounters death before crossing back over the threshold into the known world as a master of both worlds.

The structure proposed by Campbell (Figure 10.3) is very useful when thinking about how the main character (especially in role-playing games) goes from a position of great weakness to one of great strength and resolve, gaining the power to overcome any obstacle, even death, in the long journey. The concept of a helper is also useful in that the helper only can perform a number of functions: explaining game play, advising about what to do next, offering tidbits about the game world setting and story, and even assisting in combat and other game actions. There are problems with trying to stick too slavishly to Campbell's structure since some of the stages—for example, The Meeting with the Goddess, Woman as Temptress, and Atonement with the Father—might slow down the pace of the story. Still, Campbell's book is a goldmine of ideas for designers and should be required reading for anyone interested in creating story-based games.

Open World Structure

Many role-playing games have experimented with a more open-ended structure for telling stories that allows the player to freely roam around the game world. This approach is sometimes referred to "sandbox" style because it feels like the game world is one large sandbox that the player can explore at will. The story line in such games is often episodic and nonlinear, and often the player has multiple ways to complete the game. This structure caught on with Rockstar Games' release of *Grand Theft Auto III* in 2001. It has been used in Bethesda Softworks in several role-playing games, including *The Elder Scrolls* series, *Fallout 3*, and *Fallout New Vegas*.

In these games, there is still an overarching plot that drives the action of the game, but events are broken into smaller quests and sub-quests for players to undertake in whatever order they desire. A player might visit a location in the story that is tied to the main plot but not trigger the plot because other objectives have to be completed first. For example, the player might visit a monastery where the head abbot lives, and that abbot might trigger a major portion of the story. However, the player discovers that the abbot is not available at the moment or hides behind a door the player cannot yet open. Once the player completes other portions of the overall main quest, the conditions are now right for the abbot to appear and continue the storyline.

Even though players might feel they can go anywhere in the game world, they can trigger new plot elements only in a given order. However, there are usually many subplots for players to find all around the world, and so they remain continually challenged until they have fulfilled the conditions to start the next part of the main story. Designers have to be careful about structuring the storyline, assigning plot triggers to locations, and ensuring that variables which control trigger points are changed correctly as the player completes subplots and sections of the main plot.

It is possible to channel the players to explore the game world in a desired way by placing obstacles in their path to bar entry to certain areas until the right moment. The most obvious obstacles are locked doors and barred gates that can't be opened and having important NPCs temporarily be absent from areas. Another approach is place tough enemies in the path of the players. They can try to force their way past these enemies, but eventually they get overwhelmed. Later on, when the players are stronger and have better weapons, they can defeat the enemies and explore areas of the world previously off limits to them. In many games, the main plot is relatively short, making it easier to playtest and modify trigger conditions as necessary. The richness of these games comes from having so many different locations to explore and subplots to resolve.

Linking Plot to Game Play

In a game where the story is external to game play, such as in real-time strategy games where the story works as a framework for holding the missions together, the story does not link in directly to game play. Usually, no cut-scenes appear during a mission to give more exposition about the characters or to show what is happening elsewhere in the world, unlike role-playing and first-person shooter games, which occasionally interrupt the game play for important cut-scenes that further the narrative. In games where the story acts as a framework, the whole plot can be worked out without worrying about the status of the characters controlled by the player or what plot elements they have resolved or not resolved at the start of each mission. All the designer has to do is use placeholders for the missions while figuring out the plot details. For example, in a futuristic wargame starts dealing with the invasion of Earth by alien forces, the designer would work up the initial exposition about why the invasion occurs, the aliens' plans, the current state of the player's forces, and the goal of first mission. The placeholder for the first mission simply states that the player's goal is defeating a squad of alien soldiers and capturing some of their weapons for research. The details of the mission do not have to be worked out at this point because they don't directly affect the story. The player either completes the mission or fails, and the story doesn't continue until the player wins.

In RPG and action games, on the other hand, the plot is usually more linked into the actual game play. The backstory for the game has to be written, just as for a RTS or wargame to explain what is happening in the game world up to the point the game begins and what the player has to do in the short run (the first mission, as it were) and in the long run (defeating the master villain) to complete the story. As players begin to explore the world, they might encounter NPCs who interrupt the action to explain some plot point or game mechanic. There might even be cut-scenes that give more exposition about the overall storyline. Game play is frequently interrupted during such games to further the story, based on what the player has achieved so far, and to change the existing conditions of the game world—adding allies to a party, undertaking sub-quests, buying and selling items in stores, and so on. In this case, the designer has to write the story plotline knowing that it might branch out in an open-ended world where the player is free to roam without direct guidance.

What makes the story for an open-ended game world difficult to plot is that the designer can never predict exactly the current condition of the characters when major events are triggered. Some players might work their way through the game world slowly, buffing their characters to the maximum before initiating a major event, while others plow straight ahead and trigger major events while their characters are relatively weak and poorly armed. If players have trouble continuing because their characters are weak, then they either have to go back and grind out enough experience to get to a level where they can survive or simply give up and move on to a different game.

When designing an RPG or action game, the designer has to assume that the average player will be at a certain level and have certain equipment before a new major event is triggered. The designer can tie the plot advancement directly to the player's level and accomplishments throughout the game, for example, saying the player must stay in one location of the game world until reaching experience level 3 and solving three sub-quests, then in the next location the character is expected to reach level 6 and solve four more sub-quests, and so on to the end of the game. The restrictions placed on the player should be connected to the game's plot and someone should give the reasons as to why the player cannot advance until certain conditions are met. Even if players decide to spend lots of time buffing up their characters to much higher experience levels, they will not be able to trigger the next major event until they complete the sub-quests that advance the plotline. Note that secondary sub-quests can remain open to be completed later, as long as the player can revisit those areas that have already been opened up.

It takes considerable testing with different kinds of players to double and triple check that major events are being initiated correctly without frustrating players by forcing them to build up their characters or to flail around trying to get the last critical sub-quest completed. The design team might need to add more secondary sub-quests to a game location or increase the experience point awards to satisfy players and keep them involved in the game.

Creating a Game Story

Coming up with a plot for a story should be easy for designers, since they are supposed to be creative. It helps to carry around a notebook or a cell phone that can store messages to jot down ideas as they come to mind. It can take time to figure out all the details of the plot, especially for a story-centered game. Since designing the story for an RPG is particularly challenging, this chapter will focus on the elements that go into building the story structure.

Figure 10.4. *The designers have to work with the art team to come up with different concepts of what characters and enemies look like, as in this sketch of an apelike creature created by an artist at Gas Powered Games.*

In addition to creating the main characters, the designers have to come up with a complete game world with different environments that are populated with NPCs and other entities. If different intelligent species inhabit the game universe, their histories and cultures have to be worked out at a high level, indicating why they act they way they do and how they interact with each other. The designers can fill in the details about these beings at a later time, but they should plan on working with the art team to come up with the final appearance and identifying unique actions for each race (Figure 10.4).

The master villain's master plan has to be worked out as well and the tasks the player must undertake to stymie the plan. The master plan sometimes involves the history of the game world, so the designers needs to come up with the most important events relevant to the story and, if necessary, tie them in to the histories of the races that have been or will be affected. Again at this point, the designers just need to work out the high-level concepts and leave the details for later. It is more important at this point to work out the master villain's plans in enough detail so that the major quests for the player can be explained coherently. The locations and NPCs involved in each quest have to be defined and placed on the game world to make sure that there are no problems or contradictions.

Finally, the designers have to come up with the important subplots that get sprinkled throughout the game world. The payoffs for each sub-quest should be defined, especially any that relate to major quests, and the locations and NPCs involved in each quest have to be identified. Inconsequential sub-quests can be added later after production begins to give more flavor to certain areas or to add more things for the player to do.

Paper Design Tools

At this point, it advantageous for the design team to create a world map on paper, showing the major locations of the quests and important sub-quests. The map does not have to be highly detailed, but it should show the environment, the races and creatures for each location. Ideally, the map should be fairly large and should be readily changeable and reproducible.

The design team should mount the map on a large cork bulletin board and perhaps hang another map in public where the whole team can refer to it. While working out the details of the storyline, it helps to use index cards or post-it notes to jot down information and then tack them to the map. By creating a visualization of the storyline, the designers can make sure that all the quests and sub-quests are spread across the entire game world. If some locations prove to be unimportant to the main storyline, they can either be dropped or set aside for sequels and add-ons.

Once the main storyline is set, a flowchart of the action can be created to incorporate into the design document and to print out and post with the maps. Since the details of the story can change once production is underway, the story flowchart and the map should be updated regularly both in the design documentation and on the bulletin board to reflect changes. The map and flowchart are useful tools for the testers to check that all the details of the story are correct and that the dialogue also refers to the correct locations and characters. If the dialogue is to be spoken by actors, it is important to get the details correct as early as possible since any mistakes will require the voice actors to come back to the recording studio for pick-up sessions. Moreover, if the game is to be released internationally, any changes to the dialogue will require the localization houses to bring in their voice actors as well for more recording sessions.

Even though a final paper version of the whole game is likely to be too detailed for a bulletin board, the design team should keep the design document updated as details are worked out. The updates can be done either in a word processing or spreadsheet program. The document can be posted on the company's intranet for reference by

RPG Checklist: Locations and Major Quests

Location: South Continent	Quests	Conditions to Meet	Major Characters	Reward
Great Mountain Pass	None			
Woodlands	None			
Plain of Sorrows	None			
Rescue the Gnome King's Son from the Lost Mine				
Great Falls (Town)	Stop the Gnome King (GK)	End the gnome invasion	Mayor	Clue #3 to final quest
Gnome King's Camp	Find GK's son	Search Lost Mine	Gnome King	Great Fire Sword
Lost Mine	Stop GK's mad brother	Kill GK's brother to rescue son	GK's son GK's mad brother	GK's son GK's son joins party
Find Champagne Crystal for Dark Elf Lord				
Downsling (Capital)	Give peace treaty to Lord	Have Dark Elf Lord sign treaty	King Estlor	Magic Lockpick
Forest of Quardor	Return crystal to Lord	Retrieve crystal from Gnome King	Dark Elf Lord	Signed Treaty
Gnome King's Camp	Find replacement for crystal	Bribe Bogie Chief for crystal	Gnome King	Champagne Crystal
Bogie Tower	Find Flame Egg	Aid or eliminate Flame Bird	Bogie King	Replacement Crystal
Fiery Aerie	Save Flame Bird	Eliminate Ice Goblins	Flame Bird Ice Gobline	Flame Egg

Table 10.1. *The locations and quests for a game can be kept on a spreadsheet as a handy reference during production and testing. Each quest includes the steps and conditions required to complete it, the major NPCs and the payoffs.*

level designers and artists. See Table 10.1 for a sample spreadsheet of a game location with details.

Using "Chapters" to Structure a Story

If the story for a game is epic in scope, as many RPG game stories are, then care must be taken to make sure that all the loose ends for plot elements and sub-quests are wrapped up and not left incomplete. Each quest and sub-quest should have clearly defined beginnings and ends, which are reflected in the dialogues with the many NPCs the player encounters. One method for structuring a large game story is to use self-contained "books" and "chapters," just like in large novels. A "book" in this case refers to a major section of the story that can involve several sub-quests (the chapters). The designers have to define the major plot element that begins the book and what the player has to do to finish it. Likewise, the sub-quests forming the chapter have to be laid out with their beginnings and endings.

Assume, for example, that the player is given the task of tracking down the Runestone of Thor by a powerful wizard who will in return deliver the first key to open the major villain's lair. This is the first book and the various objectives the player has to achieve to retrieve the key are the chapters of the book. To get the Runestone, the player has to undertake four sub-quests, and the wizard gives instructions on the location of the first sub-quest. At this first location, an NPC asks the player to kill a monster that threatens his village. When the monster is slain, the NPC gives a reward and directions to the second sub-quest, thus ending the first chapter of the book. The sub-quests continue until the player finally gains possession of the Runestone at the end of the fourth chapter. Along the way, the player learns from various NPCs that giving the Runestone to the wizard isn't such a good idea, since the wizard is *non compos mentis*. Still, to complete this sub-quest the player must bring the Runestone back to the wizard, which results in a battle with the wizard who is indeed bonkers. By defeating the wizard, the player gains the first key to the master villain's lair and a clue to where the next key is hidden. The *Wizard's Runestone Quest* book is now finished and the play proceeds to the next book.

Testing Story Cohesiveness

A book and chapter structure for a large storyline provides breakpoints that can be checked to make sure the internal logic for all the scripts is correct and that items are correctly added and removed from the player's inventory as required by the story. This approach lets the designers make a checklist for themselves of what needs to be done to complete each chapter and book. For example, are all NPCs saying the correct dialogue at the same time and then changing their responses as conditions of each sub-quest are met? Are locations correctly affected by the resolution of the sub-quests—for example, the mad wizard's tower in the mountain path gets destroyed during the battle and therefore blocking the passage between two areas for the rest of the game? Are the loose ends all tied up by the end of the book so that NPCs no longer talk about finding the Runestone and the sub-quest can't accidentally be restarted?

This structure works well for plots that are linear, meaning that plot elements from one chapter do not spill over into a new chapter. Where this structure works less well is when the story structure is more episodic and plot elements can overlap one another. For example, if the player triggers the "Find the Green Key" episode while the "Make My Witch Ally Happy," "Earn Enough Gold to Buy Sword of Entitlement from Dwarf," and "Find the Secret Passage to the Underworld" episodes are running concurrently, the dialogue choice for NPCs involved in these sub-quests can get very complex. It requires much greater effort by the design team to ensure that the episodic structure does not cause contradictions in the script logic or problems trying to acquire items or get to important places in the game world.

As an example, suppose that in the earlier example there are four keys the player must acquire to gain access to the villain's lair. If the player can go after the four keys only one at a time, the plot is linear and the chapter structure works well. If, however, the player can go after all four keys concurrently, then there can be considerable overlap of conditions the game logic must deal with. The NPCs have to be able to respond correctly to the current state of affairs and their dialogue logic must be carefully structured so they "recognize" which episodes are currently running and which ones are complete, and so respond appropriately during conversations.

It is also possible that sub-plots can carry over from one episode to another if they aren't directly connected to the main storyline—for example, a quest undertaken by a secondary member of a party. It is better to give these sub-plots their own book that is separate from the main plot. The timing for sub-plots can be important, so the designers might want to have a clock running in the background that allows these minor plots to start and end at times that won't affect the main plot. If the player doesn't help the party member within a certain amount of time, that NPC's sub-plot never starts. Likewise, if the player doesn't help complete the sub-plot in a given amount of time, the NPC simply refuses to reward the player.

Dialogue in Games

In games where a player interacts with NPCs, the dialogue for all characters is written by the designers, although professional writers are often brought in to polish the final text to make it sound more natural when spoken by voice actors. In games where there are no dialogue choices available to the player, the text is relatively easy to write because everything is linear. The player initiates a conversation, the NPC responds, then the player responds, and so on to the end of the chat. Once the initial conversation is over, the NPC then repeats some generic text until circumstances in the game world change—for example, if the player has completed a quest initiated by the NPC. After another exchange in which the player is rewarded, the NPC then repeats another text message until the state of things in the game world changes and causes the NPC's dialogue to change again. A given character can have many changes in dialogue, depending on

Figure 10.5. *In Bethesda Softworks'* Fallout 3, *the player interacts with NPCs by selecting dialogue options. Sometimes the player is offered the option to select from friendly, neutral, and hostile statements.*

how intricate the game plot is and how often major changes to the game world demand additional text.

In many games, the player is offered choices during a dialogue, in which case the process of writing the text becomes much more challenging (Figure 10.5). For example, if the player is allowed to show the character's mood during a conversation, there might be several choices for text: for example, one text that is jovial and friendly, one that is neutral and non-committal, and one that is threatening and antagonistic. Depending on the choice the player makes, the NPC can respond in kind and his or her responses can change dramatically based on the NPC's new mood toward the player. This type of dialogue is referred to as branching dialogue because each text choice allows a number of possible responses, which can grow over time like the branches of a tree. While this form of dialogue makes the NPCs feel more realistic, it can become daunting to write because the responses can spiral out of control into sheer confusion.

Scripting the Dialogue

A scripting system (or scripting language) is used to create branching dialogue and to change responses as the conditions of the world change. The system uses variables (or flags) to note the current conditions of game states, and when the states change the variables are incremented or decremented accordingly. For example, if the player is about to visit an NPC that will initiate a quest, the variable that tracks changes in the dialogue is set to zero, and as the player performs actions, the variable's value is changed according to the new game state. The logic for the change might look like this:

```
If (KING_QUEST_CHAT = 0)
    SAY ("The king bids you retrieve his
sword from the Bog of Doom.")
            SET (KING_ QUEST_CHAT_1)
Else if (KING_QUEST_CHAT = 1)
    SAY ("The king asks you if you've found his
    sword yet.")
Else if (KING_QUEST_CHAT = 2)
    SAY ("The king thanks you for retrieving
    his sword and gives you a bag of gold.")
            SET (KING_ QUEST_CHAT_3)
            TAKE_INVENTORY (KING_SWORD)
            GIVE_REWARD (1000_GOLD)
Else if (KING_QUEST_CHAT = 3)
    SAY ("The king thanks you again for
bringing back his sword.")
```

In the above example, the first text appears when the player first meets the king who initiates the quest to retrieve his sword. Because the quest in now begun, the variable is incremented by one (it could be set to any value used by the scripting system), and the king keeps asking about his sword until it is found and brought back. Once the sword is in the player's possession, the variable controlling the king's dialogue is incremented to 2 (KING_QUEST_CHAT = 2). At that point the king thanks the player for completing the quest, and the sword is removed from the character's inventory and the player's gold is increased by 1000. Since the quest is now complete, the king keeps repeating his thanks to the player until something else happens in the game world that causes the king's dialogue to change.

When the player initiates conversation with the king, the game engine checks the current value of the KING_QUEST_CHAT variable to determine the appropriate text to show on the screen. Other variables can be used to change the mood of the king's responses as well, for example, if the king gets more and more upset that the player hasn't yet found the sword yet, the logic for the variable "KING_QUEST_CHAT = 1" can have its own set of variables:

```
Else if (KING_QUEST_CHAT = 1)        AND
    (KING_PATIENCE_LEVEL = 0)
    SAY ("The king asks you nicely if you've
    found his sword yet.")
        SET (KING_PATIENCE_LEVEL = 1)
Else if (KING_QUEST_CHAT = 1)        AND
    (KING_PATIENCE_LEVEL = 1)
    SAY ("The king is impatient for you to
    return his stolen sword.")
        SET (KING_PATIENCE_LEVEL = 2)
Else if (KING_QUEST_CHAT = 1)        AND
    (KING_PATIENCE_LEVEL = 2)
    SAY ("The king sputters in rage about
    your incompetence. 'Where is my sword?'
    he roars.")
```

In this case, the king gets angrier each time the player speaks to him until the third response, which repeats pending the player bringing him the lost sword. It should be obvious that as using branching dialogue can get to be complicated because the number of variables that are used to measure the NPCs' temperaments can increase rapidly.

Reducing Dialogue Options

While branching dialogue can add considerable flavor to a game, it also makes the task of testing more difficult. It is easy to forget to modify the value of a variable, resulting in the wrong text appearing, and when the text options grow exponentially in branching dialogue, it is almost inevitable that problems will arise. Add to this problem the fact that the game might be translated into multiple languages and the task of testing the dialogue in all versions to guarantee that every character says the correct text at the appropriate time can become overwhelming.

There are several ways to reduce the clutter produced by branching. One approach is to reduce the number of dialogue choices the player can select or to use them only in the most important circumstances of the story. However, the sudden addition and reduction of text choices not only breaks the convention used for dialogue but also can confuse a player who is suddenly expected to make an important decision that has repercussions on the plotline.

Another approach is to limit the number of actual responses by NPCs to what the player says. For example, if the player always has the option to select a pleasant, a neutral, or an angry text message, the NPC might respond with the same text to the pleasant and neutral choices and respond differently only to the angry text. This reduces the number of branches from three to two, making it much easier to write. Of course, players might wonder why they were given three text options, since NPCs respond only one of two ways.

It is also possible to simply have the NPC stop responding if the player is acting abusively. Each time the player selects an angry response, a variable is incremented and after a certain threshold is reached, the NPC simply stops responding to the player, either temporarily until another dialogue is triggered or permanently until conditions in the story change. Of course, it can be important plotwise to employ angry messages to get stubborn or undecided NPCs to give up some important information. In this case, the text should be written so the player knows the NPC is slowly opening up from intimidation and not just shutting down out of contempt.

Gating

Another method for limiting branching is "gating," which forces all the dialogue decisions either to be resolved at the end of a chapter or to be tagged by a variable to continue into the next chapter. In effect, the end of the chapter is like a wall and only the correct text messages are allowed to go through the "gate" into the next chapter.

When using this approach, each branch of text messages can include a variable that identifies it as starting in a certain chapter. When the story element that concludes the chapter is finished, the text variables for the current chapter are all reset to "0" except for those that are still available in the next chapter. It then becomes easier to check all the NPCs to ensure that their text dialogues end correctly. This method can be used to change the text messages for generic NPCs when major conditions in the game world change. A nice tool the programming team should consider building for the design team is a simple text editor that allows changes in dialogue to be tracked throughout a chapter or even throughout the text in the whole game.

Flowcharting NPC Dialogue

Another tool the design team can create for themselves is a flowchart for the text responses by each NPC, especially if using a branching dialogue structure. The chart can be created either in a word processing document or spreadsheet, and the designers should settle on an appropriate format structure for NPC responses. The real text can then be plugged into the format structure so that the logic can be worked out ahead of time before trying it out in the scripting language.

Here is an example of a format structure for an NPC initiating a quest:

- *Greetings.* Personal introduction and start of the quest.

- *Waiting.* Response while quest is underway.

- *Payoff.* When player completes quest and gets reward.

- *Follow-up.* Chat after quest is over (until some event triggers new dialogue).

Many NPCs have no direct influence on the events of the game and are used as simple window dressing to make the game world feel more populated. In such cases, these NPCs are given a single line of text that is repeated throughout the game. In some cases, however, these NPCs are given multiple responses, even if the player isn't given multiple dialogue choices when first initiating contact with an NPC. These NPCs often give considerable information about the town and local environments as well as the various important characters the player will meet. Usually, a simple variable system is used to key the changing dialogue responses:

```
If (NPC1_CHAT = 0)
    SAY ("Welcome to the town of Abbadabba.
    You'll find some fine shops to the north
    of town and the famous Cave of Aladdin to
    the east.")
```

```
                SET (NPC1_CHAT_1)
Else if (NPC1_CHAT = 1)
    SAY ("It's good to see you again. I hope
    you're enjoying your visit.")
SET (NPC1_CHAT_2)
Else if (NPC1_CHAT = 2)
Else
SAY ("I've heard there's an old widow in
the forest to the north who is looking for
someone to help her find a lost brother.")
                SET (NPC1_CHAT_0)
```

Using this approach, an NPC can be given any amount of text to say to the player, and variables can be set and checked to see if the player has undertaken local sub-quests, so the NPC's responses change based on which quests have been completed. Of course, as with all dialogue in the game, the design team should keep in mind that the text will have to be translated for oversea markets, and the challenge of testing for bugs in dialogue responses grows as the game text grows.

Conclusion

Creating an interesting story that gives structure to a game is a lot of fun but is also a huge amount of work. In addition to working out details of the main plotline, the designers have to create the history of the locations in the game and the characters who inhabit them. The documentation needed to describe a large game world can take up hundreds of pages, most of which is not seen by anyone outside the team. Where a novel is completely linear with only one path from the beginning to the end of the story, a game often allows players to create their own paths through the story. Using a strictly linear story structure in a game helps cut down on the work, but can feel confining to players since they can't control where in the world to explore next. A quest/sub-quest structure allows designers to create more open-ended game worlds for players to explore while still providing specific goals for players to achieve as they work towards the climax of the story.

Likewise, the task of writing dialogue for a large game is not trivial, and requires much more careful planning than simply working out the plot, especially if the designers want to give the characters choices in their attitude towards NPCs. While using flowcharts to map out the dialogue for major character and minor NPCs might seem pedestrian, it is much better to invest the time during the design phase rather to wait for some muse to strike with the divine fire of inspiration two-thirds of the way through the development process to help resolve some plot problems. The testers will also be much happier if they have roadmaps of the plot and dialogue to check against during the long process of debugging the game.

Exercises

1. Do some research on the Internet to find three examples of games where the story was important to the progress of the game and three examples where the story was unimportant. Write up an analysis of your findings as to why the stories made some games better while other stories added little to game.

2. Draw up lists of ten novels or movies that have greatly influenced the stories in console and computer games.

    a. Create a list for each of these genres: science fiction, fantasy, and horror.

    b. Compare your lists with others and note those works you have not yet read or viewed.

    c. Read or review one such book or movie and write an essay on its effects on games.

3. Take a story structure discussed in this chapter (quest, zigzag, mission, or Hero's Journey) and write up the outline for the plot of a game.

    a. If your game project is a role-playing, real-time strategy or first-person shooter game, expand the main story you came up with so that it becomes the backbone for all game action.

    b. If your game project is a simulation or wargame, write up the historical or sociological information the player should know before beginning play.

c.   The outline should include all major locations in the game, the major characters involved, their motivations for acting, and what the player must do to complete the story.

4.   Once you have the outline from Exercise 3, create a flowchart or spreadsheet for the story/history showing the major quests/missions involved. (You don't have to include minor quests at this point.) Prepare a presentation of your story for others to critique, so you can get feedback on its cohesiveness and whether the overall story is too flimsy or too complex.

5.   Think about what players see and learn at the very start of your game project and create the opening scene or animated sequence.

a.   Create simple storyboards for the backstory or historical narrative of the game.

b.   Write up the dialogue for the characters and/or narrator.

c.   Prepare a presentation of the storyboards so you can get feedback from others to make sure the understand not only the main goals of the game but also what they need to do once they play begins.

6.   Create a short but emotionally charged dialogue between two characters where they three possible dialogue options based on their changing emotional states.

a.   Draw out the responses as branches on a dialogue tree, making sure that each response is unique. Use an "if-else if-then" structure to determine the logic for the responses.

b.   Test the dialogue by running through every variation.

7.   From Exercise 6, you probably were aware that your dialogue tree quickly grew massive and unwieldy after a number of exchanges. Now use "gating" to reduce the number of unique responses to a more reasonable number. Test the dialogue again to see that all the responses make sense.

8.   Include two versions of the story or background information for your game design document.

a. Create a short summary of the plot/history for the first section of the document, which is aimed at management and marketing.

b. Start working on a longer version where you go into more detail about the plot/history and also the environment, the characters and the important items in the game world. This longer version can appear as an appendix.

CHAPTER 11

DESIGNING PLAYFIELDS

Most commercial console and computer games are set in three-dimensional settings inside large worlds for players to explore. However, a number of games, especially those designed for less powerful platforms or as casual games, still use two dimensional playfields where figures are flat and animate against flat backgrounds almost like cartoons. Three-dimensional games are much more interesting visually, but they are also much more challenging to design and build. While most designers can quickly learn to use 2D map editors to build flat playfields, it takes additional skills and artistic talent to build 3D levels in a graphics program like Autodesk's 3ds Max or Maya or using commercial game engines like Epic Games' Unreal Engine or id Software's Tech 5.

Whether in 2D or 3D, the playfield for a game has to be appropriate for the game world and enjoyable to explore. There should be surprises for players to stumble upon as well as dangers to face. There should also be logic to the way the playfield is constructed so the players can figure out how to get through the map without getting completely lost or having to retrace their steps in search of some unobvious path to a new area. Secret paths, of course, can lead to hidden areas with extra goodies, but the main pathway through an area should always be obvious. Good map/level design can make or break a game, so designers must understand the basics of what goes into building a playfield.

For purposes of clarity, the term *map* will be used to refer to two-dimensional playfields, whether shown top-down or from the side. The term *level* will refer to three-dimensional playfields, both inside buildings and other structures as well as external environments. *Playfield* will refer to the type of map used in a game, be it 2D or 3D. These terms are often used interchangeably, but their usage is restricted in this chapter to differentiate 2D maps from 3D levels under the rubric of playfields.

2D Maps

Two-dimensional flat maps come in a number of flavors. There are games that use top-down perspective in their maps, so that it seems the player is hovering over the playfield watching the action. This perspective was used in such games as the early versions of Maxi's *SimCity* and BMG Interactive's *Grand Theft Auto*. Depending on how the art for the map is created, the map either looks totally flat or it can have a pseudo-3D look to it by using forced perspective. All objects in the game world are basically on the same level, and terrain objects form barriers that moving objects must go around.

Side-scrolling games also use flat maps, this time with the player viewing the action from one side of the setting as though watching a play or movie. These games allow a character to move left and right as well as jump up and down on levels or platforms. They have been a staple of games from Atari's *Pong* in 1975 to the latest version of Nintendo's *New Super Mario Bros. Wii* in 2009. The artwork can either be completely flat or it can contain elements made in 3D graphics programs to give a sense of depth to the playfield.

Another approach to two-dimensional maps is to show them tilted at an angle and viewed from above the ground plane. This view uses isometric projection to give a sense of pseudo-3D to the playfield and dates back in games to 1982 with the release of Gottlieb's *Q*bert* and Sega's *Zaxxon*. Sometimes the terrain features are solid, and moving objects are forced to go completely around them to get to the other side. More recent games, such as Ensemble Studios' *Age of Empires: The Age of Kings*, use transparency when moving objects go behind terrain features, so the paths are shorter and more realistic. Using isometric projection gives games a sensation of being three-dimensional but without all the extra math computation involved in showing overlapping 3D objects moving around in real space with realistic lighting effects.

2D Map Editors

To create the background for a 2D game, an artist could create a large piece of artwork that extends beyond the screen and then have the characters move around in front on it. However, the background

Figure 11.1. *In Weiring Software's Tile Studio, the tile set is at the right side of the screen, and tiles are selected and placed on the map to build 2D maps.*

might wind up being so large that the art file takes considerable time to load into memory on less powerful game platforms like some cell phones and other handheld devices. The long load time can prove annoying to players. One way to get around this problem is to break the background up into smaller tiles that can be put together to form a repeated pattern across the screen or assembled to create larger terrain features like lakes. It takes much less time to load the smaller tiles and show them on the screen. Also, if the artwork is cleverly created, the tiles can be put together in many different ways, allowing the designers to create multiple playfields that each looks unique, all the while using the same set of tiles.

Tile sets can be used to create playfields for top-down and sideways-scrolling games, and there are a number of simple 2D map editors available that can be used to create such maps. Some examples include Tile Studio (http://tilestudio.sourceforge.net/) as shown in Figure 11.1 and the map editor in Code Project (http://www .codeproject.com/KB/game/mapeditor.aspx). In most simple 2D map editors, the main screen shows an empty grid with sets of map tiles adjacent to it. The designer clicks on a tile and then on an empty grid space to place it. The process is somewhat like creating a jigsaw puzzle by placing appropriate looking tiles next to one another.

The tiles themselves can be programmed to have special attributes, for example, lava tiles that destroy anything that moves onto them or river tiles that prevent movement from one bank to the other except at bridges. The designers need to work out with both the programmers what effects are needed per tile set and the art team to decide what terrain features are available per tile set. Usually, a tile set is used to build maps of a single environment, but the editor can contain a number of different terrain sets. The designers might want to have different tile sets for such objects as trees, rocks, water, and buildings that look the same in all environments, and they can tab between the tile sets to select which objects to place on the current background.

Although 2D games take place in a flat world, it is possible to give them a pseudo-3D look by using parallax scrolling. This technique was first used in games in 1982 in Irem's arcade game *Moon Patrol*, and it involves having multiple flat, overlapping pieces of art move across the screen at different speeds. Objects in the distance, such as far-off mountains and the sky, move very slowly horizontally or vertically while the next art layer moves a bit faster and the next layer move even faster until one reaches the main art layer where characters move around and interact with one another at normal speed. It is also possible to have additional art layers appear above the main action level, for example to show clouds floating by above the playfield or characters walking behind trees. Each layer of art has areas of transparency that allow lower layers to show through. The whole effect is almost 3D and gives a sense of perspective to the artwork.

Another useful feature for 2D map editors is an invisible overlay grid that fits over the map and is used to place objects on the playfield and to define paths of movement. This invisible overlay can also be used with a scripting system for defining simple AI routines, such as patrol routes for units, areas affected by off-screen artillery barrages, locations where moving platforms travel to, and so on. The designers should work closely with the programmers developing the map editor tool to make sure that all features they need are included, that the tool is simple enough for everyone to use, and that it is thoroughly debugged.

3D Levels

While 2D maps are relatively easy to build once designers have mastered the map editor, 3D levels are something else entirely. Because so many games are produced in 3D, a new discipline has arisen to deal specifically with building the game environments—the level designer. Sometimes this title refers to a person who is trained in using complex 3D graphics programs specifically to model and texture the environments (for example, Autodesk's 3ds Max and *ia*Maya) and sometimes it refers to someone who designs interesting levels in conjunction with 3D artists who create the graphics and programmers who script the action. In either case, the person needs to understand not only how to visualize game worlds in three dimensions but also what makes games fun to play.

Unlike 2D games which use paint programs to create tile sets and animating character, the environments and characters in 3D games are created using mesh models on which 2D textures are overlaid. Characters and objects that move around in the world have their motions worked out and recorded for use in the game. Then the locations for the models are positioned in the 3D environment, and the models are lighted and cameras positioned to track the movement of objects through the environment. Building the models and environments requires many more software applications and specially programmed tools to make everything look and move correctly in a much more photorealistic game world (Figure 11.2). It

Figure 11.2. *In Bethesda Softworks' Fallout New Vegas, the world is depicted in a photorealistic style that makes everything look three-dimensional.*

takes considerable training for artists to become proficient in the 3D graphics programs used to create the meshes and then apply textures to them so they don't tear.

The process for creating 3D games is comparable to filming movies while creating 2D games is rather like creating cartoons. However, where actors portray the characters in a movie and move and act as the script requires them, in games the player controls the actions of the main character (or racing car or professional athlete or some other object) while the AI code module controls the actions of all other beings and objects in the game environment. These AI-controlled entities have to find their way through the 3D world, avoiding such things bumping into buildings and having to deal with unexpected piles of rubbish caused by explosions. If combat is involved, they also have to know when to detect players, fire weapons and chase after them should they try to escape.

3D Level Tools

When creating a 3D level, the team responsible for building it discusses what game events happen in it and what terrain, entities, and items they need to make. One or more artists work on the environment model, whether inside or outside, while other artists create the models for entities and items appearing in the environment. Once the basic mesh models are finished, the texture artists create the "skins" that are mapped onto the models. Moving entities are animated by creating skeletons inside the models (called rigging), moving the skeletons and recording the results, and then checking that the skeleton joints move smoothly and that textures don't tear. The various elements are then assembled in the graphic renderer to see how they look inside the game, and changes are made as necessary to the models, the animations, or the textures. Special lighting effects like moving shadows and ambient occlusion (how light reflecting off an object affects the brightness and color of other nearby objects) can then be added and the correct camera positions worked out fro how the player will view the environment and character.

One approach to creating a level is to have the artists create everything from scratch, basically starting out with a standard geometric shape like a cube or cone and deforming the mesh until the model winds up looking like the desired object or entity. The final art model, after it is textured and animated, is then put into the scene and rendered to the screen. This process assumes that the

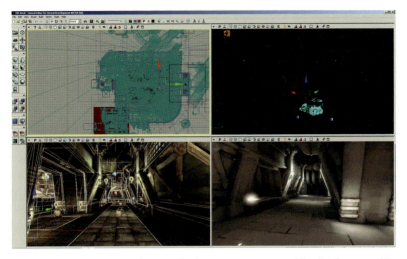

Figure 11.3. *Epic Game's Unreal Editor is a commercial level editor used by many companies to build 3D levels.*

development team wants to create all the artwork from scratch to use in a proprietary game engine.

There is, however, another approach to creating levels and that is to import original artwork into such a commercial game engine. These engines are licensed from company that created them, although it can be expensive to license such an engine. Epic Games' Unreal Engine, for example, is a complete game engine that developers can lease, and it comes with a suite of tools that are used to animate 3D models, create cut-scene animations, write scripts to define entity actions, handle the audio requirements, and much more (Figure 11.3). It does not include a 3D graphics program to build the models, however, so artists have to use *3ds Max, Maya* or another program to build the original models to import into the Unreal Engine.

A game developer leases a commercial game engine to save time and money so it can concentrate primarily on content rather than technology. One problem with these engines, however, is that the programming team sometimes has to spend time modifying the code to make entities behave the way the design requires. Another problem is that the game developer might have to pay royalties as well as leasing fees to the engine's owner. However, since it can taken years for a company to build a 3D game engine from scratch, leasing a commercial engine can prove more economical and time effective.

A third approach is to use the artwork that appears in a game to create more levels for the game, using the same art and development tools that the game publisher makes available. It is even possible to create new artwork and important it into existing games. This approach is known as modding, and it gives amateurs the opportunity to create new levels to show off their design skills. A number of popular games have such construction sets available. The interest in modding blossomed with id Software's *Doom* in 1993 and continues today with such games as Bethesda Softworks' The Elder Scrolls Construction Set for *The Elder Scrolls IV: Oblivion* and Valve's Hammer Editor for *Half-Life 2*. The tools provide enough flexibility to allow gamers to modify some of the code and artwork to make unique looking mods. However, the mods created with these tools cannot be sold commercially, although they can be made available online for free download.

Designing Playfields

One way to approach the design of a map or level is to think of it as having a story to tell. There is a beginning (the point where the player first appears on the playfield), a middle (the events that transpire as the player explores the playfield), and an end (where the player leaves). The path through the playfield can be linear, meaning there is only one direction forward, or branched, meaning there are different paths leading to different areas that may or may not overlap one another. A linear playfield is much easier to design since there are no overlapping pathways, and in a 3D world, the path can go up and down and diagonally as well as vertically and horizontally. The terrain features can change as the player progresses through the playfield, too.

For example, suppose the player starts a level at the mouth of a cave. The area around the cave mouth is one area of exploration, but the only path forward is into the cave. If the designer wants the pathway to be linear, the cave would be like one long tube, twisting and turning up and down and possibly having short side branches to explore as well. The cave might end up connected to the sub-basement of a large building, which the player can then explore floor by floor to the exit door that leads to the next level. Even though there are side branches in the tunnel and multiple rooms in the building to explore, the pathway from start to finish is linear. To make these levels branched, the designer could design the cave with multiple passages that lead to different exits at different levels inside the cave. Likewise, the building could have a number of different exits that lead out to different buildings that are all connected by staircases and elevators.

Depending on how powerful the game platform is, there might be opportunities for offering breathtaking panoramas at certain points so the player gets a fuller sense of what the whole game world looks like. If the game platform has limited graphics capabilities, for example, as with handheld platforms and some cell phones, such panoramas might not be possible because they would slow down the frame rate too much. It helps to have the artists and programmers review a 3D level design so they can give advice about what concepts work and what ones need to be revised.

Multiple Pathways

A playfield can also contain multiple pathways that open up at different times in the game. For example, there might be locked doors players can't open until they find a key somewhere else in the game. Once unlocked, the door leads to a new pathway through the same area they have already explored. In this case, however, the designer would want to make the new pathway challenging, perhaps by introducing new enemies or other obstacles the player must overcome to advance. One advantage of this approach is that it lets the level designers create new places for the player to explore without necessarily having to increase the total amount of environment art requirements.

The designer can also give the player a tantalizing clue about the new area, perhaps showing a new weapon or quest object on the other side of an unbreakable window or on the ledge of a floor the player simply can't reach. In this case, it's a good idea to let the player know that this area can eventually be reached—for example, an overhead light that illuminates a door into the room or a flapping window shade drawing the player's attention to the jutting ledge where the quest item is found.

When building multiple pathways, it is important to keep things fresh for the player. If the pathways are all available at the same time, then the obstacles along the paths can all be of the same difficulty. If the pathways open at different times, then the later ones should contain more demanding obstacles than the earlier ones so players continually find new things during exploration of the game world. If there are restrictions that can't be overcome—for example, the maximum amount of data about enemies that can to be loaded into memory at one time—it is up to the designers to figure out how to the make the new areas interesting while using existing game objects. Some ideas might be to include ambushes in the new area where enemies suddenly appear on all sides, an environment change such as an ice cave suddenly melting because of a volcanic eruption, or making progress through the new pathway be dependent on solving puzzles instead of fighting monsters.

Placing Objects in Playfields

As important as figuring out the layout of the playfield is the task of determining where items and encounters will be placed. Obviously, these game objects cannot be placed on or behind impassable terrain or players will never get to them. Putting a treasure chest on a small offshore island that can never be reached, for example, is cruel because players will try every method to get to the isle. In such a case, it feels as though the designer is thumbing his nose at the players. Placing game objects in difficult to reach locations is different matter, though. As long as players can get to the location sometime during the game, they will be satisfied. Putting objects where they can be seen but not yet reached is a good way to make players thoroughly explore the playfield.

Object placement on the playfield can also act like a trail of bread crumbs, luring players along the desired pathway. If players see some NPC or item in the near distance, they will try to get to them. If another object then appears beyond that point, players will continue on as long as new game objects are available. This process can continue until the players arrive at a location that kicks off the next part of the story.

Whether items reappear after they have first been gathered depends not only on how often players are expected to backtrack over a visited area but also on how often the player needs to get supplies. In many games, the player acquires items and armament by visiting towns and spending cash to buy things in stores. If players get only a little cash each time they defeat an enemy, they might be forced to "grind" for a while—that is, repeatedly going to areas to fight low-level enemies to get the money and/or experience they need to improve their characters. MMORPGs are particularly noted for forcing players to spend a lot of time grinding to get the cash or experience points to improve their characters.

If players go through certain supplies quickly—for example, health potions—it can help tremendously for them to find health items or healing stations on the playfield that they can either take with them or use to refresh themselves. For example, in a desert environment, there can be chests containing healing potions, water holes where characters can heal, and oases where they can rest for the night and completely heal. Likewise, ammo refills are often sprinkled around levels in action games where players use projectile weapons frequently. During the testing process, designers should listen to the complaints of the playtesters about the availability of items in the game and provide enough materials so that even slow and clumsy players are well provisioned at all times.

Scripting Languages and Playfield Design

Game worlds are often populated with NPCs who are willing to talk with players. Sometimes the NPCs start chatting as soon as a player draws close and sometimes the player has to activate a character to start the conversation. As discussed in the previous chapter, the changing text for NPCs is handled through a scripting language. Item placement can also be handled by scripting. For example, while an item exists on the playfield, it can have a variable set at "1," and then when the player gets the object, the variable is set to "0" or "2." When the player exits the map or level, the variable value is then changed. If the item can reappear again the next time the player enters the playfield, then the variable of "0" is reset to "1." If, however, the item can only be gathered once, its variable value of "2" remains, and so the item does not reappear.

It is possible to set variable values to change the identity of items found by the player as well. If an item's presence is indicated by a generic symbol of some kind—for example, a large red "?"—its actual identity can be determined randomly when it is gathered. A Treasure Table can be created per playfield with all possible items that can be collected on it, and the outcomes can be weighted so that some items are available more often than others. The same idea applies for items that are found inside other objects—chests, barrels, crates, and so on.

One thing designers should keep in mind is what happens to items if the player discards them. The easiest answer is to have them disappear entirely—that is, use 'em or lose 'em. This approach could be problematic if the player tries to discard a quest item, but then a variable could be set to prevent the player from actually discarding it. Another possibility is to have the item be universal so that if it is dropped anywhere in the game, it remains at that location until the player picks it up again. Using this approach, the scripting language has to be structured to allow variables for items to be "local" (meaning they apply only while the player is on the playfield and then get reset when the player leaves) or "global" (meaning their values apply all the time and change only when the designers want them to be different). Thus, if the designer wants an item to remain on a playfield where it is dropped, a global variable can be used to indicate the item has been dropped and save the coordinates for where it was dropped on the playfield to the current Save Game file. If the designers want the item to disappear when the player exits the playfield, the variable can be local, and the position of the item will then not be added to the Save Game file.

Enemy Encounters

While some games such as "dungeon crawls" and other RPGs include random combat encounters, most action games have set-piece encounters where the player meets an NPC or creature that is important to the storyline. The random encounters allow players to accumulate some cash, experience and low-level items, but the important encounters are all scripted and occur when the player enters the enemy's space or an adjacent space. In some cases, the designer might want to allow the player to engage in combat repeatedly with an enemy but to receive a vital item or weapon only once. For example, the player has to enter a nest of spiders to retrieve a golden chalice, but the chalice can only be found once while the spiders remain in the nest at all times. After the initial combat is won, the variable determining the enemy's treasure is changed, and the new value can indicate that some random item from the area's Treasure Table becomes the enemy's loot (see below). Also, the amount of cash and experience points rewarded to the player can be adjusted using the same variable.

In wargames and RTS games, the enemies behave differently because they actively scout the player's forces and then engage them in combat. Because enemies are controlled by the game engine, their actions are determined by the game's artificial intelligence. The designer can sometimes create the AI routines using a scripting language if they are simple enough, but any complex behavior should be handled by the AI code because it is normally much faster than the scripting language. The AI might have to continually figure out what paths the enemies are to use when approaching the player as well as determining where and how best to attack. In this case, the design team should work closely with the AI programmers to describe the behavior they want the enemy to exhibit. Having a simple interactive model of the game allows the designers to test out the AI behavior and to suggest modifications to the programmers.

Point-of-View in Playfield Design

In addition to figuring out how the playfield will be laid out, the design team must consider what point of view works best for the game. A first person point-of-view looks at the playfield directly ahead through a character's eyes and limits the amount of information the player receives about events happening to the sides and behind. This viewpoint is excellent in games that try to keep the player in a state of suspense, for example, in FPS games and some recent RPGs like Bethesda Softworks' *The Elder Scrolls III/IV: Morrowind/Oblivion* and *Fallout 3*. It is easy to set up ambushes where the player passes a certain point on the level, unleashing a horde of monsters from hidden areas.

A similar sensation of claustrophobia and dread can be created for third-person shooter games that keep the camera view just over the shoulder of a character. Capcom's *Resident Evil 4* and *5* use such a viewpoint. The player has a slightly more open view of the surroundings and can see events ahead in a bit more detail, but the view is still restricted, allowing for ambushes and other surprises. Occasionally, the these games include action sequences that pull the camera back to show more of the playfield, when it was important that the player see what lay ahead while moving and/or shooting.

Most third-person action games tend to pull the camera back even more, allowing the player to see a good deal of the playfield. The ability to see more of the terrain as well as oncoming enemies is important in platform games where players have to judge distances when trying to leap from one terrain feature to another. The game can actually include several camera angles, for example, first-person (through the eyes of the character) and third-person (from a distance), allowing the player to select whichever mode is best for the moment. *Fallout 3*, for example, can be played in either viewpoint. Many simulation games use a similar mixture of viewpoints, for example, in racing games that let the player view the action from inside the car as the driver or outside from behind as an observer.

Some games work best with a third-person view where the camera is far above the playfield. Real-time strategy games are played on large maps where the combat units are small but still easy to recognize by type. It is important in these games for the player to be able to see the whole battlefield at a glance to know where to send reinforcements or to attack an enemy's weak point. But there is a limitation to the view in such games. The field for a major battle might be far too large to show on one screen, and therefore the player has to scroll around the map to see everything, as in Firaxis' *Sid Meier's Civilization* games. Including a strategic map in these games helps the player grasp the scope of the playfield but doesn't necessarily reveal in detail what friendly and enemy units are in the area or what terrain features are available for cover. Games with really large playfields are best served if they are turn-based rather than real-time, so that players can review what is happening and what needs to be done without worrying about enemy actions while they are pondering what to do next.

The size and viewpoint of the playfield are important features to keep in kind when approaching the initial design of a game. Depending on where the camera is placed and what it can see, the game can feel intimate and restricted in scope (with a first-person viewpoint) or detached and large in scope (with an overhead third-person view). The designers might ask the programmers to create different camera views early in the technical review phase to check out their assumptions of how the game will look on screen. They can then make whatever design changes that might be needed depending on the desired viewpoint.

Visualizing the Playfield

The design team can help the environment artists by including a thorough description of game locations in the design documentation. The description for each major location should include ideas on the plants and wildlife for outdoor locations or the buildings, parks, playgrounds, and other urban highlights for town and city locations. Any major enemy or NPC encounters should be listed as well as any important items that can be picked up while exploring the location.

It is particularly helpful for the art team to have the documents include a visual collage of the designers' ideas for what the locations

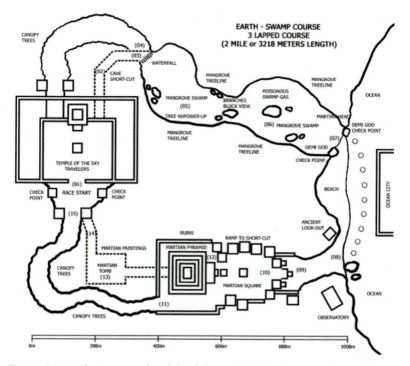

Figure 11.4. *This is an overhead sketch by artist Ed Williamson of a track in an unpublished racing game that the author helped design. It shows the major features to be found on and around the track. The storyboard (Figure 1.3 on page 13) visualizes the entrance to the Martian Square, marked 10 on the map sketch.*

might look like. While it is easy to find photos and pictures of real-world locations on the Internet, coming up with visuals for fantasy and science fiction locations is a bit more challenging. There are many websites that showcase the imaginative works of artists and these can be mined for images that match what the designers have in mind for the overall look of different locations. It is very helpful to keep a list of websites where the art came from so the art team can check the originals and perhaps find other examples that work just as well. While these images can be circulated internally as references for the artists, they should never be made available to the public without getting permission from the original artists because of copyright issues.

The design team should discuss their ideas with the art team but let the artists come up with their own ideas on the environments (Figure 11.4). Everyone on the development team should want the art to look original and unlike anything others have created (unless, for example, the desire is to have a level that specifically looks like it's straight out of Hieronymous Bosch). The art team should be encouraged to come up with a number of visual ideas that can be discussed with the design team and management in order to select the right visual style for the locations in the game. Of course, this same approach should be taken for all art in the game including locations, characters, enemies, NPCs, and items.

Problems in Playfield Design

There are a number of problems that arise during the playfield design process that should be avoided. First, it can be frustrating for the player if movement through the playfield is too restrictive. There are times, of course, when a pathway has to be restrictive, either because of game engine considerations (for example, not having too many models appearing simultaneously on the screen that slows down the game) or because the player's suspension of disbelief will be shattered. Players will explore the playfield thoroughly and try to find other possible routes through a level or map, so having only a single path can be a letdown.

Likewise, making a playfield too expansive can cause problems. If the current location is a vast African savannah and there are no landmarks available for determining position, the player can wander around aimlessly for a long time or go around in circles before accidentally finding the exit point to the map or level. If a lone NPC with an important quest stands around on the savannah, the player can spend unnecessary time trying to locate the person (especially if NPCs in the game have AI routines that cause them to wander around).

Another problem is expecting the player to get around a level by performing difficult maneuvers the game engine doesn't easily support. Some examples include creating 2D platform games where the player has to be at the very last pixel before jumping to the next platform or else must blindly jump off a high platform in a leap of faith that there will be some unseen terrain feature to keep the character from plunging to his death. In 3D games, the designer might want the player to jump around from pillar to post across a lava landscape, which can be very difficult if the camera automatically jerks up automatically when the player moves forward. While such design decisions make the game more difficult, they don't necessarily make it more fun.

A minor problem is to have anachronistic elements in the playfield that are out of place in the overall game world. It could be a bad mixture of architecture styles, for example, placing Greek temples on an alien world, or it could be inadvertent usage of objects from different time periods, for example, having ancient Egyptian hieroglyphs decorate medieval cathedrals. If players notice such inaccuracies, they can be yanked out of their immersion in the game.

Trying to be too atmospheric can lead to other problems, especially in games with 3D levels. A level can be so dark it is impossible to see anything more than a few feet away, or it can be lit dramatically but in such a way that important items blend into the scenery. Players should be able to change the overall lighting value in the game to make things brighter or dimmer as they choose. Mood is important in level design but the level shouldn't get so dark and gloomy the player can't find a pathway around the terrain.

A final problem that should be addressed early in the design process is how games will be saved. Most computer games allow players to save their position at any time and also easily reload a saved game. Today's video games are often stuck with the old concept of using Save Points, which are the only places on playfields where games can be saved and occasionally reloaded. When consoles had memory restrictions, there was a reason to limit the ability to save and load games, but nowadays with most consoles having a hard drive, the Save Points are almost archaic. If the design team still wants to use Save Points, their locations should be determined early so testers can let the designers know if there are enough points in the game. It is a poor design that sets the last Save Point at a location where the players has to continue playing for more than five minutes before reaching the final confrontation with the main villain. While such a tactic makes a game more difficult, it also makes players extremely frustrated if they have to replay the end sequence repeatedly before beating the villain.

Planning Before Building

It helps tremendously to think out a map or level before committing art, programming, and design resources to build it. Creating a model of the playfield on paper helps a designer figure out where to place encounters and items for the player to find. It is possible to play out the whole game on paper before any other teams are asked to work on the assets, and problems can become manifest and resolved early in development. Having a paper prototype of the whole game is also incredibly useful for testing to make sure that every portion of the map or level is checked out for possible bugs and problems and to help testers speed through a long game by highlighting important items and encounters.

2D Map Prototypes

When creating the paper prototype for a 2D map, the designers can initially draw out their design concepts on plain paper and then switch to graph paper for the last iteration once all the problems have been worked out. They can work out the pathways through the level on the plain paper version and where items and encounters are to be placed, and then they can use the graph paper to ensure that the scale is correct. Of course, once the designers create the real map, they might find that changes have to be made because items are hidden by terrain features or pathways become impossible to find. It is a good idea to either scan the final graph version of the map into a computer or use a graphics program to translate the paper version into an electronic one. The final maps can be collected in the appendix of the design document for reference by team members, testers, and whoever is hired to create the sequel and add-ons.

3D Level Prototypes

While creating a paper prototype for 2D map is relatively easy, creating one for a 3D level is more challenging since parts of levels can overlap one another. It is still useful to draw out the original concepts for the level on plain paper so game play can be tested. Creating a realistic version of a level on graph paper is challenging because the extra dimension of height is more difficult to map out. It is possible to create multiple overlays with each overlay being a set distance (say, 20 feet) higher or lower than the next. Connection points between entrances and exits on each overlay should be duly noted. Using graph paper forces designers to use a standard measure of distance per grid square, so any distortions can be detected early on. It is useful to transfer the graph paper layouts to transparencies so they can be stacked atop one another to check for inconsistencies and gaps. Once the models are created in a 3D graphic program, the level designer should create screen shots of the level from multiple projections to help during testing. Adding all this information to the design documentation can make for a very heavy tome, so the designers and testers should work together to figure out what depictions of the level are most useful and revealing.

Another point to consider when building 3D levels is what spatial requirements are needed by the AI-controlled entities. The AI module has to figure out paths through the level, and the entities have to move naturally in the environments. Having too complex a structure can cause slowdowns as the AI module goes through repeated iterations trying to find the best routes to travel. Likewise, designers should pay attention to how entities move in the 3D environments. For example, if a creature has a long tail, it needs lots of space to be able to pivot around correctly so that parts of its tail don't go through walls. Of course, narrow pathways can provide players some hiding places that large creatures can't enter, but it is important to work out with the art and programming staff how AI-controlled entities will move and behave inside each level.

Conclusion

Coming up with interesting game playfields is part art and part science. It is difficult to come up with totally original ideas for playfields since games have been set everywhere in the known and unknown universe. Still, while locations might seem be familiar to players, the way they look and their layouts can all be original. If the game has a well-developed storyline, the ideas for locations and what encounters and items are to be found in them should arise naturally from the documentation and visual suggestions provided by the designers.

The actual process for building the playfields is more rigorous and uses map and level editors, 3D graphics programs, scripting languages, and specialized tools created by the tool programmers. Learning to use such tools is daunting to anyone first getting into design, but they are so important to the craft of building games that learning them is almost a prerequisite for getting a design job. Map and level editors are available for many commercial games, and anyone seriously interested in getting into the industry should learn how they work. However, simply understanding how to use the tools will not make a good designer. Knowing how to build interesting playfields that advance the story and are fun to explore is equally as important. The craft of building levels requires both skill and art.

Exercises

1. Search the Internet for five 2D map editors and compare the features each one offers.

   a. Download at least two editors that can be used or tested for free and try them out by creating some simple 2D levels.

   b. Write up an analysis about their ease of use, what major features they include, and what other features from other map editors that could be incorporated to improve them.

2. Design three 2D maps on paper and build them using one of the map editors you downloaded.

   a. The levels you design should use whatever tile sets that come with the map editor.

   b. The layout for one map can be relatively simple and stand alone, but the other two maps should be more elaborate and connect with one another.

3. Search the Internet for four 3D level editors and analyze their strengths and shortcomings.

   a. Compare the features set for each level editor:

      i. Does it allow artists to build the game environment inside the program, or do they have to import the artwork from a different graphics program such as Autodesk's 3ds Max or Maya?

      ii. Does it include a built-in scripting language, or will a programming team need to create one.

      iii. What additional features (AI, physics, 3D sound placement, etc.) are provided for programmers, artists, and audio engineers?

      iv. Estimate the difficulty you would face in learning how to use each level editor as a professional game designer.

   b. Select the level editor you think is most useful and write up a summary in which you defend your reasons for selecting it.

4. Create a multi-story 3D level for a first-person shooter game in paper prototype.

   a. The level does not have to be very large but it should contain at least three connected areas at different elevations.

   b. Depending on your art skills, either create the level on graph paper, showing the different heights on several sheets, or build a 3D model from paper or cardboard.

   c. Indicate throughout the level where encounters occur and where items and puzzles are located.

   d. Have others test the level to provide feedback on its overall design and play value.

5. Create two different versions of a large 3D level for a first-person shooter game. You can design the levels on graph paper or build 3D models of them.

   a. Each versions should have at least two pathways through it.

      i. The first version should have all pathways open and available when the player first enters the level.

      ii. The second version should have one pathway available at the start with the second pathway opening later in the game.

   b. Populate the level with enemy entities you created from the exercises in chapter 6 and use your Combat Table from chapter 5 to test the level.

6. Using one map you created in Exercise 3 or Exercise 5, set up at least five encounters (NPC, combat, puzzle, etc.) on the map or level.

   a. Have at least two encounters be linked: that is, as the player satisfies the conditions for resolving one encounter, the conditional variables for the second encounter get altered and vice versa.

   b. Work out the logic using "if-else if-then" statements for each encounter.

7. Assume you are working on a science fiction, fantasy or horror role-playing game and have been assigned the task of creating one 3D level.

   a. Design the layout for the level in paper prototype (as in Exercise 4). The environment of the level should change at least three times throughout the level.

   b. Once you have the prototype done, search the Internet for visuals that match your concept for each location. You should gather visuals for the architecture, environs, items and entities at each different area on the map.

   c. Create a document containing the visuals and describe how they relate to your mental picture of what the level looks and plays like.

8. Create at least 3 maps or levels for the game you are designing using graph paper or graphics software.

   a. Include a terrain key for each map/level.

   b. Indicate per map or level where all the items, encounters, entities, quests, puzzles, resources and so are placed.

   c. Write up an outline indicating what transpires as the player moves through each map or level.

CHAPTER 12

INTERFACE DESIGN

The user interface is the link between the player and the game. The interface includes the game controls, the different screens and menus that appear both inside the game and out, and the feedback received during play. A well-designed interface is seamless and intuitive, and allows the player to become fully immersed in the game world in just a few minutes. If a game doesn't have a good, intuitive interface design, players might soon hate how sluggish the controls feel or complain about the clutter of icons on the screen.

Spending the time to come up with a workable interface design might be considered time that could be better spent on level design and fleshing out the story, but that is a mistake. Beginning designers are primarily concerned with what information appears on each game screen and are less concerned about the game controls and feedback. Experienced designers are just as concerned with how the controls feel and what feedback the player receives throughout the game as with what the player sees while playing. It is well worth the designers' time to work out the details of the user interface early on with the programmers and then spend more time with the interface artist making sure that information the players need is always only a click or two away. A really good user interface is transparent. A really bad user interface is always irritating.

Graphical User Interface

The visuals the player sees on the screen during a game are referred to as the *graphical user interface* (GUI). Every screen that appears, from when the player first inserts a DVD/CD to install the game to when the player finally quits, is part of the graphical user interface and should work together as a visual whole. It is important for designers to include as complete a list as possible of the screens, pop-up windows, menus, and other visuals in the game in the design documentation and to update the information as the final assets are completed. All this materials can be gathered in an appendix for reference, but the functionality of each screen should be described in detail in the document itself.

There are two groups of screens in games: the first are the *in-game screens* that are used during the course of play and the second are the *shell screens* that are used outside the game. Some screens are accessible both in-game as well as outside. For example, a pause screen is a shell screen but it can be brought up during play, and active options such as computer hot-keys allow players access to other shell screens during play to save their game, check their score, change audio levels, and so on.

In-Game Interface Screens

The in-game screens include the main playfield, the inventory, the combat screen (if different from the main playfield), and any windows or menus with lists of items, spells, weapons, character statistics, and other relevant data. The information on these screens might be *static*, meaning that the player doesn't directly act with the data, or *active*, meaning the player can select some options or move things around. For example, a screen showing the player's current character attribute values is static, but one that allows the player to assign points to these values is active.

These in-game screens are viewed continuously during play and the information presented on them should be obvious to players at a glance. If players have to search for information on the screen or bring up an extra menu or window in the midst of on-going events, they might gets distracted from the action and lose the game. If the events are less frenetic, such as selling or buying items, the screens and menus can include more information since players have time to consider their options. Imagine engaging in fierce combat with multiple creatures in an action RPG and suddenly having to deal with a peddler popping in to sell his wares. Sometimes for simpler games, different areas in the game world can be shown together on one primary interface screen, such as in TikGames' simulation game *Cinema Tycoon 2: Movie Mania* (Figure 12.1).

The amount of information appearing on any interface screen and how much the player interacts with it should be based on where the screen appears during play and what functionality it serves. The main playfield screen should include the most important functions

Figure 12.1. *In TikGames'* Cinema Tycoon 2: Movie Mania, *several areas of the game world are shown on one interface screen, which reduces the amount of time the player spends moving between areas.*

used while playing—for example, movement, character information like health and mana, resource availability, strategic map, and so on. Other information that needed occasionally can be assigned to secondary screens, for example, inventory, spell lists, journals, character attributes, experience points, etc. These screens can appear during play when the player wishes, for example, during combat, but the player should decide when they appear.

Shell Interface Screens

The shell screens are not used to play the game. They include the installation screens, the main title screen, the game options screens, the pause screen, top scores screen, and the end of game screens. All these screens have important information about the game, but they aren't directly used when the action begins. Players can sometimes halt the game action to bring up these screens to save their current position or load a saved game or change the settings for the game, but these changes don't directly involve how the players interact with

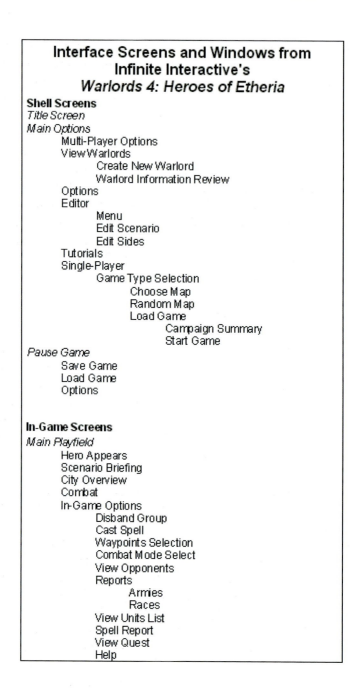

**Interface Screens and Windows from
Infinite Interactive's
*Warlords 4: Heroes of Etheria***

Shell Screens
Title Screen
Main Options
    Multi-Player Options
    View Warlords
        Create New Warlord
        Warlord Information Review
    Options
    Editor
        Menu
        Edit Scenario
        Edit Sides
    Tutorials
    Single-Player
        Game Type Selection
            Choose Map
            Random Map
            Load Game
                Campaign Summary
                Start Game
Pause Game
    Save Game
    Load Game
    Options

In-Game Screens
Main Playfield
    Hero Appears
    Scenario Briefing
    City Overview
    Combat
    In-Game Options
        Disband Group
        Cast Spell
        Waypoints Selection
        Combat Mode Select
        View Opponents
        Reports
            Armies
            Races
        View Units List
        Spell Report
        View Quest
        Help

Figure 12.2. *This is a list of all the interface screens, both in-game and in the shell, appearing in Infinite Interactive's* Warlords 4: Heroes of Etheria.

the game play. Some shell interface screens provide multiple options to the player—for example, an options screen that lets the player set the difficulty level, remap the game controls, change the audio levels, and start/save/load a game. The visual style for all these shell screens should share a common visual theme with the artwork for the in-game screens.

The number of screens in a game can get to be overwhelming. As a game gets more complex, the number of interface screens rises. In such a case, players ideally get introduced to the different in-game screens in an extended tutorial so they can absorb the information over time rather than having it all dumped on them right at the start. See a list of all the screens appearing in the Infinite Interactive's *Warlords 4: Heroes of Etheria* game in Figure 12.2 for an idea of how complex the graphical user interface can get.

Designing the GUI

The design team is responsible for defining the functionality of each game screen, indicating all the information that is to appear on the screen and whether it is static or active. The design team works with the interface artist and programmer during the development phase to nail down the actual layout for each interface screen and where the interactive areas are to be located. Extensive testing by new players is needed to ensure that the final layout of the in-game screens is easy for most players to understand and use.

Many game genres have a fairly well-defined graphical interface system. For example, the main playfield screens for all FPS and car racing games tend to look the same, because the play for all games in these genres is very much the same. Designing the main playfield screen for such games is relatively simple and straightforward. For other type of games, such as puzzle and simulation games, the interface screens have to be unique since the game play is so different, and it can take time to get all the elements placed on the screen in the correct locations where they are easiest for the player to understand and access. Other games, such as role-playing and real-time strategy games, are often play similarly to existing games in their genre, but they can require more effort to get all the elements correctly placed on the screen. It makes a big difference in an RPG, for example, if the player controls a party or a single character because the information for the party members can take up more screen space than for the lone character.

Screen Locations for Information

Deciding where to put the most important information on a screen can be time-consuming not only because what the designers initially consider important data might prove be marginal for players during play but also because the size of the data is either too large or too small. If the data displays cover too large an area of the screen, players might have difficulty seeing what is happening on the playfield. There are graphic tricks that can be used to improve how the data appears, such as making the artwork for the data displays transparent (Figure 12.3) or only appear when the data changes, but these tricks can be problematic. For example, if the designers of a shooter game decide that the data for weapon, ammunition, health, and shielding appear only when the values change and otherwise fade away to reveal more of the playfield, players might not be able to retrieve this information easily and so not notice when their health level is very low. They will resent the cleverness of the fading data displays that can be fatal. The players would be better served if the important data were transparent to begin with so that playfield could be seen behind the numbers and then faded somewhat but still dimly visible, brightening only when the data changed.

Figure 12.3. *The graphical user interface for CCP Game's Eve Online is organized to show considerable game information to the player. However, the displays are transparent, so the player can look at the model of the spaceship while reading the text.*

Another major decision is where to put the interactive areas on the screen. Interactive areas include such things as pictures of party members that bring up that character's attributes when selected, items on the playfield that can be picked up manually, or icons along the screen edge that can be selected to bring up various game options. The player might have no idea initially what areas are interactive, so it is helpful to point them out either in a tutorial or by changing the brightness or shape of the cursor when it moves over an interactive area or even having interactive objects in the playfield become highlighted when a character draws near. For example, the cursor in a computer game that is normally an arrow might change into a hand when there is something on the playfield to interact with, and the object itself could be outlined in different colors to indicate if it is useful or damaging.

The amount of information that has to be shown on any screen should be limited so that the player is not overwhelmed or confused when the screen first appears. Many games try to jam too much information on a screen, either resulting in very small labels that are difficult to read or flooding the screen with text and numbers that are difficult to grasp at a glance. Early computer and video games suffered these problems when the screen resolutions were small—for example, the VGA standard in the 1980s for computers that allowed a resolution of 320 × 200 pixels in 256 colors or the pre-HD televisions with their loss of scan data near the edges that forced video games to include buffers on all sides, thereby reducing the area on screen where interface information could be shown. While HD television and high-resolution video cards have removed the limitations for showing data on a screen, the underlying principle that too much information can be overwhelming should not be ignored. Screen information the player needs during the game should be kept to a minimum, especially in action games, and more descriptions and details can be assigned to secondary screens that the player can read over in leisure.

Information Presentation

The designers have to decide how best to present the information on each screen. Should they use icons and images or buttons with words? Should character attributes like health and mana levels be represented by numbers or by icons like thermometers? The advantage of primarily using icons is that they can be used for an international audience without having to be translated, although some symbols can mean different things in different countries. However, a sword is a sword in all languages and probably has something to do with combat. Because of its long association with the Red Cross, a red cross icon usually has something to do with health, but in countries with large Muslim populations the red cross is often replaced by a red crescent.

There can also be problems if there are a lot of interactive options on a screen for the player to operate. If each option has an icon for the player to select, then it can be difficult coming up with artwork that clearly represents what each option does. Players can usually remember a few odd icons once they've selected them a few times, but having multiple options can become confusing during play, especially if the action is nonstop.

Sometimes it's better to use words instead of icons because their meanings are clear. A button that reads "Inventory" is easier to understand than one showing a backpack or other icon. There is a problem, however, in using text on the screen if the game is to be sold internationally. A German translation of the English text, for example, might become too long for the button since German often combines shorter words into larger words. For example, using the German word "Warenbestand" for "Inventory" adds an extra four letters. Likewise, the button artwork might be too thin for countries that require diacritical marks above or below letters, like the acute accent (the mark over the "e" in é), cedilla (the mark under the "c" in ç) in French, or the tilde (the mark over the "n" in ñ) in Spanish and other languages.

Dealing with numbers on the screen can also be problematic, especially large numbers. In RPG and RTS games, the player wants to keep track of various information such as Hit Points, mana level, the amount of damage done by a hit, resource levels, time remaining for something to happen, and so forth. This information can be shown by numbers, and some players who are detail-oriented prefer this approach. So, in RPGs character attributes are usually shown numerically along with cash available, experience points, multiple copies of an item in an inventory, and other game information. But during battle it can be distracting to see a bunch of numbers fly by, especially late in the game when weapons do considerable damage and enemies have lots of Hit Points.

Some games have reduced or eliminated numbers in favor of showing information graphically. Health and mana levels are sometimes show as red and blue thermometers or other symbols, and as the player takes damage or uses magic, the thermometers empty out until death occurs or the player can no longer use magic. The best thing about showing the information graphically is that the symbols can be tied in thematically to the rest of the game and feel more natural, rather than watching weird numbers fly around the screen. However, it can be alarming for players to see their health or mana thermometer suddenly empty out because they received a critical hit or cast an expensive magic spell and not know exactly how much health or mana they have left.

To find out which approach works best, the designers should work with the programmers and artists during the technical review stage to test iconography versus text or numbers as the best way to present information. If there are only a handful of things on the screen for the player to track, then using icons and symbols might be best, but if there are multiple things for the player to track, then either straight text/numbers or a mixture of icons and text might work out better. Even though the development team might be happy with their decision, it still needs to be tested by new players to see how quickly they grasp the information presented on each screen.

Menus

One problem with data-rich games is presenting information to the player quickly and easily, so that the flow of the game isn't interrupted by repeatedly having to bring up other screens for relevant information. One standard for many years has been menus that pop up either by key/button input or by moving the cursor over a hotspot on the screen. The menu contains a list of the relevant information (spells, weapons, armor, and the like) from which the player selects. The advantages of menus are that options can be grouped by type for easier reference (for example, swords, bows, armor, and so on), each menu can contain a variable amount of entries, and the information on each menu can either be very brief (just a name) or wordy (usage costs, number available, and so on). The disadvantages of menus is that players have to stop what they are doing to deal with the menu, that they take up screen space and block what is happening behind them, and that they can force the player to switch gears mentally from "action" mode to "decision" mode.

It can be annoying for players to have to bring up menus repeatedly to perform some action such as healing or replenishing

Figure 12.4. *In Bethesda Softworks'* Fallout New Vegas, *a radial menu is used when interacting with non-player characters (NPCs) who join forces with the main character. The menu includes options for talking to the NPC, assigning orders and checking their inventory.*

ammunition. Many games allow players to assign certain functions to hot keys/buttons, so the function automatically occurs when the key/button is pressed. This answer works better on computers than consoles because there are more keys available on the keyboard than buttons on a video console. However, more console RPGs are experimenting with this approach to reduce the number of times menus must be accessed.

Another approach is to use pop-up radial dials instead of menus (Figure 12.4). A dial appears when the player moves the cursor over a hot spot on the screen, and the dial contains several options for the player to select. There can be many different dials in a game, each with its own options, and each dial can bring up secondary or tertiary dials with other choices. The idea is to keep the process relatively smooth, where the player moves the cursor over the hot spot and then over options on the dials until the desired one appears. Sometimes the dials are smart and only show the options that are currently usable, and then they expand as new options become available. The dials also reduce the amount of space required for pop-up menus and can add to the ambiance of the game by having artwork that matches the game's genre (futuristic, fantasy, horror, etc.).

It is also important for designers to consider how much real estate menus take up on a screen. While a menu system can be sprawling for games played on high-resolution monitors and televisions, even offering multiple options per screen to reduce the number of menus overall, the same approach does not work well for smaller televisions and monitors or for lower-resolution screens used by handheld and mobile platforms. For these platforms, the menu system should include more layers, with only a few options being offered per menu but with more menu screens for the player to page through. To port a big computer or console game to a handheld or mobile platform might require extensive rework to reduce the number of options available and thereby reduce the number of menus the players must deal with.

As a rough rule of thumb, menus tend to work better with turn-based games than action games unless the action stops while a menu is open. While this approach allows tired players to pause the game for a few moments, it does break the flow of play. However, because of the inherent complexity of games like RPGs, using a menu system might be the only way to offer players many different options during play.

Game Controls

Another major choice that has to be made early in the design process is the game control scheme—that is, what buttons and keys the player pushes to cause actions to happen on the screen. For some game genres, such as first-person shooters, the control scheme is relatively easy to map out since the game actions are almost always the same from one game to another. When playing an FPS on a computer, for example, the keyboard is used to move the character while the mouse is used to control the camera view of the playfield and the left mouse button is used for firing a weapon (or manipulating an object). On a console, the joysticks and directional pad are used to move the character and change the camera view while one of the four action buttons fires the weapon. More commands and shortcuts can be assigned to the remaining keys/buttons, depending on what actions the character performs in the game. For video games, the ability to perform extra actions is limited by the number of inputs on the controller.

For other types of games, such as puzzles, simulations and RPGs, designing the control scheme requires more effort because game play differs from other games and therefore there are few, if any, templates to draw from. Coming up with a completely original control scheme takes time and is dependent on the number of actions available to the player during play. If there are only a few actions, the controls are relatively easy to figure out, but if the player is to have a glut of options, mapping the inputs for all them can become a nightmare.

Defining Control Interactivity

The designers also have to decide whether controls are used *directly* to interact with objects on the playfield or on areas of the head-up display (HUD, the area superimposed around or over the playfield with the displays needed during play), or *indirectly* to perform game functions without touching anything on the screen. For example, in RTS games, players use the mouse to select units directly by clicking on their images and then moving them around by clicking on an area where they are to move to. Players also select items on the HUD with a mouse click, for example, selecting a building to place on the playfield and then selecting a location on the playfield with another mouse click. An example of indirect control would be moving a character on the screen in an FPS game via keys or the directional pad and firing a weapon by clicking a button or key. Players don't interact directly with the characters on the screen or the HUD information.

The best approach is to work out the functions for every screen in the game and every action that occurs on each screen and then see if there is a commonality of action per screen. If so, one button or key could be called the "action" key and can be used to perform the most important actions per screen—for example, firing a weapon, opening a door, activating or selecting an object, and so on. Eventually, the designers should be able to decide which actions are performed most often in the game and then assign buttons or keys appropriately. If it turns out that there are more actions available than buttons (for controllers), then the number of actions should be reduced. The more controls the player has to remember, the harder it is to learn the control scheme and the more likely the player is to make mistakes.

One interesting approach to allowing more game inputs for consoles and handheld platforms is to use context-sensitive controls, where the player has to push certain buttons or keys in the order shown on the screen at certain times to perform special actions.

These actions are sometimes referred to as Quick Time Events or Action Button Events. In Capcom's *Resident Evil 4* and *5*, for example, there are times when special actions are available to the player and the buttons that perform these actions flash on the screen. If the player successfully pushes the buttons in the correct order, the character performs the action and continues on—for example, rapidly pressing the "A" and "B" buttons to make the character run away from an oncoming avalanche. This approach allows additional game mechanics without having to support them continually throughout the game and therefore cuts down on the clutter of data the player has to remember during play.

Non-Traditional Game Controls

Most gamers are long accustomed to controlling game action through the keyboard and mouse (or touchpads) for computers or a controller for video games. In recent years, different kinds of game controls have been introduced, such as touchscreens used by various mobile platforms where users interact with the platform by touching it with their fingers; the stylus used with the Nintendo DS and some mobile platforms where inputs are made with a small plastic stick on a pressure-sensitive screen; the remote and nunchuk used with Nintendo's Wii where players move the devices around and the motions are detected via BluTooth and translated into movement on the screen; and the new Kinect remote peripheral for Microsoft's Xbox 360 and Move remote peripheral for Sony's PlayStation 3 that behave like the Wii remote. Because these game controllers are so different from traditional ones, it takes time to figure out the best methods for interacting with objects on the play screen.

Before plunging into production, a development team should nail down all possible platforms their game will be played on, since the input schemes for the non-traditional controllers are so different. The team should be concerned with how large interactive areas on the screen are for platforms with touchscreens and styluses. Obviously, a thin stylus requires much less surface area than a finger, but if the game is supposed to run on both platform types, then using the larger area required for touchscreen input should be the standard for both versions. Otherwise, if a game is supposed to run only on the Nintendo DS, the designers have to be aware that while control interaction is handled by the stylus on the bottom screen, there is also a second screen on the top of the device that can be viewed but not directly manipulated by stylus.

The whole development team should become experts with whatever controllers will be used for their game since they have to determine if the controls react quickly enough or if there are restrictions to how hard a player has to touch a screen with finger or stylus to get a response. Motion-sensitive controllers like that for the Nintendo Wii have had a different problem. While it is relatively easy to measure the movement of a controller back and forth along the x,y-axes, determining depth distance along the z-axis can cause problems if the player's movements are relatively small. The game logic has to determine what game actions the player is performing, and the final decision has to be made in milliseconds, so it sometimes happens that the game misinterprets what action the player is trying to perform. As a result, there can be a delay when the game engine corrects the error. This delay problem has been greatly improved by the introduction of the Wii MotionPlus, a device that supplements the remote's capability to sync player motion with what happens on the screen.

Problems with Game Controls

There are some problems with using any control scheme. The worst problem is lag time between when a player presses an input and something happening on the screen as a result. The ideal lag time is a few milliseconds between action and response. Any longer and the player feels that the controls are sluggish.

There are several reasons for this lag time. One is that the module controlling the inputs is poorly coded and some bugs are slowing things down. If a slowdown in response time occurs, the program team should do a thorough review of the code for the controls to look for any errors like memory leaks or mistimings. Another reason controls can get sluggish is because of problems with the overall memory management of a scene. If there are too many polygons being drawn to the screen, older game platforms can suffer serious lags, resulting in slow response time for all game systems. There can be other problems with the art that cause slowdowns as well, so if the controls appear sluggish in only a few areas, it would be prudent for the art team to check over all the artwork in those areas for any problems. Another potential problem is the use of a scripting language to handle certain game actions. It takes longer to process a scripting language than standard C++, and this delay can affect the control responsiveness, especially if the scripting language is used to manage very complex AI routines.

A mistake designers sometimes make is to redesign the whole control scheme from scratch, just for the sake of novelty. Unless there is a very good reason to break a standard control scheme, designers should try to match the controls of other games in the same genre. Forcing players to relearn the controls can be irritating and cause them to make many mistakes until they learn the new system.

A final problem is giving players only a single, predetermined input scheme for the controls. Unless one is designing for a hand-held or mobile platform where memory constraints impose limitations on what can be stored in saved games, there is no reason that players shouldn't be allowed to change the controls at will to suit their preferences. Some games include multiple versions of control schemes for the player to select from, but even these schemes can lack the control mapping that players prefer. With computers and consoles having huge storage capacity, there is no reason not to let players map out the controls as they choose.

Feedback

One part of the user interface that is often overlooked during the initial design phase is feedback, the signals the player receives during the game about right and wrong actions. While this oversight isn't catastrophic, it can lead to some problems down the road once the game is in full production and all the teams are working on the individual assets for the final product. If the designers realize that the players aren't getting enough information about combat results, for example, they might ask the art staff to come up with some visual sign that a combatant has taken a hit, and this change can lead to delays as the artists discuss the issue and are forced to bring in programmers to see if what they want to do is allowed by the game engine. The audio staff might also make suggestions about audio feedback during the combat which works in tandem with the new visual effect, and again the programmers would have to make sure the game engine supports the new audio demands.

It is much easier for everyone on the development team if the designers make suggestions early on in the documentation about how feedback will work in various areas of the game. They should keep in mind that feedback covers both visual and audio clues for players and is both positive (reinforcing what the player is doing) and negative (warning the player that something is wrong). If the player accidentally presses a wrong key or button, perhaps a warning

Figure 12.5. *In Gust's* Mana Khemia 2: Fall of Alchemy, *players get both audio and visual feedback when combat is resolved. In this case, the attack has done some significant damage, taking away lots of Hit Points.*

message pops up and a buzzing sound effect plays when the message appears. If a character is close to dying, the health bar on the HUD might start flashing to draw the player's attention.

One primary intent of feedback is to let players know when they are doing things both right and wrong during play (Figure 12.5). Players like to be rewarded when they do things right, but it is also important to alert them if they do something wrong. Ideally, the feedback feels natural and part of the game world, but it might become necessary to break the ambience if problems become severe. During hand-to-hand combat, for example, the damage totals might flash on the screen every time a combatant takes a hit. If some of the team object that the flashing numbers break the mood of the game, they still have to show something—either a combatant staggering for a second or flashing strobe-like effect to indicate a hit occurred or an audio effect such as a grunt to indicate someone took damage.

When working out the functionality of all screens in the game, the players should include suggestions for both visual and audio sound effects. For example, if the player presses a button in the shell interface, the player would see the button momentarily change color and hear some audio effect. Likewise, the feedback for actions during the game should be indicated as well. Even if the feedback winds up being far different than the designers originally imagined, including it as part of the design documentation alerts other teams to work they will have to do to implement the feedback system.

Conclusion

Although working on the interface sometimes feels like grunt work, it is just about the most important element in a game. Players are much more willing to forgive games with bad stories if the game plays like a champ, but they are much less tolerant of games that are hard to control or take too long to learn how to use, no matter how compelling the story. Designing a new interface takes a lot of time and effort and requires new eyes continually testing the game and offering feedback on what works and what doesn't. As development teams get larger, there are more specialist positions opening up at developers, including interface design, programming and visualization.

Throughout this book, an emphasis has been placed on thinking things through ahead of time and putting ideas down on paper to circulate to the whole team for their review and suggestions. During the development of a game, the design team puts in a huge amount of work up front, coming up with the game concept and fleshing out the details in the documentation. Once everyone on the team has agreed to the final design and worked out the technical details for how things will be done, the designers can relax a bit until it's time to test interactive prototypes or build the levels. Getting to build assets and see the game come to life as envisioned is thoroughly enjoyable for designers.

The last portion of the process—testing and debugging—is just as important, although it can become tedious to the point of tears. However, at the end of the line, when the game ships and the team can hold the final boxed product in their hands, it all becomes worthwhile. The process of designing and building complex, data-rich games is hard enough without trying to improvise what the content will be and how functionality will work halfway through production. Good designers are good planners and attentive to detail to the Nth degree. One designer spoke the truth when he quipped, "I'm so detailed-oriented I spell anal-retentive with two hyphens!!"

Exercises

1. Analyze a complex video or computer game (role-playing, real-time strategy, simulations, etc.) and make a complete list of all the interface screens in it.

   a. Begin the list with the first screen that appears when you initially start the game and go all the way through to the final screen when you exit.

   b. If the game can be played over the Internet, include all the screens that appear in this mode (assuming you can access them).

   c. Include any pop-up windows, menu systems or special interfaces (for example, Action Time Events) you find.

   d. Determine if each screen falls into the category of in-game screen or shell screen.

   e. Once you have the full list, write up an analysis estimating the amount of time a player spends looking at each screen during play.

2. Search the Internet to find walkthroughs or reviews with screenshots for at least three different role-playing games (console or computer).

   a. Analyze how the main playfield interface works in each one.

      i. How many different pieces of information are displayed on the screen?

      ii. What interface objects does the player directly manipulate during the game and what objects are simply information displays?

      iii. Does the game use a cursor for interacting with objects on the playfield or not?

      iv. What are the controls for moving player-controlled objects around the playfield?

   b. Prepare a presentation of your findings, explaining how well the control scheme works for each game and if there are any problems with it.

3. If possible, try to play a Nintendo Wii game or a game using either Microsoft's Kinect technology or PlayStation's Move motion controller. If you can't get your hands on these new controller systems, then look on the Internet for reviews and personal opinions about them.

   a. Write up a comparison of the controller you tested vs. the standard console controller or computer keyboard/mouse you've used in other games.

   b. What types of games work most effectively with the new control technology and what games have problems with it?

4. Play a complex video or computer game for a few hours and make notes about the visual and audio feedback during play.

   a. List the sound effects that are attached to game objects and entities.

   b. Create another list of the ambient sounds that occur as you move around the playfield.

   c. List the visual effects that are attached to game objects and entities when you interact with them.

   d. Create another list of the visual effects that occur as responses to using the game controls both during play and in the shell interface.

   e. Note how the music changes while you play the game.

   f. Combine all this information into a single document or spreadsheet.

5. Go through the list of the interface screens you created for Exercise 1 and write down the control scheme used with each screen.

   a. Note all the menus, option buttons, sliders, and other interface objects available to the player per screen.

   b. Note what controls (buttons, keyboard keys, mouse) the player uses to interact with each interface object.

   c. Put this information into a spreadsheet.

6. Create a simple schematic of the primary playfield interface screen(s) for the game you're designing either on paper or in a graphics program.

    a. In addition to the playfield itself, include all the information displays the player will see during play.

    b. If there are pop-up windows or menus that appear over the primary interface screen, create additional schematics for them as well.

    c. Find screenshots on the Internet from other games showing objects at the scale you think is right for your game.

    d. Prepare a presentation of your schematics so you can get feedback from others.

    e. After you make revisions, include the schematic(s) in your game design document.

7. Determine the control scheme and the feedback for the main interface screen(s) you created in Exercise 6.

    a. Indicate what objects the player interacts with directly on the main playfield.

    b. Assign controller or computer inputs to each type of interaction. (Do either a console or a computer version of your game, not both.)

    c. Make lists of the visual and audio feedback (sound effects, music and voiceovers) associated with the primary interface screen(s).

8. Come up with a list of all the interface screens you think will be needed for the game you're designing.

    a. Include both the in-game interface screens and the shell screens.

    b. Once you have the list of interface screens, determine the controls and visual/audio feedback per screen, as you did in Exercise 7.

    c. Write up this information as a document or spreadsheet and add it to your game design document as an appendix.

CHRIS TAYLOR

Figure 13.1. *Chris Taylor, Company CEO and Project Manager of Gas Powered Games.*

Chris Taylor (Figure 13.1) is one of the leading designers in computer games. He was born in Canada and started working at Distinctive Software in British Columbia in the late 1980s. While there, he designed his first game *HardBall II* in 1989, which won an award from the Software Publishers Association for the best sports game of the year. He went on to design *The Duel: Test Drive II* in 1989 and *4-D Boxing* in 1991 for Distinctive Software. After that company was acquired by Electronic Arts in 1991 and renamed EA Canada, Chris designed *Triple Play 96* in 1995.

He moved to the United States in 1996 and joined Cavedog Entertainment where he was the designer and project leader on the real-time strategy game *Total Annihilation* which was released in 1997. That game went on to win 57 awards worldwide and was named Best Game of All Time by PC Games in 1998 and the #1 Real-Time Strategy Game of All Time by GameSpy in 2004. He also created the first expansion pack *Total Annihilation: The Core Contingency* in 1998.

Chris left Cavedog Entertainment to found his own company—Gas Powered Games—in 1998. Their first release was the action role-playing game *Dungeon Siege* in 2002, followed shortly thereafter by the expansion back *Dungeon Siege: Legends of Aranna*. In 2002, Chris was named the 30th most influential person in the game industry by GameSpy. The sequel *Dungeon Siege II* appeared in 2005 and an expansion pack *Dungeon Siege: Throne of Agony* in 2006. The game became the basis of the movie *In the Name of the King: A Dungeon Siege Tale* in 2008. Also released that year was a science-fiction RPG, *Space Siege*.

Chris returned to real-time strategy games in 2007 with *Supreme Commander*, a futuristic game in the tradition of *Total Annihilation* (Atari currently owns the rights to *Total Annihilation*). An expansion pack, *Supreme Commander: Forged Alliance* appeared later that year, and in 2010 the sequel, *Supreme Commander II,* was published.

In 2009, Gas Powered Games released *Demigod*, a game that combines RTS and RPG elements in a game that focuses heavily on multiplayer competition. The company is currently working on a new RTS game set in a medieval world called *Kings and Castles*.

Having worked on both role-playing and real-time strategy games, Chris has vast expertise about game design. He took time out from his busy schedule as company CEO and project manager to grant this book's author an interview in which he talked at length about his experiences and his design philosophy.

Introduction

MEM: What is the role you play at Gas Powered Game?

Chris: The first half of my career I worked for other people, at large companies, so I didn't have to worry about running a business, and all the complexities of legal, banking, and other random stuff. Now, I get to be in charge of making the games here at GPG. There's a design document that has to be created, generally at a high level. There's the big marketing hooks, the things that make people say, "Wow, I've never seen that before!" And I get to build the design team that work on the project, and they start to do all the nuts and bolts of the design, a lot of the detailed, tricky stuff. And at that point, my job then is to make sure whatever they do plugs into the overall vision of the game.

So I have this interesting job. It's a fun job, it's a hard job, and it's a job with a lot of responsibility. Ultimately, if the game succeeds or fails, I have to take the responsibility for the design; and we can all share in the success. At the end of the day, the whole process of building the game is a team effort.

Back in the old days when I was doing *Hard Ball II*, teams were super small, even one man. If you talk to David Crane (he started at Atari and founded Activision), he did all the art, sound, programming, and AI for his games.

Today there are so many people involved in the game. I get the creative director and lead designer jobs, but when it comes to the details I can't go to the wall and draw out diagrams and algorithms and specific mechanics because these are areas of deep expertise for people on the team.

MEM: Do you enjoy designing or managing more?

Chris: I actually enjoy both parts of the process, but if you left me all alone to myself, I would be a designer. I would end up designing games that are things that I code, that I can put my hands on. I've written code since I was 14. That's 30 years ago... slap me!

I got my first computer in 1980, a Radio Shack TRS-80, and wrote all kinds of programs for it, mostly games. I just love programming. But you can't play all the position on the field, especially on the bigger projects, so you have to give some things up. I gave up one of the things I love but I got something else that I love, the design. And the team spirit, the team dynamic...although that is difficult and sometimes can be very disappointing. You don't get the results you're looking for guaranteed, like when you're working with a computer. The algorithms, the design, the team management, they're all much harder. Sometimes I think it would be good just to go back to working with the computer. It's so much friendlier, and you're guaranteed to get the results you want out of it! (Laughs)

Chris's Background in Games

MEM: What kinds of games did you play before getting into computers?

Chris: I think my enjoyment of family games—*Monopoly*, *Risk*, *Careers*, and *The Game of Life*, or any game you can teach someone to play in a short period of time—comes across in my design sensibility, I was sensitive to the fact that if someone taught me a game that was very complicated, they might beat me at it right away. I'm very competitive, and I don't like to lose.

I don't think very many people like to lose. And I think that was a harbinger of things to come. What do we love playing today? We call them comp-stomps, or players vs. the environment. And then there's cooperative play against the AI. There are scenarios where you just play against the AI, there's you and your friends against the AI, and there could be four of your friends against four AI. And that's really fun because you're on a team and doing stuff together.

Back in the old days, all those games were head-to-head. They were competitive. They probably weren't as fun as they could have been if we had come up with the idea that you could play against a computer, or should I say, beat up a computer! Back then, I loved those games because they were simple. You could learn them. I loved the hex-based games, those sophisticated paper games, but I was too young to understand the nuance of them. Computers came along just as I got old enough to understand the hex games, and probably had the disposable income to start buying them, but I was spending every last second of my life and every penny on the computer. And the computer games were simplified versions of the games you could play on paper anyhow... so I guess it all worked out in the end.

Of course, the Commodore 64 came along, and you really saw the home computer game revolution take off—Atari ST, the Amiga, IBM PC—and games went in every single direction. I never had the chance to pull out a board game again. We were full-time, full-on computer gaming. Those games didn't always turn out to be the complicated hardcore games, either. They were simple, fun games. I remember *The Olympic Decathlon* by Microsoft that came out in 1981. It was so much fun, but it was more akin to an arcade game, which is where I spent all my times since the late 70s before I got my computer... arcades!

If computers hadn't been invented, I might have become a paper game designer, although back then it was very hard to make a career out of it, so it's a doubtful idea.

Total Annihilation

MEM: Did you have an overwhelming love of RTS games before starting *Total Annihilation*?

Chris: I didn't know anything about RTS game other than playing *Dune II* when it first came out. And I loved it. (*Dune II: The Building of a Dynasty* was created by Westwood Studios in 1992.) I knew that there were tons of things about it that could be improved from a pure mechanical implementation standpoint. I was waiting for *Command & Conquer*, the next game coming out of Westwood. (*Command & Conquer* was created by Westwood Studios in 1995.) I don't think I've ever been so excited about a game before it came out.

When I started playing *C&C*, the wheels had already been turning in my head since *Dune II*, and I felt there were a lot of things that could be done to create more flexibility and freedom and make the game more dynamic.

I was frustrated that you ran out of resources at the end. I used to say that the game started off with some tanks, built into armies of tanks and helicopters and this cool stuff, but then ended with a couple of tanks because all the resources were exhausted and wasn't replenishing. I wanted to do a game where that was not the issue, one that would build to a crescendo of over-the-top spectacular warfare.

I had been doing games in 2-1/2 D with the baseball games where I modeled the ball and the physical space of the stadiums in 3D, so the ball would move accurately. These old system couldn't draw 3D graphics; they could only draw 2D sprites. We started prototyping what became *Total Annihilation*, and we started on a real-time 3D terrain system, and the frame-rate was so terrible with a software rasterizer that we knew the fastest computers would never run it. We came up with a system of prerendered 2D terrain that had a 3D height map under it, and then we rendered the units in 3D on top. That gave us tremendous features that 2D games couldn't do.

When we started the TA project (before it was called *Total Annihilation*), the name was "Really Cool Wargame." We didn't have a name. We didn't know what the hook was. We didn't know how it was going to be better. It was just moxie. I'll go and start working on it, and I'm going to make it better from sheer willpower.

So, the vision was we know we can make it better, and in truth we never did. *C&C* maintained its position and continued to sell 5 and 6 million units, and we sold 700–800K units. This was good, because we did it so inexpensively, but we didn't have any of the money those guys had for a big PR campaign, and we didn't have an established franchise. We were battling the economics of game development even back then.

It's a real testimony to what you can do when you think about game development as a craft. When you've been developing games for a number of years, when you have all these skills, you know how to put things on the screen, you know how to write the code, but you don't quite know how your game is going to compete in the market. I think we are seeing a return to those old times now.

Preproduction Phase

MEM: What affects your decision to do this game or that one?

Chris: If you're independently wealthy, you can make whatever you want. You probably would chase your design whimsy, the thing that really excites you and maybe the people you work with. Because you want to motivate them. You want to wrap them up in your vision.

But if you have to go raise money, you have to have a lot of sensitivity to what's in the market. And you have to say here's an opportunity for us in the market.

If you don't think there's any chance, you could probably throw away those designs or make them your little pet projects when you go home at night. Try to do them on an iPhone or an iPad, or do a Facebook game. Then you would try to make it into a big commercial endeavor.

Ideas for Games

MEM: How do you come up with the idea for a game design?

Chris: Where do the ideas come from? When you sit down to make a game, anything is possible, but we're not too different from General Motors saying, "Well, ya know, Skidoos are doing really well, but we

Figure 13.2. *Gas Powered Games'* Demigod *is an unusual melding of a real-time strategy game and role-playing game.*

make cars. So we're probably going to stick to making cars right now. We've got assembly lines to make cars and all this other stuff that makes cars."

I have a whole bunch of code, I've got tools, I've got expertise, I've got pipelines, I've got all this momentum. And I've got ten million dollars in software technology that I can leverage, which means that the game I do make with this technology will really shine.

Our industry has a habit of staying on a pretty straight line, but we've done some alternative things. We did *Demigod*, which is like an RTS but not a conventional one (Figure 13.2). It's something that we could fit into our wheelhouse but it was a little different. We've done some other games, some that never saw the light of day, frankly.

In this economy…the economy plays a factor. It plays a role in how creative and wild you can be.

MEM: Do you ever do whiteboarding with the designers?

Chris: We brainstorm all the time. In fact, we were just in here brainstorming today.

I've gone to a system where we use giant sheets of paper, where we can draw patterns and formations and pinch points, and sometimes I doodle, but then I can turn the page instead of having to erase or transcribe the whiteboard.

Going to something that's a little more solid than newsprint. Stuff on the easel—it's kind of sloppy. This pad becomes a permanent record and intellectual property of the company. More than what we've seen historically.

Game Design Documents

MEM: Do you create design documents for your games?

Chris: When we started GPG, we had a fully articulated design document for *Dungeon Siege*. We had all these things that we were going to do that were broken out line-by-line, and each was going to be something to raise the eyebrows of the customer looking at the back of the box. And from day one, we started engineering and building those things.

Total Annihilation took 20 months to make, whereas *Dungeon Siege* took nearly four years. So it was harder because we had more ambitious goals, but we had more wind at our back. We had more support to go and build something big.

MEM: What about *Supreme Commander*?

Chris: On *Supreme Commander*, we had a design document talking about all the cool things we were going to do. Of course we knew from the start it's very much a spiritual successor to *Total Annihilation*, so we started off with a solid list of ideas that we wanted to add since doing *Total Annihilation*. Since then, every game has followed in that tradition. We knew what we wanted to build and we went after it.

Sometimes we couldn't do what we wanted to do. There were setbacks, but we still persevered and did the best we could.

It's still a crapshoot to some degree. Just because you have a really good idea or a finely articulated plan doesn't mean that you're going to make a successful game. Or you're going to hit your budget or you're going to get it done on time. Or that you can bring the right team members together. There are still a lot of variables that can get in the way of making the game you want.

I've seen great games that have crappy designs and crappy games that have been great because of great people. So, you have a great idea that survives and makes it to the market from a team of people… they're not terrible people, but perhaps they don't enjoy one another's company, don't know how to work together, or don't have a creative relationship or that magical dynamic between them. Because these are key things, and how do you create them? How do you build teams that know how to work well together? This is almost as hard as coming up with a great game design.

MEM: Do you do much internal documentation? Documents for the publishers? Do you have to sell publishers with your documentation?

Chris: Different publishers have different requirements for documentation. Some believe in a living design document, one that has a foundation at the beginning that through the course of development grows and grows. And some firmly believe it's not a finished design until the game ships or until two or three months before the game ships.

Others adhere to the notion that you must have a fully articulated game design somewhere in the first three or four months of the game, and others are okay with ninety percent of the design being delivered in the first three or fourth months and the last ten percent during. Every publisher has a different creative director who has come from a different background, has a different philosophy about how game design is approached. I hope we never put them all in a room because they definitely don't agree with each other's philosophies.

MEM: (Laughing) They'll go after each after.

Chris: There's something valid about every one of those approaches. There's nothing like asking a designer to sit there and type out an entire design.

If you have a design vision, you'd better sit down and type it out. When doing an RPG, for example, there's really no need to type out all 783 weapons. It's not a leap of faith that you'll be able to do it.

You're also looking at the résumé of a designer. If he just came off another RPG that you just played (because you did your due diligence), and it had 512 weapons and he tells you, "I'm gonna want to make a bigger one this time. I'm going for 750 weapons!" If you really enjoyed his game and you enjoyed his weapons, you're not going to his abilities to pull that off.

But if you really want to make a big RPG, try to make a smaller RPG first. It shows a competency in how you can solve problems and how creative you are.

Prototyping

MEM: Do you ever do any prototyping for your games?

Chris: Yes, we do preproduction, which is kind of like a sophisticated prototype.

"Prototype" is a tough one. Often when you build a prototype, it's like you're intend to throw it all away when you're done. So, you're not making things that are productions versions of the game. If you make a prototype car, you're not going to sell that actual car because it has too many hand-machined parts and so on. But in video games, a prototype can often turn into the actual shipping game. You can have code that ships because it's software.

In our business, we have a concept phase, a preproduction phase, a production phase and a post-production phase. We try to keep the costs down by doing as much work in the concept and pre-production phases as we can before we flip the switch and go into production. We know we're spending money responsibly because it's all been figured out. Game play mechanics, what have you, and it all takes place in preproduction. We might use white-box art, we might use temporary sound, we might use a programming script that's hacked together and isn't terribly efficient but it gets the job done for the preproduction phase. What if we don't like it? Then we throw it away, and I say, "I'm sure glad we didn't spend time polishing or optimizing that code." We do a lot of that in preproduction so that when we're ready to go, we throw the nice coat of paint on the game with final art and final assets.

Production Phase

MEM: Do you use spreadsheets for your games?

Chris: Oh, God, yeah! We have spreadsheets up the wazoo.

MEM: For charts and table?

Chris: For everything. Over time analysis of the weapons, the spells, everything. Back on *Dungeon Siege*, we had a spreadsheet for all of this stuff, and frankly for all our games. We have whiteboards full of data; this is where we start. When we started out with GPG, we didn't have much money, so we went down to Home Depot and bought tile board. We just nailed tile board up on the wall. We had the whole progression across the whiteboard of all the regions in the world and all the different levels. We mapped it all out. We had holes, and we said we have to fill that hole before we get to that part of the world's development.

A month or two before the team started producing content, we had to map out every monster, every weapon, any kind of story plot that happens in there. We tend to think about the story too little and too late. The overall story had to be laid out because you had to decide if you're coming across the Goblin Inventor, what is the Goblin Inventor's job? What's he doing? Neal Hallford, the writer on the project did a wonderful job of making sense of our insane *Dungeon Siege* world.

MEM: Do you create the charts and tables that drive game play?

Chris: No, that role has been filled by different individuals on the projects I've worked on.

On *Total Annihilation*, I said the Commander has a D-gun (a super powerful weapon capable of destroying almost anything in the game). Rick Smith came into my office one day and said the Commander must have another weapon because the player may not be able to use the D-gun. What about another lower-power laser that is always available? And I said great idea!

So, hearing the idea and making sure the idea fits in, rather than Rick (a designer on the project) going to a content engineer and saying, "Hey, just go ahead and put a laser gun on the Commander." It had to come through me; I approved it. Then it went to Jake McMahon, who tuned the game and decided how much power that secondary laser gun should have. That's an important question. Will that gun fire off the other arm? What's the range? How frequently does the gun fire? Those are all questions that are part of another job, which is tuning and balancing.

I was the person who said that the D-gun has to be able to destroy anything it hits. That might not have been the first thing out of someone on the team's mouth. They would have said that's a big powerful gun, but it will still take time for a Commander to take its target down. No, I said, it's a short-range weapon and it does tremendous damage and will kill anything that it comes into range with, even another Commander. This was a very bold design stake to drive into the ground. This is where the leadership component comes in because the team may not have thought that was a good idea. If you took that to a committee of people, they might have said that's a little wild. That's a little crazy. There's a little risk-taking there.

Big risks come from individuals, not teams. The individual can then convince the team this is a good idea. That's an example of how I'm in there, I'm in the mechanics. We'll have nukes that can fly anywhere on the map. We can have anti-nukes that knock them out of the air with 100% accuracy. *Total Annihilation* is an example of where I designed the game mechanically. I had Jake tune and balance, but I was very involved in the detailed mechanics of the design.

But today the games are getting much more sophisticated; I have taken a step back and spend more time on the higher-level stuff. For a game like *Kings and Castles*, I lay out a plan for having new kings and queens come out every month after the game ships. A question comes up like, should we have an inventory system for the king or not? The team really loves the idea, and I'm kind of on the fence about it… so I say, let's see how it plays and make a call on it when we've collected some data.

RPG and RTS Game Design

MEM: What are the main differences between RPG and RTS game in terms of design approach?

Chris: An RTS game is different because, unlike an RPG, you design an experience that happens all at once together… the rules, the experience, it's a complete idea, and has no attached timeline, whereas in an RPG, this is very different.

With an RPG, it's like a movie or filmstrip that moves under the player's eyes. You have anywhere from 10, 20, 50 hours—BioWare games reach out into hundreds of hours—which meant that as a designer you created a game that you knew would be experienced over time. It's a very different thought process. You knew the player started out with the Rusty Butter Knife and they would end up with the Dark Sword of Oblivion that has flames shooting from it, that slices and dices, and that can kill everything in the room with one hack. You knew that you had to get the player from the Rusty Butter Knife all the way to that Dark Sword of Oblivion, and you had to do it at a certain pace. And you couldn't bore them, but you couldn't spoil them. And everything ties to that experience: the terrain that's moving under their feet, the characters they meet, the things those characters say, the monsters that they fight, the capabilities of those monsters, the puzzles that they solve, everything is going along under this sliding view port, that takes place on a timeline.

MEM: That makes them more difficult to design?

Chris: Well, it's much more exhausting creatively. You get to the point where you start to make it up: "Oh, it can have a horn… and it spits acid… and I think it rears up on both its hind feet… but maybe not." And the poor people who are animating the monsters are like, "Uh, what does it do?"

It's fun in practice to be sitting around the hamburger joint saying we're going to create this RPG because you're imagining these key moments, how awesome they're going to be. But then there's the laborious task of coming up with all those hours of content, all the stuff that's going to fill this enormous fantasy world… that's the hard part.

MEM: Plus you have to create the whole back world—the races, locations players go to, items. It's different with a first-person shooter game where there might be maybe 15 items in total in the game.

Chris: Exactly, if you're designing a *Quake* or *Doom*…let's take *Quake*. All those id Software games were very well designed. The design beauty came down to every weapon was an understandable weapon. They weren't algebraically expressed weapons that were generated from a spreadsheet. They were like a shotgun, chain-gun, rocket launcher, to name a few. So what happens there is that you understand the inherent tradeoffs, and you accept them as a player.

MEM: You have quantum leaps between this weapon and this weapon. In RPG, there's this overlap where I have a sword that can throw a fireball but it doesn't do that much damage.

Chris: When you're working on that game for 18 months, you're staring at those seven weapons for 18 months. Hmm, shotgun could do a little bit more damage. Let's change the reload time on it. Over here, the rocket jump… let's increase the health of the character so if they're near the explosion, they can fly across the room with it. That'll be funny. Oh, a little more damage and it kills them, not enough damage and people are abusing it and jumping everywhere. This is how the process works; it's very specific.

You're playing with these seven weapons the entire time and when you go to your next game, you don't throw away those seven weapons. You take those seven weapons with you and you refine them even more. If you do anything to them at all, you better know what you're doing with them.

When you design the Rusty Butter Knife, you want to get to the next weapon to come along. It's a sharper knife, or it's a sword. What you want to avoid is no-brainer decisions. Any time you say to the player this is not a thinking decision then you're doing something wrong or that could be improved. You always want to make them pause and think, "Oh crap, if I do this, then I lose that." That's a trade-off.

A trade-off is what I used to run around ten years ago spouting from the rooftop. If you want to be a great game designer, you have to understand the concept of a trade-off. If the player never has to make a thoughtful decision, there's no game play dynamics. That is a key concept in an RPG. That is a key concept in a lot of games. But what we actually think now is that games are getting to the point where they're more amusing. We like to give the player choices, but we don't like there to be a "fail" choice. It's just choices because it's your entertainment.

MEM: I step over here and fall to my death.

Chris: Yeah, we don't let them fall to their death anymore. But we say, if you go through door number one, you get this thing. If you go through door number two, you get something else. You may be left wondering what was behind the other door, but you don't get punished for it.

Punishment was widespread in gaming. I remember playing Sega's *Sonic the Hedgehog* on a cartridge. I think it was partly because there was no save system in these cartridges early on, but if you died and lost your last hedgehog, you had to go all the way back to the beginning and you were like "Oh, no!" So unless you were a total die-hard gamer, we call these players hard-core gamers now, you would lose interest and go play something else.

Back then, we had another aspect to gaming… you only had that one game to play. So you might have walked away, but then you spun around and came back because that's all you had to play. It's like being on a desert island and saying "Oh, I think I'm going to have bananas and coconuts today"—cause that's all I get!

Today, gamers are so distracted with a trillion things going on that we really can't afford to punish our customers and make them go away, because they won't come back.

So, game design has now changed from the old classic RPGs that were deep and rather complicated, to something way easier to understand. And we saw the incredible success of *Diablo* that simplified the core mechanics to a surprising level. (*Diablo* was created by Blizzard Entertainment in 1998.) We knew that people really loved the action and the quick decisions and to keep moving forward quickly exploring new areas, new weapons, and encountering new monsters…and with very few puzzles to slow the player down.

But the intellectual was taking part in a different experience. It was still there. The player was choosing weapons and deciding when to go back to town and when to empty the inventory. Do they sell that really cool item or do they wait until they're at a much higher enough level to use it? Those are important decisions that players have to make.

Rewards and Inventory

MEM: What about rewarding players after combat in an RPG?

Chris: Loot drops are a whole different thing. You've got to drop stuff that is relevant to the player, that will be relevant to the player later on in the game, or something really spectacular that it's almost like a stone in their shoe. They have to carry it for six hours before they get to use it. It's going to use up that precious inventory space. And then you give them some junk to carry that they just haul back and sell. But is it better to use that inventory space for something better? So they find a rare item, and they throw the junky thing out of the inventory and leave it on the ground. They leave it on the main path so they can pick it up later. They put it someplace in case they want to make a junk-collection run if they're desperate for money.

MEM: And then you have the pack mule (in *Dungeon Siege*). Here's a spare inventory for me.

Chris: The *Dungeon Siege* pack mule scratched a big itch for people, but it used up a character slot in the party. Do you want someone who fights or something that carries your loot? You didn't get punished when you used the pack mule in different ways. It was a nice game play tradeoff.

There were times when all my party members were dead and the mule would keep fighting. And the one monster that finished me off would go on fighting the pack mule, and the pack mule would win! And because you had a surviving member of the party, all your characters would slowly regain consciousness. And it's like, "Oh, my God, the pack mule saved me!" It was an experience most people had at least once that was very memorable.

That's emergent behavior. You build a bunch of cool rules in certain ways that things happen that please you and surprise you, but you never sat and typed them into the design document. Later on, as we've gotten more sophisticated in the craft of game design, we kind of know how to encourage that kind of gameplay. Bring the physics system in—where flying parts can do some damage in the environment. That's a perfect recipe for emergent behavior.

But when you get things like a pack mule saving the party, that's just wonderful surprise, something that falls out of the game play systems naturally.

Pacing in Games

MEM: Do you enjoy real-time, fast-paced games as opposed to turn-based games like *Sid Meier's Civilization*? (The original *Sid Meier's Civilization* was published by MicroProse in 1991.) Where there are so many actions to perform, you can't do them all at the same time?

Chris: I loved the faster-moving games, but as I get older, I like to be able to set the pace because I don't want to have my entertainment set it for me. I want to be able to control this. Real-time spoke to me. I'm a big *Civilization* fan, I've got most of the *Civ* games here in the office someplace, but there's something about real-time that captures my imagination and speaks to me.

What is it about real-time? It's like you are watching a real battle take place, and the things that happen in real battles are exciting. For example, someone fires a shell from a tank at a moving target. However, let's say the target it fired at moved or moved in an unpredictable way, so it would miss. You don't get this in turn-based games. You get dice rolls, and to me, a dice roll was always the thing you did when you had pen-and-paper or counters because you didn't have a computer to simulate it. Why on earth would you want to roll a dice when you have a computer that can simulate it essentially with a very sophisticated dice roll? Why would a tank miss another tank unless a human being is controlling it?

MEM: But there is still some randomization.

Chris: If I'm firing a shell at a tank that's rolling in front of me, I can lead it. In real life, I can lead the target, fire the shell, and compensate for every variable using a sophisticated targeting system. But if the driver of that tank suddenly stops, the shell is going to miss. And that comes through in a real-time strategy game with a simulation model. Turn-based games don't capture any of that energy. And that energy is good. It's fun to watch. It's fun to watch play out!

It's like watching a game of *Supreme Commander 2*, where the Pull-and-Smash (i.e., the Pulinsmash unit) is deployed and its spinning away, and there are ships crawling up to the shore and they start to shake and—whoosh!—get sucked into the Pull-and-Smash and are destroyed. That's unbelievable. How did it do that?

It's because it's a simulation, and there's a value assigned to the destroyer and there's a value assigned to the Pull-and-Smash, and it says, "Hey, if it's a certain value, it can pull it in." It's emergent but it's part of the simulation, and it's something you don't get in a turn-based game. Those systems only come alive in a real-time game.

AI for Games

MEM: Do you work on the AI, or do you specialists who just work on it?

Chris: We have specialists, absolutely. Jeff Petkau wrote the AI on *Total Annihilation*. It was fairly straightforward compared to the games today, but at the time it was state-of-the-art. It would build units and sent them out in groups. He had some pretty cool things he was doing back then.

Since then, there's reconnaissance, and the AI scouts you and builds different mixes of units based on what you're building, and it finds areas to concentrate its attacks. There's an influence map created that overlays the board that shows areas of danger and areas of safety for the AI, so it knows where it can move its troops and forces and then attack the enemy—the enemy being *you*—in various ways. It's very sophisticated.

We use sort of a programmatic AI today, where the person who writes is putting their own personality in, or versions of their personality. A turtler version, for example (that is, someone who builds strong defenses and doesn't attack as aggressively). And then there's some of the AI that's built around neural nets, where we teach them by letting the game play a hundred thousand times. Then when the AI goes to do something, it defers to what would the neural net would do based on "experience". This creates another level of sophistication.

MEM: Do you help at the beginning in defining the AI? Saying what you expect each unit to do?

Chris: Not really. What's great is when you hire people who are experts in RTS AI. They're already been playing our games. When we went to do *Supreme Commander 2*, we brought in Mike Robbins to help out. He had already been playing the first version of *Supreme Commander*, and he knew our AI system better than we did, at least that's what it felt like. In fact, he wrote his own versions of the AI, which he released to the community. So, we hired him and said, "Hey, maybe you can help us out here instead of over there, and do better AI for our games going forward."

I'm seldom telling these guys anything they don't know. They're way ahead of me.

Scripting Language

MEM: Do you use a scripting language? Or do you have your own proprietary engine, such as Epic Games' Unreal Engine, created for your games?

Chris: We've always built our own engines. I've built my own engines since I started in this business, going all the way back to the beginning. I've never used a proprietary engine.

Having said that, we just recently built a prototype using Unity (the Unity Game Engine by Unity Technologies), and that was really great. What we'll do now is we'll build the engine that takes us through the production phase, but it was really great to use the Unity Engine for preproduction.

MEM: Do you expect your designers to go in and build levels? Do you have a scripting language that can be used by a designer who is not really a programmer?

Chris: What we tried to do in the past is use tools that could be used by right-brained people, people who aren't necessarily technical. What we've discovered over the years is that there's nothing like a highly technical person who's both left- and right-brained, who can roll up their sleeves and do scripting, or use complicated, half-baked and buggy tools.

Trying to turn this business into a factory—where you can bring in people and plug them in like an assembly line worker who doesn't know how the engine works but can bolt on the intake manifold—isn't something that has worked for us. And it's not something we aspire to. We love people who wear multiple hats, and are specialists and know how to get into the game code and systems.

Final Thoughts

MEM: Is there anything you'd like to say in conclusion about being a designer?

Chris: To create an analogy—I like a good analogy and metaphors too!—our craft is sort of like the Wright Brothers building that first plane and now trying to build the new Dreamliner. Our industry started with a couple of guys following their passion. It was exciting. I got involved in the industry after that, after the first plane left the ground. The game industry was rolling along. There was a retail presence.

But by God it got complicated rather quickly. There can be hundreds of people working on projects, with budgets in the hundreds of millions of dollars. It's insane when you think back to where it all started.

MEM: It's like we're a factory now.

Chris: Yes. And I just don't get to stick my hands into the juicy stuff as much nowadays. There was some romance lost.

But now we're in a sort of resurgence of that romance where you can get your laptop computer and you can download incredible tools and have your game that you made on the weekend up on the Apple Appstore or available from a website. It could be the next *Doodle Jump* (by Lima Sky) or the next *World of Goo* (by 2D Boy), or the next *Angry Birds* (by Rovio). It's driven by inspiration and not a budget—convincing a big publisher that they need to give you 5, 10, 100 million dollars.

Advice for Budding Designers

MEM: If someone came to you and asked how to become a game designer, what would you say?

Chris: Don't run your own game company right out of the gate, because it's just throwing another challenge onto the already tall stack of challenges. First things first, get on a team somewhere. You can aspire to be a lot of things in life, but start with something you can do. Bite off a little more, then bite off a little more.

You can get on the production team. Quality Assurance (QA) people can become designers. Or you can be a junior artist. Just getting your foot in the door is key. There's QA, engineering, art, production to name a few teams involved in making games. In every instance you want to get into the company. You want to see a game being made. You want to witness it first hand.

Once you're there, you start to ask yourself, "Who's the person in the company driving the design?" If they don't like you or vice versa, find another company. Find someone who does like you and start to work under their wing. Find your mentor.

It's one thing to have a mentor who lives on the other side of the country, or you could read a magazine article about them, but what you need to do is find a mentor who will work with you every day. Listen to them. Interact with them. Put in those three, four, five, six years. Get that junior design position. Be on the team. Be in the meetings. Watch the other guys work who have experience.

You can be the best designer in the world but you don't get to go right to the top. You're going to work your way up through the ranks.

Casual Games and Innovation

MEM: Do you think independent games, casual games are driving innovative game design?

Chris: Yes, it's like the Amazon rain forest, supporting all these new species of life, or rather, genres of games.

There's more happening in the iTunes store than anywhere else, frankly. I don't see it happening as much on Facebook, but I think it requires quite a few more moving parts to get a game up and running there. Which is surprising, since the technical requirements are lower, but the overall complexity of launching and getting it to run it is higher.

So the app store for the iPhone or iPad is where it's running riot. And it's wonderful. It's so much fun. It's like I told someone I don't ever want to pay $60 for a game again. I like 99 cents a game. That's fun.

MEM: So does that mean you future games will be .99 cents?

Chris: Probably not, but they won't be $60 either. But that's not for me to say at this point… but I'll predict that games get less expensive, by a huge amount.

MEM: Thanks very much for your time, Chris. I'll let you get back to building *Kings and Castles*.

CREDITS

Gears of War and *Unreal Engine* used with permission.

Gears of War © 2006, Epic Games Inc. All rights reserved. Gears of War®, Marcus Fenix™, the Crimson Omen™, and Unreal® are registered trademarks or trademarks or of Epic Games, Inc. in the United States and other countries. All rights reserved.

Eve Online is used with permission of CCP Games.

Demigods is used with permission of Gas Powered Games.

Disgaea 2 and *Mana Khemia* used with permission of NIS America.

©Nippon Ichi Software, Inc. Disgaea is a registered trademark of Nippon Ichi Software, Inc. All rights reserved. Mana Khemia is a trademark of GUST Co., Ltd. All rights reserved.

Bejeweled 2 © 2004, PopCap Games, Inc. Used with permission. All rights reserved.

Fallout® *3* © 2008 Bethesda Softworks LLC, a ZeniMax Media company. All rights reserved.

Fallout®*: New Vegas*™ © 2010 Bethesda Softworks LLC, a ZeniMax Media company. All rights reserved.

The Elder Scrolls IV: Oblivion® © 2006 Bethesda Softworks LLC, a ZeniMax Media company. All rights reserved.

Portal, *Half-Life 2*, and *Left 4 Dead 2* are used with permission of Valve Corporation. © Valve Corporation.

Victoria II is used with permission of Paradox Interactive. © Paradox Interactive. All rights reserved.

Cinema Tycoon 2: Movie Mania © TikGames, LLC. 2009. *Interpol: The Trail of Dr. Chaos* © TikGames, LLC. 2009. *Word Cross* © TikGames, LLC. 2008. All rights reserved.

Lock On: Flaming Cliffs 2 used with permission of Eagle Dynamics. Copyright © 2010, The Fighter Collection.

Zombie Swarm used with permission of Ahmed Hakeen. Screenshot provided by Ahmed Hakeen (medsgames.com).

Artwork and sketch for GSR Racing Game used with permission of Ed Williamson.

Tile Editor used with permission of Wiering Software.

Sallet image used with permission of Albion Swords (www.albion-swords.com).

Senet used with permission of P. S. Neeley.

INDEX

Inactive NPC 151

Index cards 280

Indirect control of game objects 326

Indirect fire combat 114

Indirect line of sight 112

Inductive reasoning 245

Information holders 198–199

Information presentation on screens 321–323

Information screen locations 320–321

Infrared detectors 197

In-game interface screens 316–317

Initial equipment 139

Initial magic spells 140

Initial skills 140–141

Initiative 96, 115, 156, 175, 220

Insignias 197

Intelligence. *See* Wisdom

Interactive prototype 9, 16, 19, 30, 68, 74, 82, 87, 90, 120, 236, 331

Interceptor body armor system 191

Interface design 315–331

Inventory 24, 25, 32, 81, 82, 92, 94, 107, 139, 140, 150, 165, 166, 167, 168, 169, 170, 172, 173, 175, 176, 183, 190, 191, 192, 193, 194, 195, 196, 198, 199, 200–204, 205, 206, 209, 223, 252, 255, 282, 285, 316, 322, 346, 349–350

Inventory interface screen 204–205

Invisible overlay grid 296

Isometric projection 294

Item

   Categories 165–170

   Chart 171–176, 217, 219

   Name 173, 218

Map items 81–82

Slots in inventory 203–204

J

JavaScript 47

Jeopardy 246

Jewelry 196–197

Jigsaw puzzle 169, 242, 244, 248, 296

Journal 175, 198, 199, 250, 252, 317

K

Karma. *See* Luck

Katana 135

Kepi caps 190

Kevlar 190, 192

Keys 199–201

Kings and Castles 336, 346, 355

King's Quest 256

Kite shield 193

Knight 134

Knives 179

Knowledge. *See* Wisdom

Kobolds 131

L

Lab gloves 192

Lantern 198

Lara Croft and the Guardian of Light 256

Leadership ability 112

Leather helmet 190

Legend of Zelda, The 264

Leisure Suit Larry 256

Lemmings 243

Use (skills action) 94, 153

User Interface 15, 18, 252, 315–331

V

Vambrace 192

Vampires 132, 227

Variables in scripting 50–51, 276,
284–286, 287, 289, 303–304

Victoria II 61

Video tapes 199

Visual feedback 74, 223, 250,
329–331

Vitality. *See* Constitution

W

Warcraft 60, 108

Wargames

Attributes 110–113

Movement 61–67, 69, 70, 71–75

Traditional 92, 107, 108–109

Wario Land 250

WarioWare 250

Warlords 4: Heroes of Etheria 318,
319

Warrior. *See* Barbarian

Waterloo: Napoleon's Last Battle
109

Waypoints 64

Weak characters in game stories
266

Weapon (item) 166–167, 169, 170,
172, 173, 174, 175, 176–187,
195

Attack value 97, 98, 99

Chart 176

Range 112

Weight level attribute 111

Werewolves 132, 227

Wheel of Fortune 243

Where's Waldo 244

Wii Remote 327

Wing Commander 109, 228

Wisdom 129

Wizard (class) 134

Wizardry 128

Word Cross 243

Word games 243–244, 247

World map. *See* Strategic movement map

World of Goo 353

World of Warcraft 93, 108, 128

Wreaths 197

Z

Zaxxon 294

Zigzag story structure 271–273

Zombies 132, 222

Zone of control 64–66, 75, 112

Zork 256, 264

ABOUT THE AUTHOR

Michael E. Moore worked in the game industry for almost 25 years. The first ten years were in board games, primarily wargames and role-playing games. In 1979, he was hired as an assistant editor at Simulations Publications, Inc. in New York, and soon he took on the role of a developer. This role was unique to the wargame industry and involved him working with a designer to simplify or rework game mechanics as necessary to make the game more transparent and accessible for players. He also became the Managing Editor of several SPI magazines, including *Strategy & Tactics (S&T)*, *Ares*, and *MOVES*.

In 1982, Michael joined TSR Hobbies in Lake Geneva, Wisconsin, the company that published *Dungeons & Dragons*, after they acquired the assets of SPI. He continued as Managing Editor of *S&T* until he was given the opportunity to return to New York to work at Victory Games. That company had been set up by former employees of SPI who wished to remain together in New York once the company folded. Michael joined Victory Games as a developer, and over the next six years he worked on the *James Bond 007 Role-Playing Game* series and numerous wargames. In addition to helping develop the games, Michael edited the manuscripts and supervised the production of the final products. He finally had the opportunity to do hands-on design work with the mass-market board games *Dr. Ruth's Game of Good Sex* and *The Game of Good Cooking*.

Deciding that electronic games were the wave of the future, Michael started searching for a position in that industry. Fortunately, it was just at the point where companies were beginning to hire designers as new team members instead of letting an artist or programmer also handle the design duties. In 1989 Michael got a job at Infocom in Cambridge, Massachusetts; Infocom was known for its text-based adventure games. He was soon transferred to the parent company Infocom/Mediagenic in Menlo Park, California. While there, he designed the military missions for *BattleTech: The Crescent Hawks' Revenge*, designed the puzzle game Dragon's Eye in *Shanghai II: Dragon's Eye*, and wrote the story for the adventure game *Circuit's Edge*. He also was the producer of Westwood Studios' science-fiction role-playing game *The Mines of Titan*.

He then co-founded a new development company, Tsunami Productions (soon to be known as Ybarra Productions) in 1990.

There he designed the fantasy action game *SpellCraft: Aspects of Valor*, the pioneer massively multiplayer role-playing game (MMORPG) *Shadow of Yserbius* and its sequel *The Fates of Twinion*, and the strategic adventure game *Alien Legacy*. He went on to design and produce games at several other companies, although these projects were cancelled for one reason or another. Among these projects were the multiplayer action game *GenePool* for The 3DO Company, a first-person puzzle game called *Big Brother* (based on George Orwell's novel *1984*) for MediaGenic, and an arcade racing game *GS Racing*.

In 2003, he joined the faculty of DigiPen Institute of Technology in Redmond, Washington where he taught game design and project management. He was chair of the Game Software Design and Production Department between 2004–08. There he wrote *Introduction to the Game Industry* (with Jen Sward) for Pearson Education in 2007. He retired in 2009 and turned to writing, producing *Game Development Essentials: Game Industry Career Guide* with Jeannie Novak for Thomson Delmar Learning in 2009.